Framing

Manchester University Press

Framing

The social art of influence

Mikael Klintman

Manchester University Press

Published by Manchester University Press
Oxford Road, Manchester, M13 9PL

www.manchesteruniversitypress.co.uk

British Library Cataloguing-in-Publication Data
A catalogue record for this book is available from the British Library

ISBN 978 1 5261 7041 5 hardback

First published 2025

Typeset
by Cheshire Typesetting Ltd, Cuddington, Cheshire
Printed in Great Britain
by Bell & Bain Ltd, Glasgow

Contents

Contents

Acknowledgements

A heartfelt thank you to the many people who have contributed to this book in various ways – through critique, support, wisdom, and inspiration. I am particularly grateful for the generosity that afforded me something increasingly rare: the opportunity to focus.

To Alun Richards, Anika Binte Habib, Anna-Lisa Lindén, Cheryl Fung, Daniel Klintman, David Andersson, David Appleyard, David Wästerfors, Emma Ejelöf, Erik Brattström, Eva Warensjö Lemming, Felicia Hedetoft, Freja Morris, George Gaskell, Göran Finnveden, Hanna Eggestrand Vaughan, Hanna Eneroth, Hans Lindgren, Helena Sandberg, Helle Margerete Meltzer, Håkan Johansson, Ingegerd Lindgren, James Druckman, Jamie Abrams, Joanna Doona, Joe Haining, Johan Sandberg, Jonah Berger, Jonas Nässén, Jonatan Järbel, Jörgen Larsson, Karin Bradley, Karin Gustafsson, Katarina Eckerberg, Kim Walker, Kristoffer Berglund, Lea Fünfschilling, Liam Guilfoyle, Linda Soneryd, Lillemor Klintman, Lisa Broberg, Lisa Eklund, Magnus Andersson, Magnus Boström, Magnus Johansson, Magnus Karlsson, Marie Liu Klintman, Martin Rein, Matthias Gross, Matthias Lehner, Mikael Linnell, Mimmi Barmark, Monika Berg, Naja Yndal-Olsen, Norbert Schwarz, Oksana Mont, Ola Persson, Oliver Scott Curry, Olle Frödin, Pernilla Hagbert, Rolf Lidskog, Roman Frigg, Sam Fraser, Sara Karimzadeh, Sara Sharp, Dame Sarah Whatmore, Tobias Linné, Viktor Mayer-Schönberger, Vishal Parekh, William Gamson, and Åsa Svenfelt – your thoughtful comments and encouragement have left a lasting mark on this work.

Acknowledgements

I also want to express my gratitude to the Swedish Foundation for Strategic Environmental Research (Mistra) for their financial support through Phase 2 of the Mistra Sustainable Consumption Research Consortium (2022–2025), and to Göran Finnveden and Jörgen Larsson for their responsive and supportive leadership.

Lastly, to my dear wife Jenny and our wonderful boys Leo, Bruno, Fred, and Matti, for the frame that defines our little 'we', and for sharing with me the constant and delicate exercise of drawing boundaries between what truly matters and what can be gently set aside.

Introduction

Several years back, I came across a simple yet striking black-and-white photograph in a magazine. The image captures a moment frozen in time on the streets of Amsterdam in 1980. It features a woman in a somewhat awkward stance, bending over a large piece of plywood. The plywood measures roughly 1 × 1.5 m and has the silhouette of a bicycle cut out from its centre. Standing right in the heart of Amsterdam's bustling city centre, the woman looks as if she is on a mission. Behind her, the evidence of her endeavour is clear for all to see – three bikes stencilled onto the street with white paint, each spaced about 2 m apart. This line of painted bicycles is neatly framed by white-painted four-leaf clovers dotted along the street. A curious ensemble of bystanders linger on the sidelines, their expressions a mixture of intrigue and indifference.[1] They are witnesses to what will later be recognized as part of a pivotal chapter in Amsterdam's transformation into the world's cycling capital. Yet, in this moment, they seem oblivious to the magnitude of what they are seeing.

Maybe, in the days that followed, some of those very bystanders found themselves pedalling along the fake cycle path they had seen being created. In using it, they would have been participating in a transformative framing process. What began as mere illusion, a stroke of defiance and creativity on the part of the woman and her fellow activists, eventually morphed into one of the many official bike routes that now adorn the urban landscape of Amsterdam and other cities around the world.

1

Framing: the social art of influence

Through her painted bicycles, the woman in the photo was not just altering the physical landscape; she was engaging in an act of *reframing*. By changing the lines that delineated spaces on the street, she challenged the prevailing figurative, cultural frame where motor vehicles were considered the default means of transportation and contributed to elevating the status of cycling within the urban narrative. But not only that. There was also something else going on, namely an expansion of the frame that prescribes what means are available for bringing about social change.

The key takeaway, for now, boils down to two words: *framing matters*. Artists, glass workers, carpenters, and framers – yes, it's a proud profession too – have understood this for centuries, of course. From our personal relationships to our roles in larger organizations, our ability to manage and navigate the frames that define situations can make the difference between painful stalemates, misunderstandings, and solutions. Beyond the numerous examples in this book, I would argue that in most social situations, whether private or public, the ability to decipher, navigate, challenge, and reshape the dominant frames around us is crucial (though it is not the only factor – power, money, and looks also help). However, in order to translate the examples of this book into *framing strategies* that are applicable to our own lives, when we have important things to say and where our influence is needed, we'll have to examine and address a number of deeper questions.

Consider again the photo from Amsterdam. Like any fascinating image, it raises more questions than answers. It certainly illustrates the power of framing, both physical and metaphorical, and its profound impact on the urban traffic landscape. Yet, questions arise: how did ordinary citizens in Amsterdam manage, through small actions such as painting, demonstrating, and protesting, to influence local politics, urban development, the economy, the media, and public opinion to such an extent that it led to a paradigm shift in the city's approach to transport and planning? Why have such endeavours been successful in some areas but not others? This book aims to answer such questions by identifying the factors that need to be considered and how they can be adapted to specific places, situations, cultures, and, most importantly, our inherent susceptibility to the influence of others. As you'll see, assessing which framings translate into influence is not always an intuitive process. Across a broad range of issues and examples, we'll explore the potential and the limitations of framing and how it can be better adapted to different challenges.

Take another example: healthy food and living. This is a priority for many of us, or at least we like to think so.[2] Yet, paradoxically, our society consumes large amounts of junk food. Widespread information and communication about the health risks of junk food and the benefits of a balanced diet often fail to motivate change in many groups. So how can junk food be reframed to significantly increase the chances that people in at least some demographic groups, such as young men, will improve their eating habits? The book will consult fascinating research experiments on this matter, and I believe we will find a convincing answer.

Here's yet another example. It concerns what sources of knowledge people with different ideologies trust the most when it comes to sustainability problems, such as climate change mitigation and adaptation. Since the term 'fake news' came into popular use, there has been an increasing focus on how we determine what is true and what is false. What happens to people's belief in the same set of truth claims when those claims are reframed only in terms of who is said to have made them? The answer may seem obvious: of course, we are likely to trust representatives of some groups more than others, depending on the issue in question. But who do people trust more? When it comes to fact-checking misinformation about climate change, I will show that, surprisingly, neither people on the political left nor those on the political right trust non-partisan climate scientists more than they trust politicians of any stripe.

The latter two examples illustrate that framing and reframing are processes that often elude our complete understanding and control. Framing is a social art in which we shape and reshape how others and we ourselves comprehend a situation, not only consciously but also unconsciously, across all levels of society.

From junk food and climate change it's a small step to the phenomenon of sustainable consumption. As consumers, we are increasingly expected to make choices reflecting broader ethical and political considerations, going beyond mere self-interest to extend our moral responsibility. This expansion aligns with the broadening of our role as 'citizen-consumers' when purchasing and using goods and services. The term 'citizen' implies that our decisions and habits regarding the types and amounts of goods and services we buy, use, and dispose of should be informed by considerations such as air quality, biodiversity, climate change, chemical pollution, labour conditions, and animal welfare and rights.

Through the techniques shared in this book, which I break down into the four categories of texturing, heating, positioning, and sizing, we will be able to navigate and even manipulate the frames that shape our own and others' perceptions and actions. In the context of sustainable consumption, implying that people should become actively responsible citizen-consumers, complexity can be managed by making skilful use of the full flexibility offered by the toolbox of framing.

Consider two hypothetical individuals: one lives in a suburban villa with solar panels, owns three electric cars, prefers organic meat, and offsets her quarterly flights to eco-tourism sites; the other resides in a tiny rural cottage, lives off-grid, grows most of her food, adheres to a vegan lifestyle, and uses a thirty-year-old pickup truck for trips to the city.[3] Using the framing toolbox, each could construct narratives that portray their lifestyle choices as aligning closely with the dominant frames of sustainable consumption and lifestyles.

This illustrates the richness and diversity in the art of framing, which can be liberating. Yet, this richness and diversity comes with challenges. It requires a discerning eye to identify the strengths and weaknesses of different frames. By learning and refining our framing skills, we will develop the ability not only to shape persuasive narratives to influence others, such as in the case of our life choices, but also to critically assess the various frames around us. These frames present what is 'indisputable', 'normal', and 'obvious', sometimes so convincingly that they become invisible to most people – not just to the eyes but also to the mind.

Introduction

Ultimately, this book aims to empower you to better manage the frames that shape our perceptions and actions, promoting a deeper understanding of our role as creators, recipients, and modifiers of those frames. Thus, we can enhance our ability to navigate the complex social landscapes we inhabit, leveraging the diversity and richness of framing to forge more meaningful connections and enact positive change.

Turning a blind eye to framing

Despite the influence that framing can have on us, often when we are unaware of it, its power – except for its role in marketing – is generally downplayed in society. In their book, Framers, Cukier, Mayer-Schönberger and de Véricourt even state that '[B]elief in the value and power of framing is under threat'.[4] Various organizations attempt to counter the blunt lies that appear in discussions of hotly debated topics such as those covered in this book – including food and health, climate change, vaccination, artificial intelligence, violent crime, military aggression, evolution by natural selection, cultured meat, and smoking. United Nations agencies (World Health Organization (WHO), UNESCO), fact-checking services in traditional media (the *Washington Post*'s Fact Checker and BBC Reality Check), and non-profit organizations (PolitiFact and Truth or Fiction?) are engaged in a constant battle to combat profit-hungry or politically motivated lying and disinformation.

One would expect efforts to fight manipulation to include teaching people to reflect on how issues are framed and what various types of framing do to us. However, framing processes, with their potential for misleading us in implicit, even subconscious, ways, are usually beyond the scope of such services.

The societal tendency to exclude, ignore, or downplay the power of framing on people's beliefs about problems related to health, the environment, and social wellbeing is in line with what is sometimes called the 'knowledge deficit model'.[5] This is the assumption that more and better information and knowledge are all that is missing for people and groups to avoid being deceived. Consequently, fact-checking services, myth-busting procedures, and scientific clarifications are treated as sufficient cures for disinformation, myths, conspiracy theories, post-truth, fake news, and fact resistance.

There is no reason to assume that the daily reports spotlighting blunt lies and disinformation will not remain a necessary part of any society aspiring to be democratic, open, and enlightened. We should probably be relieved that those fact-checking services exist – at least the ones that are free from disguised biases. At the same time, several studies on controversial topics, including some of the topics mentioned above, indicate that provision of facts and correction of untruths are not only insufficient, but in some cases have even been shown to be counterproductive – if anything, enhancing the polarized knowledge beliefs.[6] This may happen when facts are detached from the socially and culturally framed narratives that each group find meaningful. Later in this book, I will explain why this is the case. In sum, it turns out that learning about the phenomenon of framing is necessary for fighting both overt deception and more subtle attempts at unwelcome influence.

The purpose of this book, then, is to provide readers – the busy, educated public, students, scholars, professionals – with a broad and practical understanding of framing. I will share the 'social toolkit' by which people and groups – consciously and unconsciously – make sense of the world and influence others in all spheres of life, from the everyday to major political events. You will be given a rich array of illustrative and engaging examples and cases that help to concretize and make the toolbox of reframing applicable. Many of the cases covered in this book have been collected from areas of health, the environment, and social well-being, but we will also look beyond these.

Complementary but compartmentalized

To gain insights into how framings work in human interaction, it makes sense to conduct and consult studies in what I will refer to as the human scientific disciplines. These are preoccupied with the individual, social, political, economic, cultural, and evolutionary dimensions of society. Alas, the human sciences are anything but one harmonious family in academia. They rarely miss an opportunity to miss an opportunity to agree on even minute aspects of how humans and society work.[7]

One exception is particularly striking – you guessed it, framing. Scholars across the wide range of the human sciences share at least one essential recognition about framing: that it plays a significant role in social life, since we humans cannot make complete sense and meaning of events in the world without gathering our impressions within at least a thin, conceptual frame. Researchers ranging from neuroscientists,[8] to behavioural economists,[9] marketing scholars,[10] consumer researchers,[11] media and communication scholars,[12] sociologists,[13] political scientists, and scholars of rhetoric[14] and of cultural studies[15] consequently share an interest in studying – or at least philosophizing about – reframing processes.

The question, then, is whether various disciplines mean the same thing by 'framing'. Several definitions exist that are adapted to specific disciplines.[16] Still, I believe it *is* possible to define framing in a broad way that would not exclude any field. During my years at Massachusetts Institute of Technology in the early 2000s, I had the privilege of having numerous seminar discussions with distinguished sociology professor Martin Rein about the framing phenomenon. To paraphrase Rein and his colleague Donald Schön, framings are constructions of ways of selecting, interpreting, and organizing our complex world. Framings, accordingly, serve as 'guideposts' for understanding, acting, and persuading.[17]

I believe Rein and Schön's approach to understanding framing provides a valuable foundation for the discussions in this book. However, their definitions do not fully capture the extensive range of framing to be explored here. As such, a broader definition is necessary to match the scope of this book. This definition should encompass framing that is both automatically and strategically constructed, which can profoundly influence not only others but also us – the creators of the frame.[18] It should also acknowledge framings that not only simplify but also complicate the aspect of reality they concern. Moreover, and perhaps most crucially for a deeper understanding of framing's impact, this definition should include framing that can both clarify and obscure that aspect of reality.

For this reason, I suggest this expanded definition:

> Framing is the automatic or strategic process of selecting, shaping, interpreting, and organizing a part of our complex reality into a bounded construction that may affect both our own and others' understanding and actions.

With this in hand, we can introduce some subtlety to our discussion of how framing influences our perception of people, groups, or issues. As an example, let's visualize this with a tool beloved by us sociologists: a four-field table.

The functions of framing

	Simplify	*Complicate*
Clarify	'Are we conflating issues?'	'Let's unpack this further!'
Obscure	'It's just the way things are!'	'It depends on what the meaning of the word "is" is.'

On one axis, frames can *simplify* or *complicate* our understanding of people, groups, and topics. On the other axis, frames can either *clarify* or *obscure* our understanding of them. Incorporating both axes into the imagined four-field table reveals no consistent rule as to what a simplification or complication will do to our understanding. Not all simplifications bring clarity, and not all complications introduce confusion. Different academic disciplines often concentrate on just one or two of these four framing functions. For example, scholars in the field of 'ignorance studies' have identified what they call 'strategic ignorance',[19] several strategies that refer to obscuring the issue at stake by either oversimplifying or overcomplicating it. The former may include the tactics of a company that deliberately shifts attention away from, for instance, problematic parts of their environmental performance, oversimplifying their record by putting a spotlight on the parts where it does well.[20] Alternatively, a company may use the latter tactic, obscuring its sustainability record by overcomplicating the issue at stake, overloading their reporting with valid but raw or unorganized environmental impact data, making it impossible for auditors to fully evaluate and scrutinize.

In contrast to the study of ignorance, the research field of science communication often investigates which types of framing of scientific findings improve clarity and enhance public awareness and concern regarding issues of environment, health, and social wellbeing.[21] In addition, the opposite of uniform clarity can sometimes be highly beneficial. In artistic production and performance, such as visual art, literature, music, theatre, and other cultural expressions, ambiguity and complication are often precisely what makes them interesting and important works. By creating ambiguity and communicating with the audience not only explicitly but also implicitly and suggestively, the works can make us question what we've previously taken for granted, thereby enriching our understanding of both the artistic work and other aspects of life. The saying that 'an explained poem is a dead poem' aptly illustrates this point.

Agreeing that framing matters does not mean there is a vibrant, multidisciplinary exchange of insights into how framings work. Sadly, more often the contrary is true, although there are welcome exceptions. For instance, the path-breaking framing research work by the Nobel laureate Daniel Kahneman and Amos Tversky[22] has had a significant influence on various fields between behavioural economics and various strands of psychology – most notably in terms of human biases and nudging.[23]

Additionally, research on the framing strategies of social movements (civil rights, women's rights, peace, environment, animal rights) has had some valuable exchanges with political science scholarship.[24] In addition, framing in literary studies has influenced several social science-oriented areas.[25] These include sociology,[26] critical discourse analysis,[27] and postmodern thought.[28] However, from a broader, bird's-eye perspective of framing research, many other possibilities for mutual learning remain unexplored, even where the disciplines seem compatible and complementary, not only in how they understand framing but also sister terms, such as discourses, boundaries, schemata, scripts, and narratives. One aspiration of this book is that examining the phenomenon of framing will also shed valuable, indirect light on these related concepts and ideas.[29]

Take, for instance, the relationship – or rather the lack of relationship – between the conceptual tools for analysing how various texts and speeches strategically aimed at persuasion are framed. In the past fifty to sixty years, framing scholars focusing on the specific area of strategic and conscious rhetorical techniques for mobilizing people around a common cause have developed an intricate combination of concepts for such rhetorical analyses. Unfortunately, this endeavour has largely neglected the opportunity to benefit from the classical art of rhetoric, which, with its two thousand years of development, provides a nearly fully transferable terminology applicable to this type of frame analysis.[30]

The broader consequences of the unexplored opportunities for knowledge integration are that scholars in each discipline invent an ever-increasing number of concepts and sub-concepts describing specific ways framing can work. This is, to be sure, sometimes helpful for understanding a particular case.[31] However, it is also increasingly difficult for neighbouring disciplines to engage with these conceptual developments, even if the curiosity is there.

This lack of knowledge exchange and integration on framing is why I decided to write this book. Insights into how and why people and groups lead and mislead each other in various framing processes are so essential that they simply must be brought to a wide, public light – far outside any one field of scholarship. Therefore, parts of this book will be devoted to possible connections between the separate disciplines as well as separate cases, showing how we can learn from and integrate insights across scholarship, even where they might not be compatible in every detail. On that basis, I will provide you with my own approach for making sense of, and becoming more active in, influencing the framing processes around us.

Since the turn of the century, I have had the privilege of conducting hands-on research in the UK, the US, Sweden, and other countries, examining how individuals and organizations wield influence through framing processes at all levels of society. My research has spanned at least twenty different sectors, primarily within the domains of social well-being, environmental issues, and health. For several years, I have incorporated elements of social, economic, and evolutionary sciences in my studies. Since 2016, I have collaborated with scientists from various disciplines at the University of Oxford and other academic institutions in London, gathering their insights on both successful and unsuccessful framing processes, and how better to empower individuals and groups to become more conscious of and control the framing processes that surround them. Some of the most edifying reflections they generously shared with me will be shared with you in this book.

The outline

Chapter 1, 'Perspectives on framing,' introduces two conventional understandings of framing and its potential to improve the quality of life and society. Here, I challenge these standard views and offer preliminary insights into the book's third alternative approach to framing. This sets the stage for the book's four main sections, each of which focuses on a distinct framing technique.

Part I explores the most fundamental – arguably primitive – framing technique we all practice and experience multiple times a day, which I call 'texturing the frame'. It examines why and how we categorize things as positive or negative, true or false, pure or impure, reliable or untrustworthy, and so forth, referring to these dichotomies as 'smooth' or 'rough' frames. We trace our instinctive judgements back to our evolutionary origins, emphasizing that social influence extends beyond these basic dichotomies. Part II looks at the art of framing as it relates to adjusting the perceived intensity or 'temperature' of our perceptions, like how physical frames may need heating to reshape or cooling to stabilize. This part investigates the role of temperament, timing, and metaphors – both positive and negative – in exerting social influence. Part III discusses techniques for creating or altering the very meaning of what is at stake concerning a part or aspect of reality. For instance, framing the protection of an untouched natural area, such as a virgin forest, in terms of short- or long-term job opportunities, nature tourism, national security, or natural resources, can significantly influence different groups' attitudes and management of this natural site. This part highlights that aligning a frame with the currently dominant narrative of an issue is less straightforward than often assumed, leading to discussions on frame resizing in Part IV, the final main section of the book. This last part explores the possibilities for addressing challenges by completely changing their frame size, considering broader inclusivity or narrowing focus for clarity and predictability.

The concluding chapter reflects on framing-related questions that have arisen from conversations with various individuals, both within and outside academia. My responses provide insights based on my approach to the framing phenomenon throughout the book, intended to apply to different aspects of your life and to encourage engagement with the nuanced art of framing.

1

Perspectives on framing

Physical and figurative frames

The Danish artist Jens Haaning approached the curator at the Kunsten Museum of Modern Art in Aalborg, Denmark, with an idea. He wanted to recreate one of his previous art installations, consisting of two framed glass canvases – one large and one small. The large frame would hold banknotes representing the average annual salary in Austria, while the small frame would represent the average annual salary in Denmark. The museum found the idea exciting and assisted Haaning by providing the necessary banknotes, worth 534,000 kroner (£60,000), to complete the installation.

Within the agreed period, Haaning sent a box containing the artwork to the museum. However, upon opening the box, the staff discovered that the framed glass canvases were present, but the banknotes were missing. Inside the box, Haaning had placed a small sign with the name of the artwork: *Take the Money and Run*. In a later interview with Dansk Radio, he explained: 'The artwork is that I took their money'. The museum, perhaps understandably, wanted its money back. But Haaning refused, arguing that returning it would undermine the meaning of the art.[1]

Did the artist's effort to reframe his artwork fall short, given the museum's refusal to commend it as a 'masterful conceptual piece, deserving of the funds'? Alternatively, did Haaning's inability to sway the museum staff indicate that his reframing was, in fact, an artistic triumph, sustaining the tension with the money lenders?

Reflecting on this puzzling art affair, even *trying* to comprehend the many ways framing influences us, may seem dizzying. Fortunately, we have a toolkit at our disposal: framing, of course, in the figurative sense.

But before we dive deeper into the world of figurative framing, let's pause for a moment to consider what 'figurative' means in this context. How much can we really lean on the properties of physical frames to get a grip on how their figurative cousins work? *Take the Money and Run* offers us a lens through which to explore this. Haaning's art project nudges us to look at the parallels and differences between the frames we can touch and those we can't.

A common ground for physical and figurative frames is their boundary-setting role. Just like Haaning's frames, which were supposed to make a clear statement with banknotes, figurative frames carve out the space for specific ideas or issues, defining what's up for discussion. Both kinds of frames draw our attention to their contents – or their missing contents – making everything else fade into the background, whether it's a physical object or a concept.

Another shared characteristic of physical and figurative frames is that they don't just highlight what's inside them; they also add context. A frame around a piece of art can suggest a period or style, just as Haaning's empty frames sparked conversations about the value of art and the expectations we place on artists. It's clear that whether we're dealing with an idea or something you can hang on a wall, frames have the power to influence how we see and interpret the context outside.

One possible difference might be the extent to which they can sway opinions and perceptions. Don't figurative frames 'win' here? The way something is figuratively framed – a policy proposal, for example – can vastly alter its reception, a flexibility that physical frames don't typically possess to the same extent. However, Haaning's project gives reason to rethink this difference. He used his physical frames to achieve a significant shift in perception, questioning the intrinsic value of art and the role of the artist.

How about differences in terms of layering and complexity? While a physical frame usually encloses a single object, figurative frames can encompass multiple layers of meaning and interpretation. At the same time, Haaning's empty frames, by leaving space unfilled, invite a complex web of thoughts and discussions, suggesting that physical frames can indeed host a depth of conceptual layers akin to their figurative counterparts.

Another possible difference is the potential for many people in various roles to participate and interact in ways that influence a frame. Figurative framing often seems more open in this respect, allowing for wider participation in shaping how ideas are framed and understood. Still, as this book will show, such openness and participatory inclusion in figurative framing is far from the rule. And conversely, Haaning's art shows how physical frames can be used to provoke a broad spectrum of interpretations and debates, something that further narrows the gap between the physical and the figurative.

Pulling all these threads together, the line between what physical and figurative frames can achieve is quite thin. Thus, exploring the full extent of framing – both in the tangible world and in the realm of ideas – doesn't seem to stretch the concept too far from its original meaning.

Some further clarifications

When framing is described as a *social* art here, I am referring to the function it serves in influencing the perceptions and actions of others, either consciously or unconsciously. The ability to both influence and be influenced by framing is crucial for cooperation and coexistence. It also helps protect us from being exploited and, depending on your perspective, enables us sometimes to mislead or even deceive others – even ourselves, which isn't always bad.

By claiming that framing is a social *art*, I am alluding to its alignment with several qualities traditionally linked with artistry. Much like art, figurative framing demands a toolkit and sophisticated skills. It entails the meticulous selection and arrangement of elements – akin to an artisan working with materials – to shape and accentuate specific facets of the reality it encapsulates, often with the objective of influencing people's and society's viewpoints and actions, and – by extension – contributing to change or to maintaining the status quo. The reliance on form and structure is a trait framing shares with art in the conventional sense, encompassing both traditional and avant-garde styles. However, framing carries a distinctive function: to cohesively encase its 'object' or 'content' – a segment of reality or a specific situation – in a manner that significantly influences people's understandings and actions regarding that part of reality. This role subjects framing to even stricter formative conditions compared to literal art. Some of these forms and conditions are deeply rooted in human history, stretching back to our hunter-gatherer days. These rules are part of our collective genetic 'memory' and our individual variations.

The depiction of framing as an art, a social art, is very much in line with how classical rhetoric, with its many sophisticated techniques, has been researched, presented, taught, and used for more than two millennia. Aristotle's *Rhetoric*, developed between 367 and 322 BCE, introduces three fundamental elements – *pathos*, *ethos*, and *logos* – which are essential to the art of rhetoric.[2] These elements are frequently incorporated into the framing techniques discussed in the book. *Pathos* involves crafting messages with linguistic finesse and carefully selected stories and perspectives to evoke emotional responses aligned with the speaker's intended perceptions and actions. However, the use of strong, emotional language is not always the most effective across all contexts. *Ethos* focuses on establishing the writer's or speaker's credibility and trustworthiness. It's important to note that credibility doesn't solely depend on demonstrating superior knowledge or ethical standards. This is illustrated by an example later in Chapter 3, where neither political faction trusted impartial climate scientists' corrections of climate change misinformation. *Logos* pertains to persuading through logical reasoning and argumentation, appealing to the audience's rationality.

While classical rhetoric primarily concerns persuasion, framing's impact extends significantly further, as demonstrated by this book's comprehensive definition of framing and examples like Haaning's art project. An intriguing aspect, to be explored later in the book, is framing's ability to affect not only humans but other species as well, suggesting its origins predate humanity. This underscores framing's broader scope compared to rhetoric, hence the book's preference for the term 'influence' due to its neutrality. Framing's influence spans a wide spectrum, from unconscious, unintended inspiration to deliberate manipulation and propaganda, including persuasion and indoctrination that can foster anything from democratic to extremist ideologies. Therefore, 'influence' is the foundational term, subject to contextual nuance.

Lastly, when I say framing can be like a 'trick', I mean that it, like a literal artwork, can dramatically alter our perceptions. It's sometimes so transformative that, to an intelligent but socially inexperienced Martian observer, it might look like magic. The term 'trick' also implies that we're often unaware of when and how framing is happening, and of its impact on both the frame artisan and the affected environment. At the same time, these tricks are usually 'truthful', at least for the most part. This is because, when framing deceives us, it typically does so by subtly misleading or influencing us without our awareness, rather than by outright lying to us. We'll look at important exceptions to this rule as well.

The framing toolkit has helped me place claims found within many schools of thought on framing into two approaches – leading up to a third approach. The first one I call 'reality speaks for itself'. The second is labelled 'framing is everything'.[3] Despite appearing to be opposites, both approaches have an intuitive appeal. Many of us likely perceive human influence through one of these lenses at different times. Consider the case of British tourists Angela and Donald Lincoln, travelling in France. They may have joyfully exclaimed, 'Once again, the reality of superior French cuisine has spoken for itself', as they savoured what they believed to be a 'gorgeous pâté' from a can labelled Mousse Gourmande, only to be informed later that they'd actually eaten cat food.[4] So this ought to mean that framing – in that case in the form of product labelling – is everything, oughtn't it? But then, let's consider the case of burnout – a state of chronic physical and emotional exhaustion often linked to prolonged and intense stress, particularly related to work or caregiving activities. Burnout is characterized by feelings of overwhelming fatigue, detachment, a sense of ineffectiveness or lack of accomplishment. It may seem like certain diseases and health disorders, like burnout, named in the 1970s, are mere constructions without substantial content – illusory products of our modern times.[5] 'How come no one seemed to have these problems before the word burnout was invented?' employers started to ask, rhetorically. Yet, we discover that the specific symptoms of burnout were described in Homer's account of the Trojan War and in the Old Testament's depictions of Moses (Numbers 11:14) and Elijah (1 Kings 19) during their most challenging moments.[6] Doesn't it, then, seem that 'reality speaks for itself', regardless of framing and naming?

All of this raises profound questions about framing and its impact on us. I have distilled a vast number of questions into three key enquiries. First, how important and powerful is framing in influencing people? Second, can we truly understand what lies inside a frame – the content, if there is any? And finally, what role should framing and reframing play in enhancing quality of life and society? Throughout several chapters, we will explore real-life, practical cases to address the latter two questions. However, the remaining portion of this chapter will focus on the first one: how important and powerful framing is in influencing people. I will dig into this by introducing the two seemingly opposite approaches – that is, 'reality speaks for itself' and 'framing is everything' – and examining their answers.

'Reality speaks for itself'

Framing has an impact on us in various situations, even if the objective issue remains unchanged. Later, we'll learn more about the case of Amsterdam traffic in the 1970s and 1980s, identifying decisive factors for *how* the reality (the traffic situation and structure) could be successfully reframed – not just by painting the streets with bicycles but also through combined activities – into something so emotionally charged that it could bring about political and physical changes in the urban landscape. More examples of the power of reframing will be given from a wide range of places and spheres of life.

In many situations we tend to believe that 'reality speaks for itself' and assume no further comment or framing is necessary for people to evaluate and act accordingly. Thus, framing is often considered irrelevant or superfluous. An example of this is when public authorities provide information to encourage healthier habits among citizens. They present what seems to be neutral, truthful, and factual information about what to eat, how to exercise, and more, hoping that these unadorned pieces of reality will speak for themselves. The authorities expect people to become more aware of the gap between their current lifestyles and healthier choices, leading to a motivation to adopt healthier habits. A similar approach is taken regarding climate change, where simply learning about our large carbon footprints should be enough to impact our beliefs, concerns, and actions.

To frame truthful and self-explanatory health information, particularly with a thick cultural or identity-oriented lens, would, according to 'reality speaks for itself', divert the message away from the relevant facts and towards irrelevant aspects. It shouldn't matter for how we choose to live, for instance, if a film star follows health or climate advice. They are not experts. Furthermore, what if that film star later declares their disregard for the authorities' recommendations, deeming them foolish and patronizing? It's easy to sympathize with the belief that what's *inside* frames should be the only influencer: the content, the substance, the reality itself, free from irrelevant details like anecdotes, cultural context, marketing tricks, emotions, aesthetic trends, or political correctness, that is.

In the aesthetic domain, some of us might have sworn by this principle of letting what's inside the frame speak for itself when spending time at art museums and overhearing conversations between a gushing parent standing with their child:

> Hey, come over here and let me tell you about this amazing painting! Look at its antique, ornate gold frame, which was actually added after the painter died. It's super famous, this painting, you know – probably the most valuable one in this whole museum! And guess what? It has a pretty exciting story behind it. A few years ago, it was actually stolen! But they found it and brought it back where it belongs. And get this – it's worth millions of dollars! Now, the painter who created this masterpiece was actually quite poor. Can you imagine that? But

not only that, he was also very, very unhappily in love. It's like a story straight out of a movie! Oh, and he did something terrible to his own ear...

Even Vincent van Gogh himself would probably cringe at such a fixation on the frame. The frame, both physical and metaphorical, so often distracts from the content. Instead, the content, what's in a frame, simple and pure, is all that matters. No fluff needed. Yet, he noticed a trick people play, one that art galleries are particularly guilty of. They put ordinary art – the kind you'd pass without a second glance – inside these gigantic, showy frames. Suddenly, the artwork seems 'important'. But to Van Gogh, this was a ruse, a magic trick to make us believe in the value of something inherently ordinary:

> some paintings in their huge frames look very substantial, and later one is surprised when they actually leave behind such an empty and dissatisfied feeling. On the other hand, one overlooks many an unpretentious woodcut or lithograph or etching now and then, but comes back to it and becomes more and more attached to it with time, and senses something great in it.[7]

Van Gogh argues that what he calls 'huge frames' aren't just decorative extras, they're downright intrusive. They muddle up the image, drawing our attention away from the true essence. They're not just distracting us; they're robbing us of experiencing the real beauty and quality of the world. Put briefly, the content itself provides a sufficient basis for navigating in the wild sea of epistemic, ethical, and aesthetic claims around us.

Van Gogh's argument that content has intrinsic value that should be better expressed without a thick and fluffy frame seems convincing. It is also in line with the virtuous principle of communicating health and environmental issues in an unbiased way, without distorting reality. But classical rhetoricians, as well as current researchers from various fields, including neuroscientists and cultural studies scholars, all agree that frames are essential for making sense of the world. How does this align with the 'reality speaks for itself' approach? It fits, but only when we consider some nuance. The approach doesn't suggest that absolutely no framing is necessary for creating meaning. Instead, it argues that a thin, functional frame layer is sufficient to hold the content in place.[8] In Van Gogh's painting *The Potato Eaters*, for instance, we see soil and dust. It's not just in the ground where you'd expect it – it's sprinkled on the potatoes, brushed on people's faces, tucked under their fingernails, and smudged on their clothes. These earthy details are more than just part of the picture. They recall all kinds of thoughts and feelings – aided by the thin, tacit layer of common references that our psyches, morality, and culture have carpeted for us. In the painting, some cues are clear – the hard work, the connection to the land. Others influence our thoughts and feelings without us even realizing it.

We may also adopt the 'reality speaks for itself' approach further into the moral domain. For example, when the media informs us about a natural catastrophe that affects many people far away, wouldn't the factual information provided about the severity of the situation suffice, only thinly framed with additions in the form of the details of relevant charities accepting donations, to prompt our unhesitant action? Adding fluff to the framing – such as sentimental comments, emotional images, or showcasing others' donations – might seem unnecessary or even misleading for evaluating and responding to such situations. Similarly, when it comes to understanding climate change, it ought to be enough for us to act if we're informed about the urgency, the predicted temperature rises, and the connections with large carbon footprints, particularly those of the middle and upper classes. Likewise, in discussions of vaccination, such thin frames ensure that the logic behind health recommendations is understandable to non-experts. Relevant communication should include a thin framing that emphasizes the public health risks when a significant portion of the population remains unvaccinated.

The idea that reality – thinly framed only with 'relevant facts' – speaks for itself implies a few specific things. First, it implies that people have access, directly or indirectly, via, for instance, science, media, and other people, to reliable and unequivocal information about the issues that are *really* at stake. Secondly, people are deeply motivated to gather perceptual input and knowledge to draw accurate conclusions about the issues that matter to them. In short, people are 'issue rational'. They are fundamentally driven to reduce problems and achieve gains in areas such as material living standards, a clean environment, health, comfort, beauty, and entertainment. Therefore, the only meaningful type of framing is a thin layer of pedagogical clarification that guides individuals to see the intrinsic significance of substantive issues within this thin framing layer.

'Framing is everything'

Reality – dressed up in nothing more than a sleek, enlightening framing layer – might be all that *should* guide our actions. The fact that, for instance, Kim Kardashian has publicly vowed to boycott plastic straws *shouldn't* perhaps be the reason millions of people do the same.[9] What really should make us stop using them is that millions of these straws otherwise end up in nature, harming untold numbers of birds and fish. Yet, 'thick frames' – the 'irrelevant' layers and ornaments of cultural and social context – do play a role in guiding, misleading, and even tricking us in many aspects of our daily lives.[10] So, how significant are thick framings? Do they surpass the importance of the explicit issue at hand? And are there discernible patterns indicating what kind of cultural, ideological, and cognitive signals are likely to succeed or fail?

To make things clear, we need to provide 'reality speaks for itself' with its counterpoint, namely 'context is everything'. In the scope of this book, we'll revise that to '*framing* is everything'. This phrase may signify several things. First, it can mean that any framing effort can succeed and become culturally accepted more or less anywhere and anytime. Second, 'framing is everything' could mean that the way something is framed is what truly matters, not the content itself. This aligns with the adage that a skilled salesman can sell sand in the Sahara. In this view, how you frame something can make all the difference, regardless of the substance. Lastly, the phrase can touch on deeper philosophical issues. It can imply that we can never truly understand the 'content' enclosed by frames, or even question whether there's any real substance within those frames at all. For each case we discuss, I will specify which of these meanings I'm referring to.

Of course, many scholarly disciplines are far more nuanced than either 'reality speaks for itself' or 'framing is everything'. Still, the disciplines differ in the extent to which they emphasize the influence of the frame or its content. For instance, the insight that thick frames do influence us is the bread and butter of behavioural economists, who are always on the hunt for the cognitive biases that impact our decision-making. These biases lead us astray from making logical, issue-focused decisions. In the eyes of behavioural economics, the way a framed issue influences us – the so-called 'framing effect' – is seen as irrational, and ought to be irrelevant for our actions.[11] Behavioural economists aren't content just to uncover these biases. They also identify ways to amplify them, to create a supercharged framing effect. Companies apply such insights when convincing us to buy their products. NGOs use techniques from behavioural economics when prompting us to donate more. Picture this: you're offered three options, perhaps three waffle irons or three levels of donation to an environmental organization. One of these options is extreme in one way or another, like a waffle iron that cooks only on one side, or a donation option in which 80 per cent of your gift is swallowed up by administrative costs. Even if you don't pick the extreme option, it shapes your perception, guiding you towards a more reasonable choice (not necessarily the middle one).

Behavioural economics opens our eyes to a simple yet profound fact: we can be irrational when it comes to making decisions, especially when the way a problem is framed sways us. This understanding is a powerful tool in specific circumstances. For example, when we need a hand in dealing with a defined issue or reaching a clear goal. Imagine organ donations or substantial pension savings are the default choice – you'd have to try to say 'no'. This simple shift can help lots of us make decisions that are more aligned with the issue at hand.[12] In parts of several different framing research traditions, the potential influence of framing is often explored without acknowledging or addressing limits beyond culture, as if there were no limit to the influence of framing other than the cultural limits within which it operates. Little attention is given to potential constraints on when, where, how, and for whom framing can be influential, apart from the need to achieve 'cultural resonance', sometimes referred to as 'framing resonance'. The terms refer to the state in which the frame is designed and communicated in a way that the public feels 'resonate' with their sense of familiar and accepted culture. However, does this mean the culture shared by a whole society, or can it be a deviant part of the culture? Is a framework's compatibility with a culture – society-wide or partial – sufficient, necessary, or both for a framework to exert social influence?

Let us clarify this by relating cultural viability to one of the three approaches this book takes: 'framing is everything'. We see that this approach is relevant in some areas of linguistics, for example. Take George Lakoff's in many ways brilliant book *Don't Think of an Elephant*. Lakoff, a world-renowned cognitive scientist and linguist, is undoubtedly one of the leading experts on the intricate interplay between what our culture signals and other factors, such as the genetic makeup of human beings, that influence which frames affect us and which do not. Still, when he examined how words were used strategically between Republicans and Democrats in American politics in the early 2000s, his conclusions seemed like the 'framing is everything' approach. Lakoff highlighted how conservative framings such as 'tax relief', 'death tax', and 'entitlement programmes' crept into everyday speech and blurred party lines. The sneaky thing about these framings was how they nudged people, regardless of their political leanings, to view taxation as largely an unwanted and unethical burden – something citizens should be 'relieved from'.[13] Lakoff's account is fascinating enough, to be sure. But when he tried to dissect *why* certain framings (mostly conservative ones) have gained traction in American politics, he divided values into two 'metaframes'.[14] On one side, there's 'the strict father model' – the conservative metaframe. On the other, there's 'the nurturing parent model' – the progressive, liberal metaframe. Lakoff slots ideologically charged topics like abortion, LGBTQ+ rights, and international politics into these two categories convincingly.

But presenting reframing as if any value set or ideology that exists or has existed in a society could form the basis for the dominance of a particular frame in early 2000s American culture is like giving a description rather than an explanation of why different frames and metaframes, such as the nurturing parent model or an explicitly racist model or a complete laissez-fair model that includes neither a strict father nor a nurturing parent, hold sway in other cultures.

Our only takeaway is that people are 'irrational' – haphazardly influenced by some frames over others. Simply saying 'Because these are the norms or ideologies in those cultures' only sends us in circles. Studies on framing that lack deeper explanations for why some frames are more successful than others in a specific culture and time usually resort to obvious factors, such as that the individualistic 'because I'm worth it' framing hits home in a society steeped in greed and self-centredness. Yet again, we're not told why societies *differ* in their response to individualistic frames. Are we just supposed to throw up our hands?

However, studies on cultural framings usually don't give much insight into the reverse – but at least as curious – pattern, namely why various cultures *share* so many similarities when it comes to the types of frames that get traction.

Here are some questions routinely overlooked in framing research: why are the distinctions between 'us' and 'them' such an integral part of framing in most cultures, even when the topic seems utterly impersonal, like whether climate change is a fact or not, whether spanking is an acceptable form of discipline, or if the aesthetics of death metal music are superior to those of a combine harvester? And why is the rhetoric that underscores fairness so vital to the success of certain frames across a variety of subjects and in most cultures, sometimes even more so than the actual differences that these policies would mean for each individual or group? These ponderings about cultural similarities all lead us down the same path: it seems that the susceptibility to framing is a common trait among us humans, regardless of our cultural backgrounds. Even though the specific content of these frames might vary from culture to culture – such as what is considered fair or unfair – the underlying themes, like fairness itself, are subject to global framing.[15]

'Framing needs ancestral resonance'

Do the shortcomings of the two polar views – 'reality speaks for itself' and 'framing is everything' – mean that we must resort to an all-too-common trick: introducing two opposing, simplified, and extreme views, just to follow up with a more measured, moderate middle path? I'll try to avoid falling into that trap. It wouldn't be fair to box scholars or entire disciplines into one of the two camps. In fact, even those works that lean towards one of these extremes can provide invaluable insights, if we remember that they don't offer a full explanation or comprehensive understanding of when or why frames sway us. Taking a thoughtful, piecemeal approach – incorporating elements from seemingly contradictory studies – can be quite useful. A piecemeal approach entails, for instance, identifying specific claims that scholars have made that resemble one or the other approach, although this need not mean that these scholars could be categorized within that approach.

To understand why people and societies care about framing at all, we need to look beyond the obvious and explicit level. An avenue that may seem a bit far afield is often rewarding when trying to understand why human cultures, distinct as they are, share so many characteristics. The opening pages of this book have offered a taste of this approach. You will notice that many of the examples of reframing given throughout the book don't involve explicit framing discussions among the people involved – in these cases, people didn't mention or weren't asked whether it matters to them how the issue in question is framed. This aligns with findings that suggest we're most often swayed, consciously or not, by framings subtly implied in social situations.[16] A fascinating question follows: if our susceptibility to framing goes back to our evolutionary past before verbal communication, does that mean our capacity to be influenced by how a constant issue is framed predates even human-like consciousness and self-reflection?

For a long time, researchers in the human sciences assumed framing was a uniquely human thing. This assumption isn't exactly a compliment. After all, wouldn't it be nice if 'it's complicated' – people's standard phrase of resignation, particularly when dealing with teenage squabbles fraught with framing dilemmas where the actual issue is either invisible or non-existent – was exclusive to our species? In our less sympathetic moments, we might wonder if animals, with their less complex social structures, are spared from such energetically costly nonsense. To find out, we could turn to our animal kin – the chimpanzees and bonobo apes.

In a series of experiments, apes were given a choice between varying 'framed' fruit servings or a fixed number of peanuts. In a 'positive' setting, they were initially offered one piece of fruit, which was occasionally bumped up to two. In a 'negative' setting, they started with two pieces of fruit, which sometimes dwindled down to one. Both the 'positive' and 'negative' frames offered the same quantity of fruit. Regardless of the framing, the amount of fruit remained constant.[17] Despite this, the apes responded differently in the two settings. In the 'positive' frame, they chose fruit over peanuts. In the 'negative' frame, they chose peanuts over fruit. This suggests that apes, like us, are prone to changing preferences based on framings, even when the substantive conditions are identical. On hearing this, you might wonder what the average human would prefer in a similarly framed situation. As for me, I'm pretty sure I'd choose the same as the apes – getting one delicious piece of fruit as default with the occasional delightful surprise of a second piece. In Chapter 3, we'll find out precisely why the apes and I aren't outliers in this regard.

Each of the two standard approaches to understanding framing, namely 'reality speaks for itself' and 'framing is everything', has distinct merits that will be discussed throughout the book. However, their limitations in explaining, for instance, the universal and even cross-species limitations as to what types of framings may make a difference or not in specific situations, call for a different perspective. The way frames subtly guide us, often without our conscious realization, hints that framing may have evolved before language and full human consciousness. This two-million-year-old genetic legacy we have as collaborative hunter-gatherers, predated by fifty million years as social primates living in groups,[18] not only creates opportunities for but also imposes some critical constraints on reframing. I label this approach 'framing needs ancestral resonance'.

To indulge further in metaphor, the constraints and potentials of framing are tied not just to current or a-few-centuries-old cultures where the framings occur. Frames need to go beyond merely aligning with contemporary cultural traits. They require a connection to humanity's collective ancestral memory, the 'ancestral resonance' of this third approach. I argue that deep-seated, age-old elements – 'screws' and 'glues' – facilitate our learning and adaptation to various environments through a genetic foundation grounded in our long ancestral lineage.

Understanding why these ancestral screws and glues are crucial in framing can be better grasped by analysing the primary survival needs of our prehistoric forebears. Oliver Scott Curry, an evolutionary anthropologist, has identified what he argues is the paramount capacity among humans and most other higher primates: fostering and conforming to diverse types of cooperation in various social settings. In fact, the entire reason why all cultures have morality, and why some forms of morality are shared universally even across cultures that have never met, is that moral sentiments are crucial for advanced, social cooperation. Scott Curry calls this the principle of 'morality-as-cooperation'.[19] The role of framing is often to signal moral expectations and to obscure deviations from these expectations regarding, for instance, individuals' rights and duties in various collaborative setups, and the repercussions that follow moral deviations. Given the plethora of issues and potential resolutions to cooperative hurdles, a myriad of moralities has emerged. To dissect this further, Scott Curry has employed evolutionary game theory to outline seven distinct forms of cooperation, each presenting its own unique difficulties and solutions:

(1) the allocation of resources to kin; (2) coordination to mutual advantage; (3) social exchange; and conflict resolution through contests featuring (4) hawkish displays of dominance and (5) dove-ish displays of submission; (6) division of disputed resources; and (7) recognition of possession.[20]

These forms of cooperation are crucial to people, forming the foundation for deeply ingrained moral elements tied to our emotions:

(1) family values, (2) group loyalty, (3) reciprocity, (4) heroism, (5) deference, (6) fairness and (7) property rights.[21]

Scott Curry illustrates how moral elements can merge similarly to physical atoms, creating 'moral molecules'. These originate from the intersection of different cooperative solutions. For example, the meeting of kinship and mutualism generates an expectation of brotherhood. Likewise, the merging of mutualism and ownership brings forth the anticipation of collective ownership. Scott Curry and his colleagues explore how different types of cooperation, and their interplays require unique solutions and foster varying expectations.

To illustrate this, consider the uncomfortable silence following your question to your mother-in-law about the cost of dinner ingredients at a family gathering, with you intending to pay your share. This situation presents a conflict between familial cooperation and the market exchange principle typically applied in distant cooperation settings. Similarly, the quick dismissal as 'absurd' of a US president's proposition to purchase Greenland from Denmark showcases an unreconciled clash of different cooperative principles.

In relation to framing, my argument is that these structures and forms of morality and cooperation also shape the constraints on framing. Such framing vibrates in correspondence with our ancestral past, linking our current social cooperation scenarios with the ingrained, genetic 'memories' of past cooperative forms and associated moral anticipations. Reality signifies the specific intertwining between culture, genetics, biology, personality, and specific situations we find ourselves in. Of course, there are immense cultural differences across times and places, even within specific cultures. Yet, as I will show, cultural variation is far from endless. Separate cultures that, on the surface, may appear vastly different often, if we look deeper, share a remarkable similarity in cultural *form*, an aspect frequently overlooked in the social sciences, not least in previous studies of framing processes.[22] By suggesting that framing needs ancestral resonance, I emphasize that successful framing among us who live today must consider the collective memory of our species and translate it to the context we find ourselves in, or vice versa. As you shall see, this contrasts profoundly with both the previous approaches of 'reality speaks for itself' and 'framing is everything'.

Understanding the framing phenomenon demands a broader scientific foundation than the earlier methods provide. This book aims to integrate vital insights from natural, social, and economic sciences to fully grasp the art of framing.

Part I

Making bad seem good – and other frame texturing

Some years ago, cinemas all over Sweden showed a commercial for the classic Swedish sandwich spread Kalles caviar – a simple, pink spread with something of a 'distinctive taste'. In the commercial, a pasty Swedish marketer travels around the world trying to generate international demand for this peculiar food product. He stands in a Tokyo street and offers passers-by small hors d'oeuvres with Kalles caviar neatly curled on top. A woman takes a bite but finds the caviar so disgusting that not even her polite Japanese manners can hide her nausea when she backs up and bows. In another episode of the commercial, the influencer visits Venice Beach, California, calling out for people to come and try. Many mumble excitedly, 'Oh, caviar!' Their thoughts, of course, go to Russian or Iranian luxuries. After tasting, however, the hippies, businesspeople, and beach bums of all stripes grimace and say things like, 'You can't give this to people! This ain't real food, man!' The Swedish marketer says in his broken English, 'This is very popular in Sweden'. A woman in elegant business dress responds, 'Well, it ain't popular here, hun'.[1]

This seemingly innocuous caviar commercial embodies the most elemental frame property: I refer to this as the framing texture, which can be rough or smooth. It is the instantaneous signalling that frames can provide about whether something or someone is good or bad, positive or negative, safe or risky, reliable or unreliable. Or, in the case of sandwich spreads, delicious or repulsive. Now, imagine a keen Martian observing us from space, trying to predict and decipher what and who influences us and how we interact with each other.

Let's say the Martian is blissfully ignorant of the complexities of human interaction. In this case, it would predict that people invariably avoid things and people associated with rough frames and are always attracted to the smooth ones. This is indeed a common pattern in our life choices, but not always the rule. Human behaviour and influence are not always straightforward. Since Adam and Eve defied God, our unpredictability has made us more intriguing than angels. Human action is shaped by a multitude of factors ranging from individual personality traits, experiences, and eccentricities, to financial situations and cultural norms. Consequently, framing of what's good or bad impacts different people and groups in various ways. In the Kalles caviar ads, the typically positive Swedish frame is reinterpreted negatively by international palates, which paradoxically *enhances* consumer interest in the product, but only in Sweden.

My distinction between 'smooth' and 'rough' framing textures stems from a particularly unfortunate episode in scientific history. The terminology hints at a series of controversial and ethically dubious mid-twentieth-century experiments. Baby rhesus monkeys were isolated from their mothers for months and provided with artificial surrogate mothers – one smooth, soft, and warm, but without a milk bottle, and the other made of rough metal wire but with a milk bottle. Despite the latter offering food, the baby monkeys clung to the smooth 'cloth-mother' almost all the time. The baby monkeys only came to the wire mother for food and immediately turned back to the cloth-mother, thus sacrificing their control over the food attached to the wire mother. This demonstrated a fundamental need for comfort and contact over sustenance.[2] It was this realization that drove the scientific community to reconsider the importance of social and emotional connections for psychosocial well-being. Most mothers could have told these scientists so beforehand if they'd only asked, but that's another story.

Is the baby monkeys' prioritization of comfort over material necessity rational? Not if you assume that the only thing that matters is securing food. From that perspective, it seems irrational, just as the worldwide revulsion for Swedish caviar ironically sparking an increase in its popularity among Swedes appears irrational. Why do we, from daily life to world politics, respond so diversely to the textures of our situations that a smooth frame can make us willingly risk our material safety? And why, in other instances, are we drawn to rough frames? The answer lies in the world of social influence that extends beyond mere irrationality,[3] or issue rationality.[4] The upcoming three chapters will explore the nuances of influencing others through frame texturing and how to exert more control over how we are influenced by similar framing properties.

2

Why is our frame smooth and theirs so often rough?

Judged by their frame texture

Purchasing a sandwich spread *because* foreigners find it disgusting or, as we've seen among monkeys, sacrificing control over food for the sake of physical contact are but two examples of the many ways our rapid and instinctive perception of reality – what I call the texture of frames – can guide the actions of people as well as non-human primates.[1] But why do we place such an extraordinary emphasis on these frames, often overlooking the nuanced techniques of the people or things they encompass? The answer lies in the deep-rooted human instinct to differentiate between 'us' and 'them'. You place just about anyone in a functional MRI scanner and flash images of various faces before their eyes – each image for less than a twentieth of a second – and you'll see that their brain responds distinctly differently to 'them-faces' compared to 'us-faces'.[2] Outside the sterile environment of a lab, we exhibit a remarkable ability to identify whether someone hails from our community. We pick up on the dialects, the nuances of language, the subtle gestures, preferences, and the slightest variations in attire.[3] We're so adept at this that it's reasonable to believe that this skill has played a crucial role in our ancestors' survival throughout history.

This impulse and ability to distinguish between 'us' and 'them' allow for a healthy curiosity about those who are different from us, a quality that has fostered immense collaboration and created networks across group boundaries. In this sense, the distinction between 'us' and 'them' is not only harmless but also adaptive and enriching for both 'us' and 'them'. 'Us' represents our 'in-groups', the people with whom we share a bond of identity and loyalty, while 'them' signifies those outside our in-groups, the people we – at least initially – don't particularly identify with or feel connected to.[4] Amid all curiosity, the framing textures around 'us' and 'them' often serve as cues, hinting at who is probably trustworthy, whom we could probably influence (even manipulate), and whom to distance ourselves from in order to maintain our social standing. At the heart of this process lies a fundamental need to avoid being betrayed and deceived. Hardly anything triggers our emotions – particularly anger and sadness – as intensely as the sensation of being misled, tricked, or deceived.[5] As I will explain in depth in Chapter 8, the awful feeling of being betrayed or deceived has even been shown to make teenage boys significantly reduce their junk food intake. The frame retexturing of junk food that the researchers helped the boys to internalize serves as a reminder of how powerful framing effects can be – for better or worse.

The most sorrowful moments that have been etched onto the canvas of human history stem from a deep-seated trait we seem to carry in our genes – the propensity to draw categorical and prejudicial lines between 'us' and 'them'. However, before we delve into the shadowy depths of such divisions, it's worth pausing to consider an enlightening idea about how we might go about managing the more harmful relics of our evolutionary lineage. The source is not me, but the nineteenth-century biologist and anthropologist Thomas Huxley, a devotee of Charles Darwin and a luminary in his own right:

> Let us understand, once for all, that the ethical progress of society depends, not on ... running away from [any process in nature that causes harm and suffering] – but in combating it.[6]

Huxley's wisdom, penned in 1893, holds true today. But we have been slow to take it to heart, to weave it into the fabric of our society, especially in places where the wounds of division run deep. Consider the often-harmful narratives seen in the polarization and animosity between groups that define themselves along ideological or ethnic lines. If we are to truly absorb Huxley's proposal, it's not enough simply to wish these conditions away or narrow their causes down to one single element – be it immigration or resistance to facts – or indeed to dismiss them as irrational or unfathomable phenomena. Rather, our first task is to comprehend the long, evolutionary roots of why groups have continuously, but not always, framed each other in such rough ways throughout history. Of particular interest is why we possess this instinctive drive to see ourselves and our group – whoever we may be – in a favourable, smooth frame, while we are predisposed to place 'them' – whoever they might be – in a rough frame. So, let's try to unravel this mystery. Once we have done so, we can turn our attention to some surprisingly positive outliers, before exploring more tangible solutions to counter this detrimental practice of applying the categorical and normative 'we' versus 'they' framing.

Many scholars have provided ample evidence that the foundational 'us' versus 'them' framing is not value neutral but boils down to a smooth texture for 'us' and a rough one for 'them'.[7] It's a bias that seems quite predictable when considering the high levels of deadly intergroup violence among hunter-gatherer societies, starkly exceeding the conflict within the groups. This violence often occurred in the scramble for resources and, among men, competition for women. In an interdisciplinary effort, archaeologists have suggested that between 16 and 64 per cent of men in these societies met their end in such conflict.[8] Scholars studying human evolution make a compelling case that our species has spent a major part of its existence in small groups, living as hunter-gatherers.[9] Consequently, we've evolved to prioritize the issues and dangers that were most prevalent and perilous in hunter-gatherer societies. For instance, exclusion from one's social community or group was one of the gravest risks. It left you exposed to the high likelihood of violence from rival groups and deprived you of the collective protection of your own group. Evolutionary anthropologists and psychologists argue that this, in essence, is why 'we' so often treat 'them' differently from how we treat those within our own circles.

What does this say about the oversimplified framing that divides our social reality into 'us' versus 'them'? Does it offer clarity, or does it muddle our understanding? It might be comforting to conclude that these simplifications are solely obfuscating and wholly irrational. But that may not be the whole truth. Consider the disproportionately higher risk throughout history of being slain by people from the out-group – 'them' – than by those within your in-group – 'us'. This genetic predisposition to be suspicious of out-groups likely saved countless ancestors from a premature demise.[10] In a sense, this oversimplification might have provided clarity, following the old adage of 'better safe than sorry'. But it's also true that this 'us' versus 'them' perspective often clouds our view. It threatens to make us overlook the subtleties of 'the others'. It may prevent us from seeing the potential for relationships that can form from mutual respect and reciprocity, extending far beyond our traditional group. Moreover, in contemporary urban societies, where in-groups and out-groups intersect daily, there are compelling moral reasons to challenge our tendency to assign a rough texture to 'them' and a smooth one to 'us'.

Still, as Huxley tried to tell us in his quote above, we need to learn about the basic human constitution – also the less flattering parts – if we are to make ourselves and society better. For instance, it is common, particularly in stressful situations, to judge people from other groups with suspicion and prejudice. Take, for instance, the momentous event that unfolded in Paris on 15 April 2019 that would captivate the world for months to come. The iconic Notre Dame Cathedral, a beloved symbol of the city, was engulfed in flames, its sacred structure under threat. In the face of this tragedy, French president Emmanuel Macron expressed his sorrow, lamenting the loss of 'this part of us'. Naturally, the question on everyone's mind was: what caused the fire? Throughout history, a principle has guided investigations into such incidents. Originating from the renowned English philosopher and monk William of Ockham, commonly known as Occam, this principle is known as 'Occam's razor'. Occam's razor dictates that when faced with multiple explanations or solutions to a problem, the simplest and least speculative option should be favoured before considering more elaborate assumptions. In the case of the Notre Dame fire, many fire safety experts asserted that the simplest and least speculative explanation was an accident. The cathedral's attic, where the fire originated, was under renovation at the time. Fire engineers believe that an electrical short circuit or a discarded cigarette butt were likely causes. However, in the age of social media, conspiracy theories quickly emerged and spread globally. Baseless claims circulated, implicating the French government, Islamist groups, or even the Jewish community as being responsible for the fire. Theories also suggested a coordinated effort behind the fire in Notre Dame and those in other Western churches around the same time.[11] It's fair to say that people who unreflectively assumed the claims must be true had been tricked by various explanatory frames, unable to see and weigh up which among the different possible explanations were likely to be the valid ones.

This leads to a crucial question: what defines the 'simplest' explanation? It appears we have two interpretations. The fire engineers point towards the technically simplest explanations. In contrast, those blaming various external groups seem to favour an explanation that aligns with their preconceived social and cultural biases. In this case, certain far-right groups harboured suspicions towards Muslims, Jews, and the French government. Although I'd bet that Occam would lean towards the fire engineers' interpretation, it's clear that Occam's razor needs careful specification to prevent it from merely endorsing the most convenient accusation levelled by an in-group against an out-group. His principle, therefore, demands that we, like the fire engineers, place our awareness and reflection *between* different possible diagnostic framings.[12] Equipped with this inter-frame awareness, we have a better chance at identifying the most probable and straightforward explanation.

When we frame our own group with a smooth surface and paint the other group with a rough one, it often leads to the instinctive perception of a zero-sum game. We see their loss as our gain and vice versa. It's challenging to overlook the intense and, admittedly, gratifying feeling that many of us experience – *Schadenfreude*. Through experiments and brain scanning, researchers have demonstrated how this emotion, which causes changes in various brain regions, can be evoked.[13] The recipe for *Schadenfreude* is simple: frame people from an out-group in a story, plant prejudiced notions about them, and witness a couple of misfortunes befall them. The result? *Schadenfreude*!

Studies have also revealed that, on average, claims made by individuals with non-native accents are perceived as less credible compared to those with native accents.[14] Inspired by this finding, we can note that similar feelings of mistrust and sceptical reservations related to what seems alien and unnatural often arise between groups with opposing views on food production and the promotion or avoidance of certain foods. For instance, advocates of organic vegetable and fruit production have long used these feelings to argue against conventional and genetically modified foods. In a related context, it's hardly surprising that the meat and dairy industries, with their interest in ensuring the consistent consumption of their products, have chosen the same, ancestrally rooted framing strategy when they've invested heavily in some of the world's prime advertising slots, such as those during the Super Bowl broadcast in the United States, trying to evoke the same kind of mistrust and scepticism towards plant-based and lab-grown proteins as towards other unfamiliar things and people. In one such TV advert depicting a school spelling competition, an adult judge informs the contestant, 'Your word is "methyl cellulose".' The young girl attempts to spell it but, perhaps due to unfamiliarity more than complexity, pauses to ask, 'Can you define it?' The judge responds, 'It's a chemical laxative used in synthetic meat.' The camera pans to the girl's mother, her face a blend of disbelief and distaste. A similar sequence unfolds with another girl tasked with 'propylene glycol'. Upon faltering and her subsequent enquiry, 'What's that?', she learns it's 'a chemical used in anti-freeze and synthetic meats', evoking a disapproving reaction from her mother. Then, a confident boy with glasses effortlessly spells 'bacon': b-a-c-o-n. Concluding the ad, a disembodied female voice resonates with the takeaway: 'If you can't spell it or pronounce it, maybe you shouldn't be eating it.'[15]

Another manifestation of how we view our own group and our way of doing things through a smooth frame, while perceiving other groups and conventions with a rough one, is that people tend to attribute their own group's failures to external circumstances or coincidences. However, when it comes to other groups, similar failures are framed within a rough texture of incompetence, poor character, and so on.[16] In essence, to comprehend the significance of frame texture and the vast social dynamics between 'them' and 'us', it would be a grave error to underestimate our frequent use of rough framing when it comes to other groups. So, let's take a deeper look at it, before we delve into some signs of hope amid this seemingly bleak panorama.

Our heightened sensitivity to rough framing arises from the fact that all organisms, including humans, have a need to protect themselves from dangers such as infections and toxins. As I explored the concept of reframing between positive and negative judgements, it became apparent just how closely intertwined the value-laden binaries of 'contaminating-healthy' and 'poisonous-reliable' are with how different groups categorize themselves in opposition to others.

In his book *Behave*, neurologist and biologist Robert Sapolsky elucidates that conflictual situations can provoke not only anger and hatred but also disgust. The ideas, values, and habits of other groups, and sometimes even the individuals themselves, are perceived as repugnant, rotten, and revolting. Such reactions often persist, regardless of whether we truly believe that people from the other group are physically healthy and hygienic in their daily lives. And in an episode of the podcast *Philosophy Bites*, the philosopher Robert B. Talisse described how he had seen this play out:

> When we [Talisse and his colleague, Scott] raise this kind of issue about how we demonise the other side as a surprise to the audience of philosophers, or at least academics, an audience that will skew liberal, we pull out a 'Make America Great Again' Trump red hat, and dare somebody in the audience to put it on his or her head. And the reaction to the hat is as if we pulled out a petri dish containing a very dangerous virus, and asked somebody to sniff it or something. They're disgusted, they see it as something tainted, as something that is dirty, as something that its presence in the room seems objectionable. Often, nobody puts it on their head. Scott and I say: 'It's just a hat, people, it's just a red hat!'[17]

So, where does this sense of revulsion originate? According to Sapolsky, the answer lies deep within a brain region called the insula. This ancient part of our brain evolved long before the existence of humanity and is responsible for triggering our feelings of disgust in response to certain smells and tastes, particularly when they signify something poisonous or rotten. The insula acts as a sensory alarm, alerting us to potential dangers. Interestingly, these same emotions can also manifest in social situations that we perceive as morally repugnant, such as instances of sadism or lynching, especially when they involve individuals or groups with whom we identify.[18]

The fact that situations and people perceived as morally abhorrent can elicit physical sensations of disgust and nausea offers insight into the powerful impact of metaphors related to out-groups. Take, for example, the Nazi children's book *The Poisonous Mushroom*, which employed subconscious associations to evoke feelings of disgust, hatred, and toxicity.[19] The poisonous mushroom served as a symbol for the Jewish people, exemplifying a frame texturing that aimed to oversimplify and distort the understanding of non-Jewish German children regarding Jews.

In a series of experiments conducted in 2009, led by researchers from Canada and the United States, participants were asked to read a popular science article on immunology, focusing on bacteria, viruses, and parasites. Weeks later, these individuals exhibited less favourable attitudes toward immigration compared to a control group that had read an entirely unrelated text, such as a guide on bicycle repair.[20] People seem to be influenced by metaphors without even being consciously aware of it.

Threatened by similarity

Rough framing textures are often employed by one group to surround others, while smooth textures typically convey a sense of togetherness and similarity within our own group. Does this mean that the more we emphasize the differences between ourselves and others, the rougher and more negative our framing of them becomes?

Nowadays, there is a widespread consensus among biologists and related fields that racial distinctions are primarily social constructions. Genetic variation within races is, for the most part, as significant as the variation between races.[21] Yet, over centuries, people have made unfounded assumptions about essential differences, including psychological and 'moral' disparities, between individuals of different races.[22] These baseless assumptions have led to hierarchies of values, often determining who is deemed more or less human. Naturally, those placed at the bottom have been subjected to the roughest, spikiest framing.[23]

Yet, it is not entirely accurate to claim that the degree of difference from our own group solely determines the framing texture we assign to others. The prevailing understanding is that the most extreme and rough framing occurs when one group portrays another as less than human. Accordingly, this type of framing fuels the most intense intergroup animosity, implying that we and they are essentially different species. This perspective, commonly held by scholars and emphasized in public debates, suggests that if we can simply recognize our shared humanity and focus on our similarities rather than our differences, we will be less inclined to hate and harm one another. Deep-seated conflicts would become far less common if we acknowledged that all groups are part of one universal human family.

Take a moment and ponder this. When we look at those we deem different, does the extent of their 'otherness' really determine how we treat them? Is the line we draw in the sand one that decides whether we regard a group as 'human' or 'somewhat less than human', the ultimate decider of our behaviour towards them? Not quite, argue the psychologists Harriet Over and Florence Enock.[24] Backed by empirical evidence, they contend that the lens through which we view these out-groups certainly shapes our interactions. Yet, the animosity often lies not in their foreignness but in our penchant for oversimplifying them into caricatures. We succumb to stereotypes, reducing a group's rich tapestry of individual identities to a singular, essential trait that defines them. But here's where things get interesting. What if we see a bit of ourselves in them? Over and

Enock propose that the inkling of shared humanity could be as terrifying as the stark differences. The harsher we treat an out-group, the more we feel threatened by them, precisely because we recognize them as humans, just like 'us'.

Another psychology professor, Susan Fiske, introduces a pivotal idea to our understanding of 'them' – their competence. Think about it: we often view 'them' as loyal to their own kind, and, therefore, potentially unfriendly towards us. In Fiske's terms, that makes them seem 'cold' to us. Since they're just as human as we are, they have the same, or even better, abilities to achieve their goals – goals that might clash with ours. That can make us more anxious, especially if they seem more competent and thus a direct threat to us. Fiske points to the unfair stereotypes often aimed at Asian immigrants in North America, who are seen as being successful in education and finance but still face negative perceptions. Other examples include Jews in Europe and Indo-Pakistani citizens under Idi Amin's regime in Uganda, among others. This challenges the common notion that viewing another group as a different 'species' is either a necessary or sufficient condition for severe mistreatment. The minority groups weren't viewed as *less* than human. Instead, they were regarded as competent humans, ones who coldly competed for the same interests as the majority population in a zero-sum game that only 'we' or 'they' can win. It's this perception that led to the appalling treatment of these minority groups.

In an entirely different aspect of life, it's even more clear that the differences between 'us' and 'them' don't necessarily escalate the risk of negativity and aggression towards the others. I'm referring to people's relationships with their pets. As Harriet Over highlights, our pets are not just significantly different from us; truthfully, they are intellectually inferior to humans.[25] Despite this, people typically treat their pets with kindness and affection, often willingly spending considerable amounts of money – sometimes to a surprising extent – on their well-being. It appears, then, that a pet's status as different and less than human is neither a sufficient nor necessary condition for us to treat them poorly.

Why is our frame smooth and theirs rough?

Al and Greta

Think of frame texturing as the spectrum between really smooth and extremely rough, as a tool to sway both the people in our group and those in others. The best part? Fortunately, it can sometimes create powerful effects without stirring up hostility. This idea shines when you compare two prominent climate activists of our time: the former US Vice-President Al Gore and the young Swedish activist Greta Thunberg. For this example, the focus is solely on their climate-related work, excluding their activism for other causes. Both Gore and Thunberg have steered clear of excessively rough rhetoric when dealing with their critics. This was true even in Thunberg's unforgettable 'How dare you?' speech at the UN climate action summit in New York in 2019.[26] Like Gore, Thunberg sets up a 'we' versus 'you', not a 'we' versus 'they'. However, the frame texturing they have brought to the climate issue through their admirable work varies greatly. I realized this while exploring the children's section of a nearby bookshop a few years ago. There was one book that stood out unmistakably. Its title was *Greta and the Giants*. The cover displayed a cartoon of a girl, about 12, with braided hair, standing with her legs apart, holding a sign that proclaimed 'Strike for Climate'. Behind her, two large, shadowy figures were peeking out from behind tree trunks. The giants – one woman, one man – had small, glowing eyes oddly placed on their faces. In the greenery, another child with a placard, a fox, and a mouse seemed to be rooting for Greta.[27] The book seemed like such a no-brainer. Had British author Zoe Tucker not penned it, someone else would've. And they did. Many children's books, as well as those aimed at adults, have since been written about Greta Thunberg.

Certainly, Al Gore has written books and had books written about him. His *An Inconvenient Truth* was a wake-up call about the climate crisis that sparked significant conversations and actions. But to my knowledge, there isn't a children's book about Al Gore. The reason might not simply be that Greta Thunberg was still a child herself when she began making global headlines for her activism. Al Gore, 55 years her senior, is also a well-known figure. However, it's typically adults who are celebrated and lauded, even in children's books, when they make sincere efforts to better our world. But would it be harder to create a similar buzz with a children's book about Al Gore as compared to Greta Thunberg? Here's my humble attempt:

> Once upon a time, in a land called the United States, there lived a kind-hearted man named Al. Al had once held an important position as the Vice-President, which meant he was the helper of the country's leader. He did his job really well and almost became the president himself, missing it by just a few votes!
>
> But Al had an even bigger dream. He cared deeply about nature and the world around him. He loved the trees, the rivers, and all the animals that lived in the wild. One thing that worried him a lot was something called climate change. He knew that Earth was in danger because of all the pollution and harm that people were causing.
>
> So, Al decided to do something about it. He left his fancy job in politics and started a new mission. He wanted to bring together powerful people from all around the world to work together and fight against climate change. He believed that by joining forces, they could make a big difference and protect our beautiful planet.
>
> Luckily, Al had many friends in important places. He knew lots of people in politics and business. This meant he had a big network of friends who could help him in his mission. Whenever there was a meeting about climate change, Al would hop on his private jet and travel quickly to be there. He wanted to make sure he could have the biggest impact possible in reducing pollution and saving the planet.
>
> Al's heart was full of hope and determination. Al believed that by working together, people could make a real difference and protect the beautiful world we live in. And so, he travelled the globe, inspiring others to join him in the fight against climate change.
>
> Thanks to his hard work in teaching people, speaking up for Earth, and encouraging everyone to take care of our planet, many more people now understand how important it is to fight climate change and keep our world beautiful and safe.
>
> And that is the tale of Al, the former Vice-President turned climate champion, who used his influence and determination to make our planet a better place for all. The end.

While it may seem a little unfair given Gore's pioneering contribution to climate advocacy, anyone could be forgiven for questioning the excitement levels of a publisher asked to promote that children's book. It's not really the content, the idea, or the true message that separates Gore from Thunberg. Instead, the differences lie in their respective contexts and settings, elements that neither of them has much control over. The framing texture comes to be organically, shaped by who they are as individuals. Age, their places within the corridors of power, their personal histories, economic statuses, images, genders, and appearances collectively create the unique conditions for their framing textures that incite and motivate various demographics to act.

Greta Thunberg's smooth framing texture extends from herself to 'we', those without substantial political or economic clout (despite her now holding quite a bit of influence). 'We' includes the youth, a demographic she's a part of. As a young person, she can echo the worries of her peers about the future with unparalleled authenticity. But Thunberg's 'we' also includes those middle-aged and older individuals without much economic or political power. Conversely, the 'you' category encompasses those with the economic and political authority to effect societal change and reduce our climate impact. She paints this group as consisting of short-term thinkers blinded by power, with whom we need to forcefully communicate the urgency of climate change, demanding a more aggressive and inventive use of political and economic tools to lessen the climate burden.

My focus on the potential of children's books is not just about the youth. It's more about how children's books are closest to the narrative structures most intrinsic to us as humans. Successful children's books usually frame different characters in ways akin to folk-tales and religious stories. These stories are easy to grasp and spread quickly. Research indicates that many elements of folk-tales and mythologies have independently 'sprung up' in different times and places, suggesting an evolutionary basis to these narrative structures. Fairy tales touch something deep within us. I would argue – and many would agree – that we are inherently drawn to the basic conflicts in these archetypal stories. They provide us with valuable insights on whom we can trust, whom we can work with, whom we should be cautious of, and whom we might need to press harder, so they don't exploit us or damage our world.[28]

Making bad seem good – frame texturing

The temptation to conserve conflict

People tend to feel at ease with binary contrasts, the black versus white, David versus Goliath type scenarios. These easy-to-grasp divisions allow us to understand complex situations, albeit simply. Yet, this can be a stumbling block when people need to encourage broader collaboration and problem-solving involving both 'us' and 'them' as equal partners. In these situations, anyone involved in such endeavours needs to acknowledge the instinctive discomfort that arises when people consider dissolving the lines between 'us' and 'them'. As welcome as universal resolutions and even consensus might be, Thomas Huxley's advice should be kept in mind, namely not to 'run away from', or ignore people's discomfort and fear that 'we' and 'they' might blur into an indistinct, watered-down 'everyone'.

The power of polarization is as intriguing as it is intense. Groups with polarized views often seem so entrenched in their positions that one could forgive outsiders for thinking that they find a sense of safety and special bonding in this clear division. A candidate example is the ongoing tensions between Christian and LGBTQ+ rights groups. Over the years, each side has developed its own unique way of presenting its arguments. As we'll see in Chapter 11, some religious groups seem to be stuck in a view that relies heavily on moral politics. They often use cultural stereotypes and religious beliefs instead of hard facts to justify their stance on LGBTQ+ issues. On the other hand, LGBTQ+ rights groups use a strategy that focuses heavily on identity. They see LGBTQ+ individuals as a marginalized population that deserves special protections under the law because they believe they are constantly under pressure from mainstream society, being labelled as deviant, abnormal, or immoral.

Could it be that the members of both these religious and LGBTQ+ rights groups are victims of manipulation through framing, be it internal or external? Are they caught in a state of unawareness about their potential to change, both within their own views and in their portrayal of the other group? Is it possible for them to ease those harsh perceptions, even slightly, without sacrificing their basic values and identity?

Not only in these specific groups but also in many other conflicts between opposing groups it can be seen that each group seems to find a sense of security in adhering to its own categorical and identity-based frame. This reinforces their internal unity and creates a barrier that hinders progress towards mutual understanding. This situation mirrors the classic 'us' versus 'them' scenario, where each side clings to its narrative for comfort, leaving the tension of disagreement unresolved. While such impasses might seem safe, it's worth considering whether self-deception and unawareness are blinding those involved to the potential for navigating between their perspectives. Experience from other cases suggests that groups can transition from talking past each other to discussing the same issue. This is a crucial step in finding solutions, whether through consensus, compromise, or even concession by one side. In the following chapters, we will explore how this transition can be achieved.

3

Sanctifying sinners and sinnifying saints

Smoothing their frame of us

In many cases, we adopt a stance that is either wholly positive or negative, even when it's evident that the issue at hand has multiple facets. Take, for instance, the introduction of vegan products into a market dominated by animal-based goods. Since the turn of the century, we've seen a trend of meat producers, restaurants, and even shoemakers that were traditionally animal-product-centric taking a turn towards plant-based offerings. How do people and organizations perceive this shift? I initially guessed that non-vegans and non-vegetarians would either maintain their usual consumption of animal-based products or perhaps, prompted by curiosity, switch a few of their animal-based purchases to vegan alternatives from the same companies. And on the other side, I thought that vegan consumers and organizations would react with cautious optimism at mainstream firms introducing vegan products. While this may hold true for some individuals and organizations, the broader landscape proved to be far more complex.

Moral show-off and suspicion

Let's be honest, few of us stand on the front lines of moral innovation or blow the whistle on unethical practices. We prefer to hang out in the safe zone, sticking to our routines and taking cues from those who live similar lives. The same holds for businesses and organizations – they naturally align with others who share the same cultural values, steering clear of moral outliers. The bedrock of cooperation, trust, and predictability is this ethical calibration. Stray too far from the moral code of those you relate to, and you risk social division and exclusion. So, how do we react when someone or a company decides to strive for higher moral ground, aim for less environmental impact, or cut down on animal cruelty in production? To an unbiased observer, say an alien from Mars, this should be applauded – they're taking steps, making sacrifices to make the world a little better, right?

Companies that can make the most of these small moral strides sometimes get to enjoy the applause. There's something marketing experts call the 'halo effect' that comes into play here. Many companies initially steeped in the animal industry have widened their product lines to include vegan goods. Consumers have often rewarded this shift with a surge in sales of these new products. Now, vegan alternatives may still represent a small portion of these companies' total offerings, but their popularity is growing. Oddly enough, these companies often see an uptick in their traditional, animal-based product sales as well. Introducing vegan alternatives not only brings new customers into the fold but also prompts existing customers to purchase more of the traditional products. It is as if including vegan products creates a smoother, positive framing of the entire company and its entire assortment. UK businesses such as the restaurant chain Leon, bakery chain Greggs, and even the shoe company Dr. Martens have experienced this halo effect after introducing vegan products.[1] A bit too generous of the consumers, some might argue.

But as a rule, we're not easily impressed when people or companies signal that their moral standards are higher than those of others. Becoming a better person or company isn't a walk in the park, especially if you're trying to do it quickly. This is evident in the mixed responses of the vegan community to companies traditionally associated with animal products introducing vegan options. Sure, some vegans appreciate the effort, but others view these initiatives with scepticism, even anger.[2] When Burger King and KFC added plant-based burgers to their UK menus, an animal rights activist was quoted in the *Guardian* as saying, 'They're trying to buy us off with these products and pretending they're our friends'.[3] That last word, 'friends', is key here. Animal rights groups are comfortable in their stance against producers and restaurants known for their animal-based products. When these companies try to smoothen their frame with modest attempts at ethical or environmental responsibility, it disrupts the narrative of the animal rights groups, making it harder for them to call out these companies for their actions. Despite the veneer of new, ethically conscious initiatives, critics contend that these companies remain the same old wolves in sheep's clothing, foes of animal welfare and ditto rights.

Interestingly, the vegan movement itself has not been immune to being seen as controversial and alarmingly smug. You might have heard the following joke already: 'How can you spot a vegan at a social gathering? Oh, don't worry! They'll tell you.' Vegans have weathered their fair share of criticisms and raised eyebrows, a situation that was vividly illustrated by an incident involving the British supermarket Waitrose. The editor of its food magazine, William Sitwell, abruptly found himself unemployed after he presumably jokingly suggested the idea of 'killing vegans one by one'. Veganism often rubs people up the wrong way, especially some folks who seem to be steering in the complete opposite direction. This has given rise to the trend of una-bashed meat-eating, sometimes marked by public demonstrations such as skinning and eating raw squirrel at a vegan market.[4]

Why do we often hold back from applauding the seemingly moral and sustainable efforts of other people or organizations? We're usu-ally ready to call out opportunists, wrongdoers, and deceivers – it's an instinctual part of our moral compass. Part of this compass is tied to a particular scepticism directed towards people and organizations that broadcast their moral righteousness, whether they lean to the right or the left. One aspect of the resistance towards veganism is that it challenges our notions of personal freedom, tradition, and culture. This allows for a negative reframing of veganism, an ideol-ogy often linked to animal welfare, environmental consciousness, and health benefits.

Virtue signalling is a delicate dance. Even among those who share our moral views, we're cautious when they seem overly eager to showcase their moral rectitude. Many of us can't help but cringe at the signals of prudery and moral superiority from certain 'friends' in social media. It becomes particularly distressing when it takes the form of humble bragging – when they admit a small 'sin' while simultaneously spotlighting more significant moral accomplishments, seeming to pretend they aren't virtue signalling. Consider the instance when your social media 'friend' posts something like this:

I have a confession. I just can't bring myself to use a composting toilet.

Underneath their apparent openness about these little environmental slip-ups, there's a masterful redirection towards their greater green efforts. With their vegan lifestyle, their solar-powered homes, or their determined stance against air travel, they seem to be doing everything else right. This can put us in a bit of a tight spot, for two main reasons. First, it makes us question our own environmental shortcomings. Are *we* doing enough? Are our minor offences forgivable, or must we step up our game?

The second part, and what's more pertinent to our discussion, is the irritation we feel towards their subtle boasting. It's like they've handed us a magnifying glass, and we can't help but scan for their hidden, more substantial moral failings. We start seeking their real, unvarnished story, hidden beneath the layers of their eco-bravado. Luckily, we can hit the pause button on their social media updates, just until we've mustered up a little more emotional resilience. Our frustration with those who toot their own moral horn taps into our inbuilt wariness of deception and betrayal. This survival instinct was critical in the intimate societies of our hunter-gatherer ancestors, as it was crucial to discern the authenticity of someone's supposed moral act. Were they really taking a risk? Did they genuinely sacrifice a substantial amount of time and resources? Or were they simply inflating the 'costs'? Missing such exaggerations could cost us dearly.[5]

In the sprawling communities of today, especially on social media platforms, this hypervigilance can backfire. We risk passing judgements that are overly harsh and largely unjust. The noise around someone's good deed can drown out the act itself.[6] In our eagerness to discern authenticity, we can end up reframing a moral act as something negative if it's presented with just a touch too much self-promotion. This tendency means that a minor, spontaneous act of goodness, if modestly presented, can often signal our benevolence more effectively than a grand gesture that lacks modesty and has less than convincing 'costliness'.[7]

But here's the upside for the unabashed moralists and virtue signallers among us. While our self-righteous showmanship may indeed raise eyebrows, we also manage to spread something incredibly valuable: awareness. In my book *Knowledge Resistance*, I talk extensively about how ignorance of specific injustices, such as harsh exploitation of workers, animals, or the environment, can provide a moral escape route. Signalling ignorance can help deflect accusations of selfishness when buying a product linked to such exploitation. But as these issues gain more attention, the 'I didn't know' defence becomes less believable. By publicly showcasing our moral virtues, we increase the odds that everyone will recognize the significance of the injustices we aim to alleviate. In doing so, we've got people to re-evaluate their normal frame, which they've been using up to this point to judge the appropriateness of their current habits. At the very least, there has been a slight spread of heightened awareness, either within or across these viewpoints, and it's more likely that others will start showing their understanding and concern. This chain reaction can lead to a rapid surge not just in virtue signalling but also in meaningful action, even if that entails significant personal sacrifices.[8]

Texturing 'us' as rough and 'them' as smooth

Sometimes, we might find ourselves mimicking the morally superior folks in our group, even if their self-righteousness is annoying. We still end up adopting some of their moral habits. In a sense, 'we' have thus adopted a self-critical, ironic, or even self-loathing framing. Can this ambivalence plunge even further, causing us to envelop ourselves in a rugged frame while draping others in one with smooth, or at least rounded, edges? Yes, it can. This dynamic takes on many forms, ranging from deeply distressing and painful experiences to instances of vanity and false humility.

There are disheartening cases where people, burdened by social, economic, and racial disadvantages, find themselves constantly influenced by the world around them, resulting in a profound sense of inferiority. In the 1940s, American psychologists Kenneth and Mamie Clark embarked on a ground-breaking series of studies known as the 'doll studies' to delve into this distressing phenomenon. These studies involved segregating children based on their race, creating distinct groups of African American and white children. This racial division was repeatedly implemented, with different sets of children participating in the study. All the children were provided with the opportunity to engage in play with both white and Black dolls while expressing their thoughts and opinions about the different dolls. What emerged from these studies was deeply troubling. Both the white and African American children consistently rated the white dolls more favourably. However, it was the African American children attending segregated schools who exhibited the most striking differences in their value judgements between the white and Black dolls. They displayed a distinct preference for white dolls, finding them endearing and attractive.[9] These findings lay bare the distressing consequences of social, economic, and racial disparities in misleading both white and Black children into accepting the prevalent racist frame texturing that surrounds white people with smoothness and Black people with roughness. This frame texturing damages the self-worth and sense of identity of the latter. We see a similar pattern in cases where some LGBTQ+ people vigorously campaign against their own rights or when certain individuals of Jewish heritage express sympathies towards Nazi ideologies.[10]

Now, take a moment and think about another type of instance, namely that when people in Western, industrialized, urban society – where a belief in that society's superiority has been the default throughout history – start pointing fingers at their own character and culture. There is undoubtedly an ethical risk involved when a group that considers itself superior to another group simultaneously idealizes the other group as more natural, authentic, and even wiser. Consider how the contempt towards and devaluation of women throughout history seems to have been closer to an idealized exaltation of women as almost divine than to respect as equals. But let's take a closer look at the myth of the 'noble savage', leaving the ethical question aside for a moment, and ask instead: is the myth compatible with reality? Picture being a privileged urbanite, belonging to the upper-middle or upper class, living in the throes of the city's rush in the early twentieth century, witnessing the inequities, the greed, and violence that play out around you. This may prompt you to question your own values and those of your society. It's in such moments that the idea of a noble savage can seem especially appealing. This notion is a generalization and glorification of past and present Indigenous peoples and their 'primitive' societies, an idea that makes you consider them more authentic, virtuous, and uncorrupted than yours. This idea has been in play since ancient times. Even well into the twentieth century, certain Western thinkers suggested that past and contemporary Indigenous societies had been and were still less violent and more peaceful than industrialized ones.[11] These conclusions weren't just abstract theories; they were the product of hands-on interactions with Indigenous communities that breathed life into this romantic notion of the noble savage.

It's common for people in a certain culture and time to argue that different cultures and times were more noble than their own. One area in which this manifests is property and ownership. An idea persists that all forms of private property and ownership are relatively modern phenomena. Accordingly, the concept of ownership must have been virtually non-existent in traditional societies. We see this critique of modern society in, for instance, ancient Buddhist scriptures, even in the writings of Adam Smith,[12] and the philosopher Rousseau, later inspiring Marx and other socialist thinkers. Rousseau, a voice from the eighteenth century, went as far as to suggest that the birth of property was the beginning of humanity's decline:

The first man, who, after enclosing a piece of ground, took it into his head to say, 'This is mine', and found people simple enough to believe him, was the true founder of civil society. How many crimes, how many wars, how many murders, how many misfortunes and horrors, would that man have saved the human species, who pulling up the stakes or filling up the ditches should have cried to his fellows: 'Be sure not to listen to this imposter; you are lost if you forget that the fruits of the earth belong equally to us all, and the earth itself to nobody!'[13]

By associating humanity's destructive tendencies chiefly with the concept of private property and ownership, thinkers like Rousseau have sometimes oversimplified the origins of violence. Though property and ownership do indeed contribute to explaining some heinous acts – such as historical and current instances of slavery and forced labour in industries like farming, manufacturing, and mining – these factors don't tell the whole story. They are, certainly, linked to various wars and conflicts where the quest to own natural resources has been the catalyst. However, this view does not encompass all aspects of human violence and wrongdoing. While the emphasis on private property does illuminate some brutal events, it overlooks others, such as ethnic cleansing, the Holocaust, political repression, and gender-based violence. In these cases, private property is neither necessary nor sufficient as an explanation.

The greatest oversimplification becomes apparent when considering claims that private property is a relatively new phenomenon and that war, violence, and evil were scarce or non-existent before its establishment. This overlooks the multifaceted history of human cooperation and conflict. Research in fields like social anthropology and archaeology propose a more nuanced understanding. They suggest that even before agriculture, people had a sense of personal ownership – albeit at a basic level and far from the extent we see in today's capitalism. Imagine our hunter-gatherer ancestors, leading a nomadic life, often on the move. Their way of living was rooted in cooperation, which left little room for extensive property claims. Still, even within their simple societies, clear status hierarchies existed, suggesting that even in a world with limited material inequality, there were distinct social structures.[14]

Scott Oliver Curry, introduced earlier in this book, has, together with his colleagues identified seven cooperative moral elements innate to our social behaviour. One of these is the principle of 'possession', with the associated virtue of respect for property. This right and virtue vary across cultures and can mean anything from family ownership to common group ownership, all while protecting property from theft or destruction.[15] The definition of specific territories as belonging to a community is an age-old phenomenon, one that has been linked to warfare even before our evolution into humans.[16]

How about violence in traditional societies and modern, urban, 'advanced' ones? Firstly, let's paint a broad, universal picture of humanity. We're not completely rough, nor are we utterly smooth. We are both, and neither, a mix that can be both cooperative and competitive, each of us relating to our society's norms. With this in mind, let's look at some of the standout differences that some systematic studies have found, especially around violence. Today, comprehensive research using a wide range of scientific methods shows that the relative frequency of violence was much higher during the long period in which thinkers such as Adam Smith, Jean-Jacques Rousseau, and Karl Marx claim private ownership did not exist, and people lived in peace.[17] To be sure, it's a fact that smaller, traditional societies – current and past ones – have recorded fewer cases of unnatural deaths compared to urban societies, if we're talking about absolute numbers. But what happens when we factor in population size? It's the difference between counting the cases and considering their proportion. This change in perspective reveals that the hunter-gather societies studied have had far higher rates of unnatural death or injury when compared to urban ones.[18] Using the terms from the introductory chapter, the simplifying frame presenting a peaceful world without private ownership seems to obscure more than it clarifies.

The idea that 'the other' might be more authentic or trustworthy is a theme that surfaces every now and then. It's not only when we're looking at different cultures, but also within our modern urban societies with their myriad identity groups. Could it be that we find more truth in what a stranger from another group tells us than what we hear from our own?

In a study, researchers Benegal and Scruggs decided to delve into this curious dynamic. They wanted to see who people would trust more when they needed to correct misinformation about climate change. For their experiment, they gathered a group of Democrats and Republicans in the United States. Everyone agreed climate change was real, but what happened next was quite revealing. The researchers gave the participants incorrect information about climate change, and then presented them with corrections from three sources: a Democrat, a Republican, and a non-partisan climate scientist. You'd think that Republicans would be most inclined to trust their own, right? Indeed, they did. But here's the twist: Democrats, too, were more likely to trust the Republican non-expert than their own party representative or even the climate scientist.[19]

This might seem like a collective case of self-doubt among Democrats, but let's look at it differently. Consider this: there's something compelling about a Republican expressing concern for climate change, going against the grain of their party. Remember how we've discussed that people admire those who appear to risk something when they stand up for their principles? With that in mind, it's not a huge leap to imagine that Democrats might think that the Republican has more to lose compared to their own party's representative or a neutral scientist. That sense of risk elevates their perceived credibility.

4

The allure of rough

Taking sides in story thinking

Every living thing, humans included, instinctively categorizes its surroundings into 'good' and 'bad', 'safe' and 'unsafe', 'reliable' and 'unreliable'. The way we quickly assign things, situations, and people to one category or the other is fundamental for survival.[1] It's so instinctive that we often feel like our quick judgements reflect an undeniable truth. But consider how easily this commonsensical idea can be shaken up with some philosophizing. Let's talk about luck, for instance. When events unfold, we often instantly label them as 'good luck' or 'bad luck'. But philosopher Steven Hales throws a wrench in the works with a fascinating real-life story.[2]

Picture this: it's 1945, and a Japanese man named Tsutomu Yamaguchi is working as a draughtsman for Mitsubishi Heavy Industries. That summer, he's sent on a work trip to Hiroshima. His work is abruptly interrupted on 6 August when the *Enola Gay* drops the atomic bomb 'Little Boy' just two miles from Yamaguchi's location. He was well within the zone designated for instant death but, miraculously, Yamaguchi escapes Hiroshima with ruptured eardrums, burns, and temporary blindness. Seeking safety, he returns home to Nagasaki. Back at Mitsubishi on 9 August, as he's recounting his ordeal and unlikely survival, a blinding white glow fills the office. Nagasaki had just been hit by the second atomic bomb, 'Fat Man'.

What are the odds of being in the blast radius of the two most destructive weapons in history in two different locations? One might call that the worst luck imaginable. Yet, Yamaguchi survived the second atomic bomb as well. He went on to live a full life with his wife and daughters, working as a translator and writer, and even becoming an advocate for nuclear disarmament. He died in 2010 at the age of 93. Some might label this as the best luck. From a grand, cosmic perspective, Yamaguchi's story could be seen as extremely unlucky, extremely lucky, or perhaps neither. It just goes to show how keen we are to neatly slot things, people, situations, and life stories into categories of 'good' or 'bad', smooth or rough. But reality? It's a bit messier.

Intrigued by intrigue

What is it about certain rough frames surrounding things, people, and situations that captivate our interest and command our attention? This question has intrigued psychologists from diverse fields who have identified what they call 'negativity bias'.[3] Despite our inclination towards smooth, safe, and convenient choices, it seems that humans have an inherent fascination with uncovering the darker side of things – the bad, the threatening, the immoral, the grotesque, and the absurd. Let's imagine you're a boss and you make a complaint to your staff. According to a well-known study on successful organizations, you'll need to deliver around 5.6 positive comments, on average, to offset the impact of that single negative remark.[4] This exact ratio might not hold true in every collaborative setting, but it does highlight an important lesson: to maintain constructive and lasting relationships, we must offer more positive feedback to compensate for each negative utterance. Recognizing this 'asymmetry' is vital.

Another aspect that points to a similar trend is the high price people pay for learning about negativity. The question at hand is whether false claims or accurate information about real events spread faster and reach more people. A comprehensive study published in the journal *Science* revealed that false claims had a 70 per cent higher chance of being reposted and spread up to six times faster.[5] Why does this happen? One main reason is that the fear and disgust people experience from the content of false claims, which prompts them to share such claims, are validated by the many repliers who repost those messages. On average, false claims on social media tend to be more threatening and focused on negative traits of certain groups compared to truthful claims. Despite negative information making us feel stressed, uneasy, worried, and angry, it seems we have a genetic inclination to be obsessively drawn to it. Our evolutionary adaptation to social life doesn't seem to have prioritized pure happiness and contentment.

Even in the realm of music, scientists like musicologist Oliver Sacks have discovered evidence of a negative bias. They describe a universal phenomenon where people get stuck with an unpleasant, detestable melody in their heads for long periods – far longer and more vividly than songs they adore. Sacks suggests that these disliked tunes can feel 'dangerous' and have an oddly captivating quality.[6] Speaking from personal experience, even if woken up in the middle of the night after just one second of thought, I can whistle the entire monotonous and unpleasant melody from the vending machine in the basement of the International House at University of California, Berkeley, where we used to do our laundry as students in 1996–97. And I'm not alone in this peculiar 'skill'; the few former International House residents I keep in touch with can do it too. At its core, the stickiness of music we dislike is probably an example of how our brains are wired to remember and pay excessive attention to signals of danger.

Take a walk on the wired side

People's disproportionate curiosity about the tough stuff is sometimes used to trick them into preferring it. Consider this famous job advertisement:

> MEN WANTED for hazardous journey, small wages, bitter cold, long months of complete darkness, constant danger, safe return doubtful, honour and recognition in case of success.

This ad was supposedly placed in the *The Times* of London around 1913 by the famous explorer Sir Ernest Shackleton, who was hiring men for his trans-Antarctic expedition. According to the story, this advertisement caused Shackleton to be flooded with responses from men – some five thousand – begging to join the dangerous expedition. The ad topped a list of 100 greatest advertisements a few decades later.[7] Sadly, some historians and science journalists have broken the cardinal rule of not ruining a good story with truth-seeking, debating whether the ad was ever actually placed in *The Times*.[8] Despite the uncertainty, the point is that this story captured widespread attention. The fascination it evoked suggests something deeper than the ad's authenticity. It raises the possibility that framing messages of some jobs with a rough texture, emphasizing their hazards and hardships, can attract people's interest, not only as an avenue for learning but also as a way of life. These acrobatics of framing can be effective due to the allure of social distinction, prestige, and the fascination we feel towards risk. Embedded within these reframed messages, the last sentence of the purported ad carries significant weight: 'recognition in case of success'.

Many evolutionary psychologists would argue that the desire for recognition, often associated with vanity, has driven individuals to take risks. This drive, seen as a sign of loyalty, courage, and empathy, has shaped our social dynamics. It's important to note that, on average, there is a gender dimension – men are more attracted to reckless activities that signal courage without emphasizing loyalty or empathy. However, historical circumstances limited the opportunities for women to participate in explorations like Shackleton's. Today, we understand that the psychological differences between women and men are statistically minor compared to the variations *within* each gender.[9] The research article by Carothers and Reis aptly captures this sentiment, stating that 'Men and women are from Earth'.[10]

There are numerous factors that attract individuals, irrespective of gender, to the rough framing surrounding certain pursuits. Many seek to stand out, to forge an identity valued within their communities, and to find their place in our advanced and diverse society. The desire to belong and carve out a niche where one feels at home motivates us to explore these adventurous paths.

In today's world, much of our risk-taking is less physical and more social in nature. Fashion is one such arena where frame retexuring thrives. The phenomenon of 'ugly fashion' has gained popularity among individuals of all gender identities who eagerly embrace these recurring trends. It's fascinating how adopting ugly fashion can serve to signal cultural distinction and superiority. There are two distinct ways in which ugly fashion becomes a powerful social signal. The first approach involves openly acknowledging that the clothes we wear are indeed hideous. Examples of this can be seen in the Yeezy Foam Runners by Adidas, which resemble marshmallows, or Converse's wildly unattractive sneaker-rainboots.[11]

In her book *The Psychology of Fashion*, Carolyn Mair explores these trends, stating that fashion, much like art, seeks to challenge traditional notions of beauty rather than solely aiming for aesthetically pleasing designs. This description, however, merely scratches the surface. There's a deeper social game at play. By purchasing and proudly wearing ugly fashion, we send two distinct social signals. Firstly, we communicate to other groups that we can afford to play around with our outfits, nonchalantly admitting that these clothes may be considered unattractive. This underlying message suggests that we possess the means to effortlessly switch up our style and acquire new outfits when desired.[12] Secondly, donning ugly fashion allows us to create a façade, both for others and ourselves, that we see the profound aesthetic value and even beauty in these products. We imply that there's a deeper understanding that those outside our inner circle fail to grasp.

This second strategy is more daring and takes us into riskier territory, putting even Shackleton's brave men to shame. It echoes the sentiments conveyed in Hans Christian Andersen's tale 'The Emperor's New Clothes'. In every depiction I've come across of this story, the emperor and his officials appear proud but are unmistakably blushing, caught in their own deceit. If only more world leaders possessed the emperor's capacity to feel shame when caught in lies and deceiving their people.

The allure of rough

Whistle-blowing

The boy in Andersen's tale took a tremendous risk when he boldly proclaimed, 'The emperor is naked!' Only a select few possess such bravery. These individuals often come from the spheres outside of power, just like in the story. Whistle-blowers, a rare breed, take significant risks when challenging the prevailing frame of truth, righteousness, aesthetic value, or even inevitability that society holds dear. They dare to question the established order of power and societal norms that the rest of us take for granted.

Whistle-blowers can create awareness about organizational activities in two distinct ways. The more common approach is to spotlight a significant discrepancy between the normal frame of organization and the actual 'content', the operations *inside a dominant frame* that the whistle-blower also accepts. Misconduct in a healthcare department, wrongdoings in a political party, or a car company's manipulation of emission data are examples. Another equally critical form of whistle-blowing, vital for democracy, involves contesting *the whole, dominant frame of normality* within which a group, organization, country, region, or the entire world operates. This entails challenging and exposing harmful norms that are often overlooked or unopposed. It's about complicating the current framework and bringing attention to potential alternatives. Slavery, child labour, severe working conditions in mines, environmental waste disposal, and inhumane animal farming have long been a part of the accepted norms, fitting within what's known as the supply chain. Many elements of this dominant supply chain frame are still exploitative and damaging, persistently requiring whistle-blowers who can view the larger context and question much of what we consider normal.

History has taught us two valuable lessons in this regard both about whistle-blowers enforcing the status quo and whistle-blowers fundamentally questioning the status quo. Firstly, whistle-blowers often face harassment from those who feel exposed or struggle to cope with their beliefs being questioned. Secondly, many societal changes that we now embrace required the initiative of individuals who stood strongly against mainstream norms and practices. Examples include advancements in civil rights, women's rights, animal welfare, children's rights to a safe upbringing, and the urgent need to halt environmental degradation. To protect these courageous individuals, several countries have implemented legal safeguards for whistle-blowers, particularly in workplaces and organizations.[13]

If things go well for a whistle-blower, their experience can be likened to the journey of starlings in autumn. Just as one starling may suddenly change course upon spotting a threat that others fail to see, like a predatory bird, the whistle-blower might question the organization's path and defy conventional ways. Over time, much like hundreds of starlings following the courageous one, other people might also rally behind this individual whistle-blower. If their brave protest and deviation from norms successfully lead others to safety, it's quite likely that they will be celebrated as a hero and saviour.

The role of a successful whistle-blower is immensely appealing for any of us. It's not surprising that some individuals continually seek it, often driven by moral convictions or sometimes just vanity. In many of their attempts, what's at risk isn't life or death, but personal reputation and, ideally, the chance to stimulate fresh public discourse. Take the case of the American writer Tom Wolfe, who in the 1990s claimed that the renowned genius artist Picasso was a fraud. The cultural frame of modernism, particularly Cubism, is as fake as the emperor's new clothes, was his claim. Wolfe stated, 'If I couldn't draw, I would have started a movement myself. I would call it Cubism.' Instead of calling out 'The emperor is naked', Wolfe declared that Picasso 'left school just before they taught perspective'. To illustrate his point, Wolfe remarked that the hands in Picasso's work 'look like the asparagus you get in the store'.[14] Wolfe's aesthetic whistle-blowing was part of a small but energetic cultural movement known as the 'Derrière Guard', which encompassed various art forms. Such counter-movements are much needed, as they expand the artistic palette and challenge what is commonly deemed aesthetically superior, thus ensuring a vivid and dynamic cultural climate. By retexturing and arguing that what the majority considers good is, in fact, bad or a hoax, we can foster broad-mindedness instead of allowing the dominant norm to remain narrow.

Sometimes, a shift in the way we see things is necessary for the sake of health and social harmony. Take, for example, air pollution. It blankets countless cities across the globe, turning skies into hazy canvases of smog for the better part of the day.[15] Air pollution in places such as New Delhi and many other megacities in the Global South is more than just a nuisance; it's a silent killer, an uninvited guest causing not only nocturnal sniffles and coughs but, more alarmingly, premature deaths, as will be explored further in Chapter 6. But while air pollution creates much suffering and frustration, the rough framing texture that people at all societal levels feel around these troubling conditions is no guarantee for concerted action. However, change is achievable, at least in theory. Just as we've transformed other seemingly immovable realities, we can also reshape the dialogue about urban air quality. Legal scholar Cass Sunstein provides a rough blueprint. His approach concentrates on the general process of reframing, understandably excluding the intricate and specific complexities of air pollution in a megacity like New Delhi:

> someone courageous has [to start saying that] the norm [that we have to live with our current air quality] is not good, which means that the second person who says that doesn't seem like a crazy person or a rebel but seems brave rather than reckless. And then once there are two, a third person can say, 'This isn't good. I agree with that.' And once there are three, and you can think of three as a metaphor for 300 or 3,000, then you can have something very large like the environmental movement.[16]

This is similar to what we observe in nature, like the behaviour of my favourite birds, starlings. When one bird senses danger and changes its path, others don't instantly follow. Instead, there's a ripple effect as one bird after another adjusts its course until they all veer towards a new direction. Although this shift happens in a split second among starlings, the principle remains the same. As per Sunstein's perspective, the tipping point arrives when it's no longer considered radical or abnormal to highlight a problem and advocate the battle to solve it. The outliers become mainstream, and whispers evolve into a roar.

Making bad seem good – frame texturing

In such a situation, the problem isn't merely seen as a rough issue. The rough frame is also warming up, becoming increasingly ready to reshape the dominant perspective of the situation. It is energizing engagement and kick-starting a process of change, ideally with participants from the government, the private sector, and civil society. The next section of the book will delve into these changes in frame temperature.

Part II

Making hot what's not – and other frame tempering

When we first cross paths with people who seem different from us, those we might label our 'out-group,' it's common to put up our guard, to be a bit wary, and sometimes even to slip into stereotyping. But if life has taught us anything, it's that things are rarely just binary. How we interact with 'them' can change dramatically over time, much like a painting that evolves with each stroke. History gives us vibrant examples of how cultures, once seen as distinct, can blend in relatively harmonious coexistence. In parts of medieval Spain, for instance, there was an era referred to as *convivencia* when Arabs, Jews, and Christians are said to have shared neighbourhoods and ideas, living in relative peace.[1] Fast forward to our modern societies, it seems that peace and collaboration outpace hostility and violence, despite ongoing conflicts and wars. This hopeful viewpoint is endorsed by scholars such and Stephen Pinker and the late Hans Rosling.[2]

Certainly, the dynamics between 'us' and 'them' are more nuanced than a simple rough and smooth dichotomy. The 'heat' or intensity of these interactions plays a crucial role. Imagine this heat as the energy and commitment that the framing has stimulated. As heating metal allows a blacksmith to shape it, heating up a figurative frame can reshape it. This is essential in order to bring about a change in cultural and political frames. For example, we might need to heat up the discussion on climate change in order to reshape it from being framed as just another tick of Earth's geological clock into a phenomenon humans have caused and can do something about.

Or concerning health, governments and civil society organizations may need to heat the debate on vaccination to reframe it from merely a personal choice to a moral obligation to society. Classical rhetoric here points to the importance of speakers and writers expressing and evoking *pathos* in order to engage the audience.[3]

How can changes in frame temperature be noticed? With heating, it becomes evident in the intensity of confrontations between groups in debates and protests. Yet, conflicts aren't confined to heating, as open, active disputes. Ask people about an ideologically charged issue and then ask their feelings towards those with a different perspective. Over the past decade, political scientists in the US and Europe have noticed an uptick in emotional animosity, usually passive, towards groups with differing views or ideologies. They refer to this as 'affective polarization'.[4] A practical example would be the level of upset a pro-vaccination parent might feel if their adult child were to marry into a fervently anti-vaxxer family, or the reverse. The worry among many who study affective polarization is not necessarily that issues become too heated. In fact, a bit of heat is often vital for engaging discussions, which are at the heart of a lively democracy. The real concern is that groups with different viewpoints might start avoiding each other altogether. In the wordings of this book, groups, in that bleak scenario, use a rough and cool framing around the other group. That's when conversations cease, compromises seem impossible, and the concept of 'us' versus 'them' becomes deeply entrenched. This kind of division results in a society fragmented by mistrust, where people from different backgrounds view each other with deep suspicion.[5] A case in point: an American study where most Democrats and Republicans admitted they'd rather take out the bins than engage in deep conversation with someone from the opposing party.[6] It's fair to assume affective polarization is at play here. As we'll explore further on, there might be additional pieces to this puzzle as well.

When it comes to altering the 'temperature' of a situation – either ramping it up or dialling it down – there are three vital elements to bear in mind. The first is temperament, a term with historic links to warmth and coldness. The second element is time. Understanding when to maintain a topic as a hot or cold issue, how long to keep it in that state, and the pace of change in the temperature can significantly influence people's responses. The last component relates to the use of metaphors and analogies for tempering the reality of a condition or situation. The implicit messages they deliver, which often vary among different groups of people, can drastically alter the perception of whether it's worth urgently taking action to change or preserve the condition at stake.

5

Temperament tricks

Fan the flames and simmer down!

From the time we're toddlers, we're constantly told to keep our cool: 'Let's take a deep breath together!' 'Remember our calm-down song?' 'Don't throw tantrums!' 'Stop making a scene!' Most parents believe this is part of moulding us into functioning adults. This call for calm continues to some extent when adults try to influence each other, even in certain cases where the situation is surrounded by rough frames signalling that it is socially unjust or exploiting. Some phrases, such as 'Keep cool, boy' (*West Side Story*), 'Come on take a chill pill' (Drake featuring Kanye West, Lil Wayne, and Eminem), 'Simmer down' (Bob Marley and the Wailers), or the old saying 'Sutor, ne ultra crepidam' (basically, you should know your place and mind your own business), all contend that calm and acceptance is the way to go. Other sayings, like 'Never take shit from no one' (anon.) or 'Workers unite' (Marx), proclaim the need for action and activism towards change. So, what's going on here? How do we reconcile these mixed messages? Let's start by acknowledging that cultures and eras differ in their preferred intensity of reactions, or 'framing temperature', to different situations. It's helpful to follow sociologists Campbell and Manning's way of breaking down cultures into three types.[1]

First up is the 'honour culture'. Here, people are constantly alert and responsive, quick to flare up at the faintest sign of disrespect from others. A slight nod from a stranger could be enough to stoke the flames and justify a forceful reaction – be it a threat or physical violence – against the ones showing disrespect. People in this culture take matters into their own hands, using their close allies if needed to counter threats. History traces the roots of honour culture to nomadic herders' strategies for dealing with their unique lifestyle challenges. The advent of horse riding allowed these herders to maintain larger herds, leading to ample food supplies and larger surviving families. However, the prosperity of these families hinged on the care of their animals and deterring theft or abduction by other herders.[2] Some wealthy men with larger herds could afford multiple wives, while others risked ending up alone – a perfect recipe for social unrest.[3] So, what kind of beliefs and conventions were behind this lifestyle? Anthropologists argue that such societies leaned towards religions with absolute divine laws and severe penalties for transgressions.[4] Beyond fearing divine punishment, men in these cultures needed their neighbours to fear them and their kin. Others in the region had to understand that any intrusion on livestock or family would lead to harm. And how to convey this message? Clear demonstrations were necessary, even in non-threatening situations.[5] The link between the challenging life of an old herdsman and today's machismo ideals across cultures, from West to East, is undeniable. Some characteristics endure: defined gender roles, a casual demeanour, a persistent need to defend one's honour, an unwillingness to tolerate humiliation without retaliation, a propensity to intimidate others 'just for fun', and a tendency to band together (preferably with kin) to assert strength against similar groups.

Continuing with Campbell and Manning's categorization, the second type is 'victimhood culture'. This seems to be the antithesis of honour culture at first glance. Where honour culture emphasizes strength and self-sufficiency, victimhood culture highlights weakness and dependence to ward off and handle perceived threats or injustices. Here, formal authorities – primarily the state supported by an ever-evolving set of educational programmes and rules against transgressions – take up the task of preventing and rectifying perceived injustices. Like those in honour culture, people here are expected to be vigilant and never tolerate even the merest hint of disrespect. Being confronted with unsubstantiated counterarguments where one's own values and factual basis are questioned can be enough to legitimize demands on society or organizations to remedy the violation.[6] Individuals and their identity-based groups are then obliged to surround the situation with a rough and hot framing, often out of loyalty to their identity group. However, in victimhood culture, it's 'society' that carries the responsibility to never remain passive and indifferent. The state and its authorities are tasked with prevention and retribution, frequently embodying a 'zero tolerance' attitude.

The third culture Campbell and Manning define is 'dignity culture'. This culture advises 'Don't sweat the small stuff'. If you feel threatened or victimized, or witness others being harmed, your first move should be to address the situation yourself, calmly and through conversation with the other party. The goal is to keep the situation's emotional heat down, as much for practicality's sake as anything else. By not making a big deal out of minor issues, challenges become easier to tackle. This less heated approach also keeps tensions from ratcheting up between groups. And what about the role of government? The dignity-culture approach contends that not until offences cross a distinct line and turn into crimes is it time for the state to step in. Dignity culture champions the idea of using the laws already in place, which are generally sufficient to address offences. Certain identity groups might call for extra protective measures. But dignity culture leans towards utilizing the existing law, designed to shield all citizens, no matter which identity group they belong to.

Campbell and Manning's categorization into three cultural types has a classic, rhetorical feel to it, showing an evident preference for dignity culture. But for our discussion, what's vital is to delve into the functions, benefits, and drawbacks of varying levels of emotional intensity, or 'framing temperatures', in specific life scenarios. This understanding will reveal when passion or composure becomes most effective in the social art of framing.

Why ever stay cool when life is framed rough?

Let's start by exploring coolness. Why do people and groups often avoid heating up the discussion around issues or relationships they feel aren't up to par? Those who take a 'reality speaks for itself' approach would reply that people and groups evaluate their circumstances – both material and social – and weigh them against the potential for improvement if they were to challenge the status quo. Lack of knowledge or skills to understand or instigate change holds them back until the situation reaches a high enough degree of unacceptability. In contrast, those who assume that 'framing is everything' see little or no correlation between the actual condition of the issues and the temperature of the discussions around them. Put differently, people are often irrational about their circumstances and goals, failing to frame them in ways that could help them improve their lot. Economists even have a term for this tendency to stick with the status quo when change could be beneficial: 'status quo bias'.[7]

Both the 'reality speaks for itself' standpoint and the belief that 'framing is everything' fall short of answering why we sometimes remain calm even when life isn't going perfectly. Stopping at mere descriptions, like those concluding that some cultures emphasize honour, others victimhood, and still others dignity can be useful points of departure for elaborating on why these three types exist and what could make each of them become more like one or two of the others. Similarly, acknowledging that people frame challenging situations differently due to different personality types that demonstrate varied levels of hot-headedness, is a valuable yet insufficient perspective for explaining why the same issue can be framed with such differences in temperature.

This book's alternative approach, 'framing needs ancestral resonance', gives a hint at why moderated reactions are sometimes favourable in challenging situations. By adopting an ancestral perspective, we find that maintaining a composed emotional response can be beneficial, especially in stable, non-threatening scenarios. From the earliest days of human history, this approach has been a

lifesaver. A simple explanation would be that this helped us econo-
mize with brain energy and, consequently, with food.[8] However,
contemporary analyses along with comprehensive critique of the
'foraging hypothesis' suggest a deeper, evolutionarily grounded role
of the human brain, characterized by navigating complex social settings through a 'theory of mind' – understanding others' intentions,
beliefs, and desires.[9] This skill set also includes advanced language
and communication abilities, a cornerstone of Robin Dunbar's
'social brain hypothesis'.[10] Rooted in evolutionary principles, this
hypothesis is vital to the book's framing approach. Over hundreds
of millennia, through natural selection, humans have become wired
to effortlessly learn and adhere to numerous rules of thumb for recognizing and dealing with risks and opportunities in hunter-gatherer
societies. For instance, most of us don't take active measures opposing the cultural norms of our society, even when they might be products of unfairness or suppression of ourselves or others. We often
don't question or even think about whether the current lukewarm
framings around such conventions ought to be heated, preparing us
for social change. By not constantly wondering whether our culture's
understanding of God is accurate, whether spanking is a suitable
disciplinary action for children, or whether Monty Python sketches
are truly as hilarious as our friends' roaring laughter suggests, we can
make our daily decisions swiftly and habitually.

Another upside to keeping the prevalent cultural narratives cool
or lukewarm is that it makes everyone's actions somewhat predictable, and this predictability fosters trust and inclusion within the
group. This trust bolsters opportunities for cooperation and mutual
support among group members. Thus, by adjusting our emotional
thermostat to match the group's feelings about an issue, we can
create an environment where everyone has a pretty good idea of
what to expect from each other. Most of us don't regularly challenge
the beliefs, norms, customs, and tastes of our social groups. And
those who do tend to find their invitations to social events drying up.
As small as that might seem, the sting of not being invited even to
that boring party harks back to a time when being ostracized usually
meant a grim and untimely end. Our ancestors likely lived in fear of

even the smallest hints of exclusion and would have gone to great lengths to avoid it. Those who didn't have this social sensitivity – this 'sociometer' – probably didn't make the cut as our forebears.[11]

Those at the top of the social pecking order, the high-status individuals and groups, have the most say over who's in and who's out. These influential folks have a vested interest in preserving basic parts of the status quo that keep them in power. They're naturally keen to spot who's for or against the established norms, because shaking up these norms could lead those further down the ladder to question their authority.[12] On the other hand, look at any novel that centres the relationship between the upper and lower classes over history, be it Jane Austen's *Pride and Prejudice* (1813), Evelyn Waugh's *Brideshead Revisited* (1945), or Kazuo Ishiguro's *The Remains of the Day* (1989). They're windows into the world of class disparities. A common thread you'll notice is the servants' nearly religious devotion to keeping the age-old rituals, the rules of hierarchy and inequality, alive and well. In *The Remains of the Day*, this is strikingly clear. There, in a discussion about employing servants at Darlington Hall, the butler, Stevens, clarifies his priorities:

> The most crucial criterion is that the applicant be possessed of a dignity in keeping with his position. No applicant will satisfy the requirements, whatever the level of accomplishments otherwise, if seen fallen short of respect.[13]

Save for some exceptionally bold characters among them – in *The Remains of the Day* the housekeeper Miss Kenton has this role – the usual pattern is that most servants seem to cling to the status quo with an almost zealous determination. Those of us who consume these stories, not least those who identify as part of the modern, educated middle class, are often a bit puzzled by this. We often miss recognizing the protection (albeit modest) and predictability (albeit of continued hardship) that may motivate the powerless to keep cool and not revolt in certain situations. Consider the expression 'He that is down need fear no fall'.

Let's turn our attention to the masters in these stories. It's quite intriguing how the kind-hearted among the masters often emerge as proponents of change. They'll say things like, 'No need to carry my bag', 'Forget the formal titles', or even 'Take a seat while we talk'. At first glance, these might seem like significant reforms. However, don't be fooled. These gestures mostly involve trivial, day-to-day practices. They steer clear of challenging the real power dynamics and the distribution of wealth that lies at the core of social inequality. What these stories reveal is a clever move by the masters. By casually discarding these insignificant traditions, they appear flexible and compassionate. The result? The master's power seems even more justified, and their place on the social ladder becomes even more secure. It's a strategic play that maintains the cool and intact framing of socio-economic inequality. The underlying structure remains unshaken.

Heating – even when things are smooth

Balancing between cool acceptance and occasional heating is essential for vibrant and healthy societies. However, the 'reality speaks for itself' and 'framing is everything' approaches view heating in distinct ways. Both approaches hold some truth. Those who believe that 'reality speaks for itself' think that people's knowledge about the objective condition at stake primarily determines whether they find it worth taking risks to heat up the dominant frame and bring about change. And indeed, in certain situations, such as medical emergencies, reality can sometimes speak for itself to all team members and doesn't require much explanation. When the medical team agrees on the problem and solution, they can prioritize the patient's condition based on urgency. They rely on the knowledge and guidelines provided by medical science and established professional rules.

For those who subscribe to the 'framing is everything' school of thought, there are no bounds to the issues you can stir up or the impact of turning up the heat. This viewpoint tends to recall classic marketing fairy tales, those of the kind through which a gifted salesperson could convince a Saharan nomad to sign up for a monthly subscription to sand. Adherents to this idea think that if you're good enough at fanning the flames, you can nudge people into re-evaluating their resources, needs, and desires. Before you know it, the desert-dwellers may start to wonder, 'Sure, we have a lot of sand, but what if we suddenly run short? Fortunately, this friendly salesperson is here to keep us from that nightmare scenario.' Much the same way, our own personal experiences often illuminate the potent effects of framing. I recall, for instance, a moment under the spell of a particularly magnetic salesperson who managed to talk me into buying a high-end gizmo – a centrifugal fruit juicer, of all things. Instore, they even whipped up a demo, leaving me with no doubts whatsoever. However, upon trying it out at home, I quickly realized the tedious process of peeling and slicing up fruit was hardly worth the resulting spritz of juice. The salesperson's talent in turning the temperature of the juicer's framing from a mere kitchen appliance to a revolutionary game-changer in my culinary routine, indeed, worked wonders on my purchasing decision.

Zooming out to the broader world, we notice how catastrophic issues are sometimes downplayed, while – again from our friend the Martian's viewpoint – less significant events that take place contemporaneously with the catastrophe may receive far more attention in the media and in the minds of us at a distance. For instance, while the mass media around the world covered Prince Harry and Meghan Markle's wedding in May 2018, a civil war took place in Yemen that resulted in an escalating yet underreported humanitarian crisis.[14] However, the power of framing has its limits. It depends on a complicated interplay between our genetics, biology, psychology, and the culture we are part of. Understanding this interplay is vital for comprehending and harnessing the truthful tricks of framing.

The hotter, the more influential?

So, what's the perfect intensity or 'heat' of a problem's framing to strike a chord in society and spur collective action to address it? Is there even one ideal heat level? Let's prepare for an answer by examining one attempt at maximizing social influence through frame heating. It's a case we've already touched upon and involves far-reaching changes in traffic planning in Amsterdam during the 1970s and beyond. While Amsterdam is widely recognized today as a 'bicycle city', it may surprise you that in the years before the 1970s and 1980s, it followed a similar trend to other Western cities. Car use grew significantly, while alternatives like cycling declined. From the 1950s to the 1970s, bicycle trips in Amsterdam dropped from 80 per cent to 20 per cent of all journeys made in the city, with a matching increase in car use.[15]

Back then, Amsterdam promoted a mixed-use system where cars, trucks, buses, bicycles, and pedestrians shared space. But this framing favoured motor vehicles over cyclists and pedestrians. Many criticized the overcrowded traffic situation, but their concerns were mostly about convenience, congestion, and general urban traffic annoyances. The traffic situation at the time sparked significant concern among several groups, all with valid arguments. The health risks from air pollution, detrimental noise levels, and traffic congestion contributed to stress and incurred considerable economic costs by eating into work and leisure time. Moreover, decreasing the number of cars in favour of less cumbersome modes of transportation was seen as being able to enhance urban aesthetics and facilitate a greener Amsterdam.

But were these framings of problems and positive visions powerful enough to trigger significant cultural and political shifts that led to tangible changes? Apparently not, given the increase in car use in Amsterdam well into the 1970s. However, there was still hope that another set of problem framings might have the capacity to stir up enough attention to catalyse change. As car use grew in the 1960s and early 1970s, so did the number and severity of accidents.[16] Within the frame of the prevailing car-dominated transportation system, heated debates about traffic violations and individual safety responsibilities emerged. By the early 1970s, traffic accidents were causing over 3,300 deaths per year in Amsterdam, including more than 400 children under 14, many of whom were cyclists.

So, what reframing turned out to be instrumental in fostering a different collective mindset and tangible changes in transportation planning? We might assume the huge, general number of accidents among the Amsterdam population. Yet, the wider issue didn't seem to provoke enough concern. Instead, the framing needed to be more heated, (even) more emotionally charged. Consequently, the protesters – many of them parents – launched a protest song: 'Stop de kindermoord!' ('Stop the child murder!'). They repeated it so often that many people – including local and regional authorities – couldn't help but associate Amsterdam's traffic problems with the provocative concept of child murder. Although 'murder' wasn't a factually correct term, this 'child murder' framing resonated not only ancestrally but also culturally in Amsterdam, leading to significant changes in traffic planning.

Does this case imply that all it takes to influence and drive change is a sufficiently hot and impactful framing of any situation? The straightforward answer is no. Firstly, we shouldn't take for granted that the most discussed problem frame in public debates and the media is in fact the most crucial or influential one. Indeed, it would be overly simplistic to conclude that a concern for children alone was enough to transform Amsterdam into a bicycle-friendly city. For example, neglecting the broader political and economic circumstances of the 1970s and 1980s would be a mistake. Oil crises, worries about reliance on foreign energy sources, and growing awareness of the public health risks associated with sedentary car use represent major underlying factors that undoubtedly played a part. This is in addition to the public outrage sparked by road accidents involving children.

We should, therefore, not expect that as long as we succeed in creating and gaining acceptance for problem framings that have highly moral overtones, we can, with a little persistence and exaggeration, create a unifying cultural resonance for our particular framing. In particular, research on high-level political conflicts within and between countries shows how moral framing, which in modern times is the default strategy for political leaders to argue that their own interests should be prioritized over those of their opponents, tends to create deadlocks and cement contradictions. What happens, for example, when a country engaged in an international conflict uses only moral arguments in support of its cause? Given what we have seen in this book about how we signal that we are being threatened or cheated by an out-group, the most that can be expected from such moral framing is that it will generate ancestral and cultural resonance only within the in-group, in this case the majority of one's own country. The same is then likely to happen in the opposing country – that is, its leaders will frame moral problems in support of why that country's preferences should be prioritized.

A large part of the deadlock that has been created is that if the political leadership on either side tries to negotiate a solution to the conflict that requires certain concessions, it will be seen in its own country as betraying the country's deeply held moral rights and thus as disloyal. This kind of impasse is so common in conflicts at various levels of national and international relations that Stephen Walt, professor of international affairs, entitled one of his articles 'Morality is the enemy of peace'.[17] Russia's war in Ukraine is one of Walt's examples. Ukraine and Western countries have framed the war from the outset in 2022 as their own moral defence of their sacred territory against a dictatorship and, by extension, the defence of Western moral principles. Russia, on the other hand, has framed the war as a moral assertion of a deep historical cultural affinity between Russia and Ukraine that must be preserved and strengthened. Walt argues that ending all wars has always required negotiations and concessions on all sides; but peace processes are delayed by political leaders' insistence on repeating their moral problem framing, which should instead be repositioned towards more pragmatic negotiating framings that bring the full range of interests – humanitarian, resource and security, economic, cultural, and environmental – to the table. Only then can counterparts begin to move away from the completely binary, zero-sum game of moral framing. This lesson from international conflicts is worth applying to conflict resolution processes in the social movements, organizations, and groups we belong to, perhaps even extending to our circle of friends and family.

Likewise, we shouldn't automatically presume that the hotter, more emotional, and more dramatic the framing of any situation, the more likely it will incite change. In Chapter 7, we'll explore attempts to reframe New Delhi's lethal air quality condition. This shift moves from viewing it as a serious health hazard to a concept as emotionally powerful as 'child murder': a 'crime against humanity'.

Making hot what's not – frame tempering

This discussion will provide a more nuanced view that goes against the idea that strong framing automatically facilitates social influence and mobilizes change. In order to have influence, any framing, hot or cold, must be selected so that its main connotations – the tacit meanings it holds – align with the meanings we associate with the problematic situation that the frame is supposed to encompass. To have influence, any framing, whether hot or cold, must be chosen such that its primary connotations align with the meanings we associate with the situation as such.

Certain societal issues are framed at their highest heat level – think about phrases like 'child murder' or 'crime against humanity' – while others are presented in a less heated manner. The act of heating a frame, either intensively or moderately, is typically done with an understanding that emotionally engaging issues are vital to incite broad protests. This, in turn, can prompt or motivate influential groups and institutions to facilitate societal change. As we navigate through this exploration of emotions, we'll focus on three essential ones: fear, anger, and hope. The way frames align with these emotions can greatly influence the success of efforts to heat a frame, thus leading to significant societal impacts. These impacts could kick-start legal proceedings, stimulate public protests, or subtly nudge cultural norms related to an issue. In the following sections, we'll probe deeper into the roles of fear and anger.[18]

Framing temperature vis-à-vis content

Sometimes our reactions to situations are more about our ancestral past than present reality. Consider, for instance, the fear of snakes and spiders. It's striking how many of us are petrified by these creatures, even more than, say, a traffic accident, which is a much likelier threat, especially in areas where poisonous spiders and snakes are a rarity. It's like my dear old grandmother, who would puff on her cigarettes all day but would break into a cold sweat at the mere thought of travelling by aeroplane. This fear, as it turns out, is deep-rooted, harking back to the days of our ancestors. In the earliest times of humanity, those who feared snakes and spiders were more likely to survive, and so passed on this fear to their children both genetically and through teaching. Fast forward to today, and we see this fear play out, even when the threat is far from us.

Let's pivot to another realm: morality. Like our primordial fear of snakes and spiders, moral instincts often drive behaviour. We see this in the well documented 'identifiable victim effect': our greater empathy and willingness to help when the need concerns a specific individual that we can identify, than if those suffering are a larger group of people that are harder to discern and identify.[19] Welcome exceptions include the record online fundraising efforts to help those affected by the 2004 tsunami in Asia and to support Ukraine in the early stages of Russia's war in 2022.[20] This disparity between our gut feelings and the reality of the situation is a mismatch between the dangers our ancestors faced and those we face in modern society. This mismatch can trick us, both as individuals and as a society, into misrepresenting the severity of threats or issues, skewing our responses to them. It's a fascinating quirk of our human nature, with repercussions that ripple through our personal lives and society at large.

Simplifications, such as 'it's just our ancestral brain', serve us well in clear-cut cases, like explaining our fear of snakes or spiders as a genetic adaptation to ancestral life. However, this same approach becomes less useful, even confusing, when applied to the complexities of our social world. For instance, attempting to trace the origins of violence, war, and exploitation solely back to the emergence of private ownership and property can distort the picture. Complex social dynamics require a multifaceted understanding. Applying a single lens could potentially blur our perspective rather than clarify it. This is particularly true concerning disparities between a disease and how it's framed over time. Take HIV, for instance. In its early days, when it was regarded as an epidemic, public interest surged, funding for its treatment multiplied, and significant institutions like the Joint United Nations Programme on HIV/AIDS sprang up. However, as perceptions shifted and HIV began to be seen as an endemic disease, the funding shrank. One possible explanation for this behaviour is our instinctive response to immediate danger.

Epidemics are perceived as urgent threats that demand immediate action. They unify us against a common enemy and attract ample funding. However, this explanation is too simplified for such a complicated issue. We should also consider that endemic diseases, although constantly present, are often associated with specific regions in the world. This tends to shift responsibility to the local areas and individuals to manage their own risks. Although an epidemic might generate more immediate action, endemic diseases, over time, pose a greater overall health burden.[21] Echoing Thomas Huxley's insights on dealing with challenges linked to 'human nature', we shouldn't resign ourselves to these psychological hurdles as 'natural', nor deny their connection to our primitive instincts. Instead, we should acknowledge this mismatch between our innate responses and the realities of our time. We should acquire and use more knowledge about this complexity to devise sustainable, long-term strategies for managing public health.

The same is true when trying to understand apparent disparities concerning other diseases and tragedies. There's rarely a simple proportionality between how roughly and hotly societies frame a disease – as measured in resource allocation, media coverage, and so forth – and how devastating it is. That's not something you can chalk up simply to how our brains have evolved.

Let's compare two devastating events from the twentieth century: the First World War and the 1918–19 'Spanish flu' pandemic. The First World War, also known as the 'Great War', was horrifying, leaving as many as twenty million dead and many more injured. Meanwhile, the so-called Spanish flu was at least as disastrous. It affected around five hundred million people worldwide – a third of the planet's population – and killed up to fifty million. The numbers are shocking on both counts. But if you looked at newspaper coverage from that time in the United States, you'd find roughly twenty-five times more articles about the war than the pandemic.[22]

Why such a big difference in media coverage? To some extent, it's likely tied to the way our brains have evolved to handle threats. We're hardwired to want to have constant updates about potential military enemies who we know intend to harm our side. Still, we're also hardwired to worry about diseases. Both war and disease are ancient threats that our ancestors had to constantly guard against. So, why were people in the late 1910s not as interested in news about the flu pandemic? We'd have to consider other factors beyond just our evolutionary instincts. Maybe it's because war is public and out in the open, while disease tends to stay behind closed doors. Or perhaps governments were worried that extensive coverage of the pandemic might demoralize people after they'd already endured four years of war. After considering these complexities, we could potentially pinpoint a handful of key factors that can help us clarify the reasons for the different levels of media coverage of these two calamitous chapters in modern history.

Hot and passive?

Most of us would agree that a particularly meaningful use of framing would be as a means towards *practical action*. But is this the only value framing holds? Does it lose its purpose if it doesn't result in noticeable improvements in the world around us? And what if we find ourselves unable to fundamentally alter the world or human nature? What if the greatest contribution we could make for ourselves, each other, and the world – encompassing nature and animals – is instead to *shift the frames* through which we *experience* life and reality? What if, by reframing our viewpoints, we could foster a less destructive and more harmonious interaction with everything around us? To get a clearer grasp of this, let's examine it from two distinct perspectives. The first contends that changing the framing temperature is as close to the action as we get. The second argues the very opposite, namely that no framing is hot if it sticks to inaction.

The proverb 'Life is not how you make it, but how you take it' is a cultural mainstay, a testament to the belief that our personal outlook shapes our world. But tweaking the frame temperature around the situations in which we find ourselves is no simple task. Here's something that sets us humans apart from other animals: we have the ability – a blessing or a curse, depending on your viewpoint – to get fired up, whether from joy or distress, not just about what's happening right now, but also about things that have occurred in the past and that might unfold in the future.

Let's picture a regrettable sexual encounter. It could happen to humans or – let's say – horses. While we don't fully understand the workings of a horse's mind, it's unlikely that the horse would stew over the incident afterwards, thinking, 'Why did I get myself into that? Now I'll have to cross paths with him every day, out in the pasture and back in the barn. What will the other horses think? This whole situation is just painfully awkward!' The neurologist Robert Sapolsky's book *Why Zebras Don't Get Ulcers* illustrates this – in both its title and its content.[23] Humans, as opposed to, for instance, zebras and horses, are the ruminating, long-term stressed species par excellence. Changing our actions to improve the outcome next time is sometimes a valid – albeit annoying – recommendation we get from our well-meaning peers. However, we can't practically modify *reality* in every area to move even close to what would be ideal. And even if we could, the framing texture and temperature with which we surround this external, 'objective' reality don't necessarily correlate with our inner experience of it.

The Swedish author Nils Ferlin expressed this in a poem:

Not even the little grey bird
That sings among green leaves
Will be there in the life hereafter,
And for this my heart grieves.
Not even the little grey bird,
Nor the birch standing white and spare: —
Yet, this loveliest day of the summer
I have longed to be there.[24]

Paradoxically, our awareness that today is the 'loveliest day of the summer' can sometimes create pressure to wrap the situation in the smooth, pleasantly warm frame it deserves. However, this pressure can have the opposite effect, turning the day painfully rough and dreadfully hot, surpassing the discomfort of an ordinary, grey day. In essence, we end up with two sources of pain: firstly, the actual discomfort, and secondly, the additional anguish, rumination, or shame we experience for feeling this pain in a situation where it shouldn't exist. Ferlin's poem suggests that even in the most wonderful circumstances, there's no guarantee we'll perceive such circumstances in a way that brings us joy or even comfort. If we fully endorse Ferlin's idea, actively changing reality, the substance inside our frames, wouldn't seem very powerful beyond mitigating the most apparent sources of suffering, such as wars, violence, disease, starvation, and extensive inequity.

Actively changing reality, the substance inside our frames, seems meaningless beyond mitigating the most apparent sources of suffering, such as wars, violence, diseases, and starvation. Nietzsche, the philosopher, takes this idea to its conclusion. According to him, our task – Herculean, possibly impossible – is not just to accept our fate, but to learn to love it, no matter how awful or wonderful it appears. He calls this approach 'amor fati'.[25] The Nobel laureate Albert Camus takes this idea a step further, drawing on the Greek myth of Sisyphus. If you recall, Sisyphus was doomed forever to grimly push a rock up a hill, only for it to roll back down once he reached the top. Camus has a different take on it, however: he imagines Sisyphus as absurdly content.[26]

So, we're left with a question: how can we enhance our feelings and those of other and other living beings? Nietzsche and Camus, each in his own way, presented us with formidable instructions about how to feel better. Their writings challenge us, or at the very least demonstrate that it's possible, not only to accept our destiny but also to embrace it, irrespective of how dreadful or splendid our life circumstances appear.

Is it possible for us to make peace with our pain – that initial 'arrow' that strikes us – rather than exacerbating our suffering by wishing that initial pain did not exist? Can we accept reality as it is, not how we'd like it to be? If framing is everything, this could be our ticket to a life of peaceful acceptance. To achieve this peace, our priority must be on putting our efforts – albeit in that effortless meditative way – into reframing reality rather than on changing reality itself. This requires us to surround our stings of pleasure and pain with a smooth and cool frame of friendly curiosity in what we and others experience. This idea predates Nietzsche and Camus by many centuries. It's deeply rooted in the Buddhist tradition, but Jon Kabat-Zinn and others have given it a modern, more secular spin.[27] Kabat-Zinn established a mindfulness-based stress reduction clinic at the University of Massachusetts, stripping mindfulness of its religious connotations.[28] Mindfulness has become a go-to strategy for many Westerners seeking inner peace and bettering their relationships. It could be as simple as closing our eyes and mentally scanning our bodies for sensations or observing without judgement our thoughts and emotions, even the painful ones. It's like taking a step back and becoming an observer of our own experiences. Preliminary neuroimaging studies have indicated that these practices have far-reaching benefits. For example, a study in the *Lancet* found that mindfulness meditation notably reduces stress and fosters resilience among students.[29] Even those sceptical of mindfulness generally admit its positive effect on well-being. So, changing the framing temperature of our reality may be the closest we can get to acting and changing the situation itself. Meditation is mainly an inward practice, demanding the individual's time, patience, and effort. However, if we practice mindfulness regularly, not only may we improve our own peace of mind, but we might also contribute to a more peaceful world, this view contends.

What if, instead, we subscribe to the idea that 'reality speaks for itself'? How would we then articulate the interplay between perceptions of the world and the real, tangible changes we can make? From this viewpoint, if this so-called 'framing temperature' means anything at all, it must signify some form of action or a transformation that pertains to reality outside of ourselves. Otherwise, we're just heating up a frame for self-indulgence, tricking ourselves that we're changing something substantive when we're not.

Earlier in the book we came across the idea that a lack of interaction with the world can be problematic – especially when this inactivity stems from fear and anger directed at out-groups. This dangerous cocktail fuels affective polarization, leading us to avoid necessary dialogue and problem-solving across different groups of thought. This escalating standoff, this fiery inertia, threatens to unravel the very fabric of democratic society. Now, let's consider another aspect of inaction. Elie Wiesel, an author and Nobel laureate, reminds us of a potent idea from earlier philosophers and writers,[30] and popularizes it in this quote:

The opposite of love is not hate. The opposite of love is indifference.[31]

This thought, which clashes with romantic notions of love versus hate, holds the weight of Wiesel's haunting experiences as a Holocaust survivor. Interestingly, neuroscience backs up this insight. Both passion and anger light up the same areas of our brainstem and hindbrain. Nestled within these ancient brain regions is the limbic system, housing two almond-shaped structures known as the amygdalae. These amygdalae light up equally, whether ignited by love or anger, fear or aggression, or even sex.[32]

The wisdom that Wiesel shares suggests that feelings of anger and fear, no matter how intense and wired, are just as lukewarm as indifference unless they drive us towards action against injustice. This viewpoint resonates with the 'reality speaks for itself' approach to one of the questions posed in Chapter 1: what role should framing play in improving our lives and society? 'Reality speaks for itself' underscores the need to change the objective circumstances of people and other beings. Framing is secondary at best; reframing reality without inciting tangible change is pointless. This viewpoint has elements of consequentialist, utilitarian ethics.[33] According to this moral stance, it's equally reprehensible to push someone into a well as it is to stand by and watch them drown while expressing deep sorrow: 'Oh, how terrible! I'm so sorry!' Your heartfelt framing of the tragedy you're passively witnessing does nothing to lessen your moral guilt; it only makes your inaction more absurd.

The strong moral stance of the 'reality speaks for itself' position, which both Wiesel and consequentialist thinking imply, is compelling. But merely focusing on morality – what we *ought* to do – isn't enough; we also need to delve into the psychology and sociology behind what might be termed 'wired coolness'. Most people with a moral compass would likely be shocked by the lack of action in the drowning scenario. However, this sort of impassive outrage is more common than we'd like to admit. Day in and day out, we wring our hands over the injustices we see, but often fail to take even small steps that could make a significant impact, like donating a bit of money or volunteering a few hours.

The pervasive 'wired coolness' is evident in the subdued outrage of groups labelled as climate 'doomers', who are riddled with anxiety. Their evident resignation or paralysis prompts one to wonder if they, in essence, mirror the views of climate change dismissivists or deniers. After all, both perspectives, albeit opposing, question the value of taking action to mitigate environmental damage: either it's too late, or climate change isn't happening at all.[34] Renowned journalist Matthew Yglesias points out in his blog, *Slowboring*, that climate anxiety discussions seldom tackle the practical actions individuals can undertake to fight climate change. These actions could be those we take as consumers pushing corporations to change, or as citizens exerting pressure on the political landscape.[35] Beyond its minimal contribution to climate change mitigation or adaptation, the passive anxiety of the doomers goes against the grain of both religious doctrine and modern psychotherapy. Both suggest easing our worries by making small, steady contributions to our communities.

But here's the twist, a real Catch-22: when it comes to individual action (or inaction) in the face of stressful circumstances, we encounter significant mental roadblocks. Let's explore this further with the following narrative.

On an icy winter morning in January 2007, Wesley Autrey was standing on a New York City subway platform, accompanied by his two young daughters. Suddenly, he noticed a man collapsing onto the tracks. Without a moment's hesitation, Autrey sprang into action. He jumped onto the tracks, laying on top of the man just as a train barrelled into the station. Autrey held the man down as the train thundered above them, missing them by a hair's breadth. The man, who'd had a seizure, was in shock. Only then did Autrey comprehend the magnitude of his act – he'd gambled his own life to save an absolute stranger.

When news of Wesley Autrey's act of courage spread like wildfire, he was celebrated as a hero, even earning recognition at a City Hall ceremony. The lavish praise he received, while well deserved, tells us something about ourselves. If we found ourselves in Autrey's shoes, watching a man tumble onto subway tracks, most of us wouldn't have reacted the same way. Our Martian friend might ask, 'Why not?'

Curiously, the mental block we run into isn't what most would expect: we often have an overload of emotional empathy. This rush of empathy, feeling the terror of the person who has fallen, can make us freeze. We become bystanders, consumed by the intense emotions of the situation. Then there's the obstacle of detached, moral reasoning. This kind of logical, morally concerned thinking has underpinned much of our moral progress, like recognizing our ethical obligations to strangers, out-groups, and non-human entities who don't necessarily elicit an immediate empathetic response. But I wouldn't bet that this kind of measured, calculated moral reasoning would lead many of us to jump onto the tracks to save a stranger. Consider Autrey's situation: he could have easily thought up a host of moral reasons not to act. By trying to help, he risked his own life, potentially traumatized his daughters, risked them losing their father, and could have faced legal consequences for trespassing on the tracks. When we apply calculated moral reasoning, we're essentially framing and reframing the situation, reflecting on different perspectives thoroughly and perhaps even systematically. By the time we've thought it all through – likely deciding against the risky rescue – it's probably too late anyway.

So, what led Autrey to act? When you look at the explanations given by him and other doers of extraordinary humanitarian acts, there's a pattern. Their reasoning is surprisingly simple, straightforward – boring, even. Consider a few quotes from Autrey himself: 'I didn't think. I just reacted. I just saw somebody needed help, and I helped ... I figured if I didn't do something, he'd get killed ... I just did what I felt was right'.[36]

You hear the same sort of thing from everyday heroes of all stripes – different ages, backgrounds, jobs, education levels, nationalities. Their words make absolute sense. They show us that this kind of extreme heroism doesn't have time for slow, deliberate thought processes or reinterpretations of the situation. These people seem to have let reality speak for itself, but in a direct and intuitive sense. There's a common thread among many of these selfless individuals: a kind of automacy concerning helping others. For many of them this automacy was developed during childhood, not least through simple, repeated sayings, rhymes, and lessons about the importance of helping others. This early moral training might be instrumental to the ability to leap 'automatically' into instant action without all the emotional calculation and deliberation that slow the rest of us down until it's too late.

Is it ever reasonable to say that our perceptions of a catastrophe are not only rough but also intense, even if we appear passive? The 'reality speaks for itself' approach highlights the similarities between not helping and actively harming others. Although there are convincing utilitarian arguments supporting this moral stance, it's important to remember a key distinction. The decision to passively allow harm or to actively cause it triggers different brain regions, resulting in distinct psychological experiences. Thus, from a consequentialist perspective, indifference and passivity towards others' suffering may be morally identical. However, psychologically, one can be passive without being indifferent. Passivity can reflect a 'wait and see' attitude, a silent readiness for resistance that can suddenly turn into fervent activity. This is often seen when an in-group perceives a growing threat from an out-group, as observed in studies on increased tensions between neighbouring groups.[37] When people silently fume over injustices, without acting on their intense perceptions of the situation, this still affects social opportunity and risk, or the 'dormant peace'. Conversely, indifferent passivity is more common when people witness threats or harm to a third group, as illustrated by Wiesel's harrowing Second World War experiences.

However, individual or cultural reactions are not hardwired in the sense of being inflexible. Both ancestral traits and cultural opportunities can influence our response to an out-group's suffering. The concept of 'altruistic punishment' is only one of several terms referring to our genetic predisposition to intervene and stop aggression against third parties.[38] Altruistic punishment can range from peaceful actions, such as a third country boycotting goods from one country that has attacked another country, to violent action, such as a third country intervening and carrying out violence against the aggressor. History is replete with examples of such efforts. Therefore, it is reasonable to argue that while the perception of miserable and exploitative situations is best understood as cool until engaging in active opposition, the rough texture of the perception can indicate either indifferent passivity – as if watching a horror movie that you don't take seriously – or intense frustration. As history has shown, the latter often quickly leads to active resistance. All this relates to how time and timing factor into our decision-making processes, as well as our awareness of the potential short- and long-term consequences of our actions. These critical topics will be further explored and dissected in the next chapter.

6

How timing is of the essence

Don't be tricked by the zeitgeist

Anyone with anger issues and who has been given the annoying, yet helpful, advice to 'count to ten' knows that time plays a crucial role in changing the framing temperature of a situation. It's not surprising that the words *tempus* (Latin for 'time'), temperature, and temperament are etymologically and literally linked. Our frames of reality take time to heat up and cool down. Furthermore, maintaining the framing temperature, whether hot or cool, requires energy and engagement over time.

Influencing others heavily relies on mastering the element of time and being fortunate with timing. Momentum must be seized to stimulate the resonance of our framing that correspond with the dominating frame of a particular issue, corresponding with larger cultural themes and therefore appearing familiar and normal.[1] Influencing through frame temperature also demands patience, allowing others to embrace our framing. We must 'read' the zeitgeist, have a sense of timing, and recognize how social norms are evolving at different speeds across various issues.

During one of my university lectures, I often pose a question that applies to individuals and organizations in various social contexts: what kind of signals do you think are most effective in convincing others to reduce environmental harm, such as driving and flying less, cycling more, or replacing environmentally damaging meat with alternative protein sources? Typically, students spontaneously respond with something along the lines of:

> People need encouragement and carrots of various kinds. Sticks make people annoyed or turn a deaf ear.

I can only guess why this response is so common, even among environmentally conscious students. Perhaps positive signalling aligns with the prevailing cultural preference for low-intensity interventions. In child-rearing, for example, psychologists recommend responding to children's heated temperaments, which lead to undesirable behaviour, with low-intensity approaches. Desirable behaviour, on the other hand, should be met with positive, high-intensity reinforcement. The low-arousal approach – using cool framing of the situation – should accordingly be the way to deal with unwanted behaviour. This ideal may also be tied to the dominant market liberal norm that shapes much of our lives. Voluntarism, encouragement, and incentives are often viewed as the most reasonable and effective policy tools, supported by policymakers from different political camps and the corporate sector. Voluntariness forms the foundation of nudging, also known as libertarian paternalism, where the first term emphasizes the voluntary nature of the approach.

When we perceive encouragement and voluntariness as the sole reasonable means of influencing others, we align ourselves with the prevailing zeitgeist. However, time also plays a significant role. I usually illustrate this to students by presenting a different form of undesirable behaviour: sexual harassment in the workplace. Suppose a workplace is grappling with employees inappropriately touching others or using sexist and vulgar language that makes their colleagues uncomfortable. What should the management do? Following the recommendations of low-intensity treatment, encouragement, and incentives, they could establish an anonymous monthly voting system to select the least sexually harassing and least sexist employee. The chosen employee would receive a badge, balloons, and cake. Unsurprisingly, every group of students I've presented this example to finds the smooth, rounded 'solution' utterly absurd. When we discuss why, we collectively conclude that the zeitgeist differs significantly across different issues. It might be acceptable, at least within our current cultural context, to award a similar prize to the most environmentally friendly employee of the month, someone who commutes by bike, leads recycling efforts, and organizes second-hand sales for employee Christmas shopping. A lenient approach may have been deemed acceptable for addressing instances of sexual harassment fifty years ago. And maybe, in a few years, the smooth, rounded approach on environmental records – only signalling encouragement – will be seen as equally absurd. There are already signs that norms in some countries are moving in that direction, such as partial increases in the public acceptance of an air passenger tax.[2] The future social norm might dictate that anyone who fails to be proactive – what we by today's standards would consider highly ambitious – in their environmental efforts as employees and commuters should face serious consequences, such as a stern conversation with the boss, reassignment, termination, or fines. That would mirror the harsh treatment that many of us today believe sexual harassment should result in. In short, determining the temperature we choose for our settings requires a keen sensitivity to the specific zeitgeist of the cultural context in which we find ourselves.

Contrary to what is often claimed in single-instance opinion polls (cross-sectional studies), people's attitudes are rarely fixed in stone. They can be influenced and changed, and each of us has the potential to contribute to this, hopefully for the better.

Why speed up frame heating?

When I'm talking with my students or chatting with managers and activists from various health and environmental NGOs, we often share a frustration. We're frustrated because changes in environmental and health policies just don't seem to happen quickly enough. Global heating needs to be reduced but, ironically, for that to happen and for other environmental, health, and social issues to be solved, we're all itching for the framings of these issues to heat up so that the world to start to care more urgently about these problems. But these shifts in the public mood, in the zeitgeist, often take decades, I remind them. We all agree, though, that this pace needs to pick up. The future can't wait – we need to see changes in years if not months or days.

But in our rush to turn up the framing heat, are we missing something? Let's consider the speed at which we dial up the urgency from a few different angles. Many scientists argue that in environmental and health issues, waiting for total certainty or undeniable proof before acting is a dangerous game. Instead, it's better to act early and adjust the framing temperature to garner political and popular support to prevent or at least manage these problems.[3] Of course, when rapidly heating the problem frame, we must accept that most of the results will be what we call 'false positives'. These are warnings that signal an apparent threat to our health or the environment, but they often end up being false alarms, or at least alarms that signal more urgency or severity than is likely to be the case. Yet, when it comes to serious matters like the environment or public health, we simply can't afford the luxury of ignoring warning signals altogether, for instance when faced with the short-term costs of stopping an activity that is highly likely, but not entirely certain, to compromise society's ambitions for the energy transition needed to mitigate climate change.[4]

There seems to be an ironic similarity between this 'better safe than sorry' approach to environmental and public health problems and the quick decisions that people tend to make based on stereotypes and prejudices, particularly when it comes to people outside our social group. Both approaches involve accepting that we'll encounter many false positives in our attempts to avoid false negatives, and thus the risk of overlooking even a single significant danger. There is a level of irony stemming from the fact that the evolution from ancestral societies to today's advanced urban communities has altered the risk proportions between them. Nowadays, in places with relative peace, it's more prudent not to instinctively flee from individuals belonging to different groups or communities than our own. This is unlike societies where sudden out-group raids could claim the lives of a significant portion of the population. Furthermore, in medical science, there is an awareness that it may be worthwhile – when all other options have been exhausted – to use medications and treatments whose side effects and risks are not yet fully understood or evident. Put differently, there is a risk of going too far with the precautionary principle.[5] Matthias Gross, an environmental sociologist, emphasizes the importance of not delaying the adjustment of framing temperature for various environmental and health issues. He and other scholars in the field of 'ignorance studies' argue that scientists and authorities should not fear uncertainty or even ignorance. Instead, they believe that embracing our lack of knowledge can help us understand and tackle environmental and health problems without being constrained by ingrained thought processes.[6]

Another compelling reason for always being ready to tweak the framing temperature of specific environmental and health concerns lies in our quest for ethical progress. Recalling the words of Thomas Huxley, we are tasked with 'combating' what he termed 'the cosmic process'. Essentially, Huxley meant that we need to challenge the human, cultural, and political biases that impede our society's progressive agility. In other words, to make forward strides, we must actively counter these entrenched biases.[7]

Many pressing issues we face today aren't as easy to wrap our heads around as the black-and-white morality tales that have gripped people throughout history. Take, for example, the problems surrounding plastics and their impact on our environment and health. In the 1990s, scientists discovered that an alarming amount of ocean waste was non-biodegradable plastic. One of several garbage patches mainly comprising such plastic waste was found to be three times the size of France.[8] Despite the clear warnings from the scientific community, the urgent framing of the plastic waste issue didn't ignite into a hot topic that spurred political action or citizen engagement for quite some time. It simply didn't stir up the sweeping response required to tackle the problem. As the science writer Stephen Buranyi puts it:

> To travel back even to 2015 is to enter to a world in which almost all of the things we currently know about plastic are already known, but people aren't very angry about it. As recently as three years ago, plastic was just one of those problems ... that everyone agreed was bad, but which few people considered doing much about.[9]

How could this be? According to the 'reality speaks for itself' perspective, there comes a point when the magnitude and severity of a problem become so significant that enough influential individuals realize that 'enough is enough'. But as this example reveals, the plastic waste situation, like many other pressing issues, does not speak for itself, at least not to the extent that it would prompt those in power to translate their awareness of the situation into appropriate action. Not even the reality of garbage patches the size of several countries nor the heart-wrenching images of suffocating birds and fish seem to be enough. According to the 'framing is everything' perspective, we should recognize that, until 2015, plastic waste was primarily framed as litter. The general feeling towards litter is that it's visible, an annoyance – indeed, something that is bothersome and may lead to unfortunate outcomes. Moreover, in cases where specific litterers can be identified, anger is often directed towards those individuals or organizations. Given the immense influence and power that the 'framing is everything' approach ascribes to framing, all these negative connotations ought to suffice for creating the framing heat needed for mobilizing widespread action.

It's interesting to note that both perspectives suggest there should have been a robust response against plastic waste well before any significant activism began. The 'reality speaks for itself' view would predict that just spreading the word about the real situation and extent of plastic waste in the environment should have been enough to provoke action. Meanwhile, the 'framing is everything' view would expect that years of presenting plastic waste as litter that's ugly, harmful to wildlife, and an overall nuisance would prompt a response. Either way, it seems action against plastic waste was justified long before it started in earnest.

However, as this book's alternative approach – the one that insists framing must vibrate in correspondence with both ancestral and current social life – points out, not all framings can be heated effectively in all circumstances. The enormity of 'plastic litter' wasn't sufficient. To figure out what would work better, we need to look at crucial social and moral factors absent in the 'litter' framing, especially when we exclude harmful and contaminating waste. It appears that moral bases related to deception, dishonesty, and unpredictable invisibility are missing from the litter frame. Plastic litter, like all litter, is seen as 'honest' because it's visible and tangible. This visibility gives us a reassuring sense of control, making it more acceptable in some ways, like a known adversary, than a dishonest friend or ally.

Our ancestrally rooted caution about unpredictable, invisible, possibly deceptive threats became apparent when the problem framing of plastic shifted from plastic litter to microplastics and microbeads. The latter – tiny plastic particles, smaller than a millimetre – were commonly found in toothpaste, personal care products, and even health-science research. It turned out that microbeads were present even in products thought to be less harmful to health and the environment from trusted companies such as the Body Shop and Johnson & Johnson. This realization of the dangers inherent in microbeads resonated with one trait that seems integral to our moral concerns in most types of cooperation, including the type that includes market exchanges: sensitivity to the other parties' failure to demonstrate the virtue of trustworthiness.[10] People seem especially eager to expose deceit in individuals and organizations with a high ethical profile, like the Body Shop. Moral outrage played a significant role in swiftly putting the issue of microbeads on the political agenda, starting in 2015. The revelation that those we'd trusted were deliberately causing substantial – and even worse, invisible – long-term damage, vibrates in correspondence with our ancestrally based caution against being tricked.

Let's speculate a bit about what role visibility versus invisibility might play in society's acceptance of risks. We can delve into this by turning to two distinct types of energy sources: nuclear power and carbon-based fuels. Nuclear power carries the threat of invisible yet potentially deadly radiation, similar to the barely visible threat posed by microbeads. Carbon-based fuels, in contrast, bring forth pollution that often manifests in visible and tangible ways. Anyone can directly perceive at least parts of the pollution stemming from carbon-based fuels. We see the pollution, smell it, and experience its effects in our itching throats and eyes.

How about the harm the two types of energy sources have caused so far? In terms of casualties, urban air pollution and indoor fuel-burning associated with carbon-based energy sources have been blamed for thousands of times more deaths than nuclear energy and nuclear waste. According to the WHO, in 2019 alone, ambient pollution from outdoor air – largely attributed to the burning of carbon-based fuels – claimed the lives of 4.2 million people.[11] Furthermore, one year later, 3.2 million premature deaths were attributed to carbon-based household air pollution from cooking and heating.[12] But drawing final, comparative conclusions based solely on the *absolute* number of deaths caused by carbon-based fuels and nuclear energy would be misleading. This is because oil, coal, and other carbon-based fuels are utilized in greater quantities than nuclear power. Instead, in order to be meaningful, the comparison must concern the relative number of deaths per generated kilowatt-hour (kWh) caused by carbon-based fuels and nuclear energy, including its waste. As it turns out, for each kWh, carbon-based fuels, depending on the specific type, have caused almost one thousand times more deaths so far than those caused by nuclear power and its waste. Meanwhile, solar and wind power exhibit similar, lower risk levels as nuclear power and its waste.[13] We should also note that these comparisons haven't even started to account for the multiple times greater climate impact of carbon-based fuels compared to nuclear, solar, and wind power. Despite these stark differences, nuclear power is banned in many countries, while carbon-based fuel emissions – setting climate change concerns aside – are permitted almost everywhere, albeit with varying degrees of regulation, carbon taxes, and carbon trade permits.

An important caveat: despite the strong argument this comparison presents against carbon-based fuels, it's important not to see it as an unequivocal endorsement of nuclear power. We can't ignore the known and unknown risks of nuclear energy, including the unresolved issues of waste storage and the connections between nuclear power and weaponry. What I'm really highlighting is that the discrepancy between policies, regulations, and attitudes towards carbon-based fuels and nuclear power is significantly larger than their respective statistical risks, even if those statistics were to change drastically. Much like visible plastic, we tend to perceive air pollution from fossil fuels as air litter – a noticeable, smelly annoyance that seems to be upfront about the damage it inflicts. Thus, it saves us from the deep-seated fear of being tricked by invisible, insidious forces or actions. It's a cool frame, perpetuated not only by the fossil fuel industry and the companies that depend on it, but also by those of us who worry about air pollution but continue to rely on carbon-based fuels.[14]

However, this cool framing temperature surrounding carbon-based fuel usage might be precisely what tricks us. By insisting on 'honesty' and visibility as a prerequisite to accepting the harm that energy sources inflict, we might overlook or disregard alternative framings that might be worthwhile considering. These might involve a framing that prioritizes the minimizing of risks – to the best of our current knowledge – over the comfort of habit and a perceived sense of honesty, visibility, and control that carbon-based fuels appear to give us. This is despite the alternative frame potentially having to include elements that have troubled us since the dawn of time – specifically, the presence of hidden, foreboding, and insidious threats. Research on risk perceptions surrounding nuclear power and its waste reveals that these hidden, ominous threats are particularly hard for the public to accept when the institutions responsible for safety declare that nuclear power and waste storage is risk-free. These absolute statements tend to amplify the public's sense of deception, both due to the inherent invisibility of nuclear power-related risks and the perception that such risks are being understated by the very institutions tasked with mitigating them.[15]

In addition to our inherent difficulty in perceiving and addressing problems in proportion to their severity at a given moment, we possess another flaw that justifies expediting the heating of problem framings for specific environmental and health issues. Our human intuitions often fail to accurately assess the rapidity and magnitude of risks and problems as they escalate. Bartlett, a physicist concerned with the issue of resource depletion, shared a thought-provoking story to emphasize the importance of recognizing problems and heating their framings much earlier than our intuition would suggest in order to mitigate or prevent damage. He presented an example involving bacteria living in a cola bottle. Imagine that two bacteria are placed in the bottle at 11 am, and their population doubles every minute. By noon, the bottle is filled. Now, the question arises: how full would the bottle be one minute before noon? Surprisingly, it would only be half-full. Most people find this calculation counterintuitive because our brains tend to perceive increases as linear, rather than exponential.[16] The key takeaway is that since various problem escalations follow exponential patterns, we cannot rely solely on our intuition to determine when it is time to prevent or manage these problems.

Of course, the relative cultural tolerance of visible plastic litter or air pollution from fossil fuels cannot be attributed solely to their inherent nature. Several social, economic, and political factors play an important role in shaping our perceptions and reactions. One important factor is 'path dependency'.[17] Most countries have long depended heavily on plastics and fossil fuels, a reliance that is deeply entrenched in the global infrastructure built around these materials. Transforming this system towards alternative solutions requires substantial effort, resources, and political willpower.[18] Nonetheless, the ability of certain groups to retain power, despite the slow progress in addressing these escalating issues, cannot be entirely separated from a heightened human sensitivity to specific types of framing over others. Therefore, the most plausible interpretation of framing's role and influence in this context is that powerful actors and organizations, who have vested interests in preserving the status quo, skilfully utilize framing strategies in conjunction with their economic and political resources.

Now or never

When it appears advantageous to rapidly heat up the framing of an issue, how can this be done? It's worth mentioning that our focus is on framing properties and techniques, setting aside the obvious benefits of considerable funding, influential political standing, or strong connections with media networks, which can instantly heat up even the coolest frames.

Consider instances where you have found yourself influenced to act, make a purchase, or engage in something that you wouldn't have done under different circumstances. Often, a sense of scarcity is at play. Retailers understand this well, which is why they offer Black Friday sales.[19] Even if the same items can typically be found at similar prices before and after this event, they capitalize on our tendency to perceive scarce things as valuable, thereby enticing us to make purchases. Auctions inherently rely on scarcity to drive bidding.[20] In many other cases, scarcity is integrated into sales strategies. A common modern experience is standing in an appliance store and casually mentioning to the salesperson that there's no rush to buy a new refrigerator, only to be met with a thoughtful gaze and the remark, 'This is the last one'. Before we know it, we find ourselves hastily loading the fridge into the boot of our car. Scarcity of time and resources amplifies the perceived value of anything associated with scarcity.[21]

Occasionally, concerns about scarcity may be purely driven by vanity. For individuals and groups who aspire to be seen as pioneers, influencers, early adopters, and trend-setters, time is always scarce. They are in a perpetual rush to embrace the new and expedite the framing of the latest trends, making it conspicuous to the outside world that they were the first to embrace what has now become the hottest thing.[22]

In travel advertising targeting the newly retired upper-middle class, messages are often framed in terms of 'now it's time to prioritize', as if life is fleeting and we don't know for how long we'll still be able to travel. Time is presented as a scarce resource. Fortunately, for many individuals in this demographic, time is not as scarce as it may initially seem. Their vitality often remains intact, even a couple of decades after retirement. When the state pension age was originally set in various countries, it was fixed close to life expectancy. For example, in 1940, when the state pension age for women in the UK was set at 60, their life expectancy was only 64, which meant only four golden years for the average woman. For men, the state pension age was set at 65, but it took until the early 1950s for the average man to reach that life expectancy. However, by 2020, when the UK state pension age was raised to 66 for both women and men, the dramatic increase in life expectancy meant that the average woman could expect to receive a state pension for seventeen years, compared with thirteen years for men. For women and men in the upper-middle class, an additional three or four years of life expectancy could be added to the state pension. The difference between retirement age and life expectancy is even higher in several countries on the European continent.[23] It might therefore be justified to say, 'This time, it's alright to travel to the other side of the world. But next time might be our last chance.'

Seizing momentum and capitalizing on favourable timing is not just a tactic employed by salespeople and those seeking to influence us. In social movements, the potential to intensify problem frames is particularly significant when groups of people sense that something is being lost – an indication that society is entering a state of crisis. This is evident in situations of apparent disaster. For example, in February 2023, when 100,000 Syrians who were trapped with no escape route fell victim to one of the most devastating earthquakes in modern times, no framing other than crisis and disaster could adequately capture the magnitude of the situation.[24] However, it's essential to note that crises are often socially constructed. A crisis seldom stems from a clear and objectively observable deterioration that, once it surpasses a certain limit, is deemed a crisis. It's even possible for influential individuals or organizations to fabricate and disseminate a heated crisis frame, often backed by scant or non-existent substance, hence tricking the public within such a frame. According to the notion that 'framing is everything', the leaders of social movement can, if they are only vocal enough, construct a crisis framing in a wide range of ways that widely resonate with the public without the need for an explicit claim of a substantive, negative change.

Still, I'd argue that the power of frame heating operates in a more nuanced manner than that. Extensive evidence suggests that a sense of loss or even a slight movement towards scarcity is crucial for a crisis framing to gain heat and, by extension, cultural resonance.

In the early 1960s, the sociologist James Chowning Davies identified the significant role played by a perception of resource scarcity in comprehensive political change. By studying uprisings in Egypt, Russia, the United States, and elsewhere, he formulated the concept known as the 'J Curve' of revolution. This pattern emerges when a period of increasing liberties or other benefits is followed by a decline, creating a graph resembling an upside-down letter J. As freedoms become more attainable, people become more hopeful. However, when there is a downturn, the fear that these freedoms will become scarce again becomes one of the motivating factors for people to revolt and fight for what they perceive as being on the verge of disappearing.[25] This phenomenon may be rooted in the strong loss aversion that we humans share with some apes. Recall the studies where a group of apes clearly prefer a 'positive' scenario in which they are given one piece of fruit and two pieces half of the time, giving a sense of a bonus, over a scenario in which they receive two pieces first and only one piece half of the time, resulting in a sense of loss.[26]

Not so fast: better play it cool?

Shortly after the main COVID-19 restrictions were removed in several countries, the Swedish comedian Simon Gärdenfors opened one of his stand-up shows as follows:

> It feels so damn good to be back, to be up and running again, you know? All this is over now, it seems. You can behave like you used to again. Yeah, it's been a pretty tough period, this #MeToo thing.[27]

Women and men alike in the audience erupted in laughter. Nevertheless, the joke – and the reactions – shed light on an important lesson learned from many instances of rapid problem reheating: most heated frames eventually cool down unless they are actively nurtured and fuelled with additional energy.

Feminist legal scholar Jamie Abrams explores this phenomenon in relation to community strategies for addressing and combating rape.[28] In several countries, rape is described as a crisis. At first glance, one might perceive this as a positive development.

How timing is of the essence

Describing it as a crisis suggests that society is finally acknowledging rape as more than just a 'personal trouble', as sociologist C. Wright Mills called it, and elevating it to the status of a public issue.[29] Indeed, the swift heating of framings in the media and politics can be seen as a strong indication that such crimes are being taken seriously. The media's focus on certain issues plays a central role in triggering policy changes and increasing financial support in these areas.

However, Abrams urges individuals and movements engaged in the fight against rape or other forms of violent crime to consider the connotations that crisis framings may carry. A rape crisis may appear to be a temporary wave that, much like an economic crisis, must be endured until it subsides, with little action taken once the crisis passes. The crisis model, therefore, runs the risk of aligning with the media logic of quick, temporary heating that ultimately cools down long before sufficient structural measures are implemented to address the problem in the long term. Abrams asserts that a better framing of rape would be less heated yet more enduring, akin to how cancer or Alzheimer's disease are framed – that is, with concrete, specific, and contextual methods.[30]

Similar scepticism regarding rapid and intensive heating of problem framings is evident in the environmental and climate field. A study on the attitudes of young people towards climate strikes reveals thought-provoking reasoning. All participants agreed on the critical importance of fighting climate change for intergenerational justice.[31] However, some who chose not to strike challenged the conventional notion where strikes and protests are seen as 'activism', while less-conspicuous, long-term, and low-intensity activities are seen as passive. Not only did the non-strikers reverse the frame of what constitutes passive and active climate engagement, seeing striking – or 'holding up signs', as they called it – as passive acceptance of the status quo. They also argued that cooler, longer-term initiatives such as litter-picking, planting trees, or engaging in ordinary political work over a longer period of time are more effective in combating climate change and environmental degradation than temporary strikes.

A couple of caveats: these arguments may stem from cognitive dissonance, which refers to the psychological discomfort experienced when individuals find themselves acting in ways that contradict their beliefs, values, or attitudes and seek to resolve the inconsistencies.[32] People may attempt to create a coherent and respectable narrative behind their choice, such as attending school as usual when classmates advocating for a liveable future climate do not. Furthermore, comparing the climate effects of participating in a climate strike for a limited period to engaging in long-term activities like planting trees and litter-picking in nature is nearly impossible to do.

However, the comment from non-striking students serves as a reminder that relying solely on media-heated approaches to address major societal problems is far from sufficient. We must be cautious not to mistake the quick, time-limited framing excitement of the media for actual solutions or consider the mission complete once the media's interest wanes.

While this temporary nature may hinder the goals of movements like #MeToo, there is a realm in society where rapid frame heating and subsequent cooling can be advantageous: retail. This phenomenon can be observed in the proliferation of fast-heating logic in various product types marketed as fashion items, such as sofas, cutlery, Christmas ornaments, and lamps – objects that were traditionally meant to be used for decades. In the realm of home electronics, the accelerated heating of products has been facilitated by barriers to repair when they break down.[33] There have even been claims that certain electronics are intentionally designed to break after a few years. Efforts are underway to pass laws that mandate the repairability of electronics and other products, something that all environmentalists should support.[34]

Is it possible to sustain the framing temperature of a societal issue to create long-term impact and change? The answer may vary depending on the specific issue. However, research on social movements and revolutions offers valuable insights. Historian Lynne Ann Harnett, specializing in Russian history, emphasizes, as we discussed earlier in this chapter, the significance of experiencing increased scarcity. The heating of frames driven by a sense of heightened scarcity has historically led to rapid mobilization, revolts, and rebellions. Scarcity could relate to various aspects, including material resources, personal freedom, and safety.

But while revolts can be dramatic, attention-grabbing, and celebrated by the media, lasting and transformative change requires something more: ideology – a profound and comprehensive vision of a better society. Messages rooted in ideology need to be framed in a motivational manner, offering a clear sense of hope that a different, improved society is attainable. This notion of 'better' often implies a society characterized by a new and fairer relationship among civil society, the state, the elite, and business.

Even limited long-term change demands more than simply invoking a sense of increased scarcity. While an entire ideology may not always be necessary, any change aiming for long-term impact must incorporate one of the key elements of influential ideologies: a straightforward narrative with powerful metaphors and similes that resonate with cultural norms and tap into people's evolutionary predisposition to respond to social risks and opportunities. The role of narratives, metaphors, and similes in heating frames and influencing one another over time will be explored further in the next chapter.

7

Metaphors as frame thermostats

God, Linnaeus and Sartre

Different stages of life come with different social expectations. In our early to mid-twenties, we often find ourselves in a sequence of impersonal networking events, bridging the gap between college graduates or job seekers and representatives from universities or workplaces. These gatherings are typically held in spacious rooms where the buzz of conversation makes it challenging to grasp more than three-quarters of what people say. Invariably, you spot a handful of competitors to yourself, skilfully navigating the crowd, captivating others with their seemingly personalized approach. They create connections and acquire exactly the information and business cards they came for.

In such settings, it's reassuring to huddle with the few faces you feel allied with and privately mull over the candid answers you wish you could give – if only you had the courage – if someone approached you and asked, 'So, what's your name?' 'What do you do?' 'Where did you study?' 'Where do you see yourself in ten years?' You would have options. You could deceive them by pretending to be immensely competent and experienced beyond your actual capabilities. Alternatively, you could downplay your achievements, taking delight in witnessing the mingler's attempts to maintain politeness while their interest in you gradually fades.

However, the coolest reply to such questions didn't strike me until much later, despite it arguably being the most renowned one in

112

Western history. As described in Exodus 3:13–14, Moses converses with God atop a mountain. At a certain point, Moses asks God to disclose His identity and name, to which God replies:

I am who I am.

It's not just profound; it's also perfect, at least for those who, like God, refuse to be confined within a frame or category. Names and occupations are often the first things people ask for when they want to assess someone's status, ethnicity, class, or cultural background. With his one-liner, God asserts his desire not to be placed in the same category as the lower-case gods worshipped in that region at the time. Remaining unnamed and unframed was the only way to maintain his unique status.

The idea that naming is a means of exerting control finds additional support when we consider the life's work of Carl Linnaeus, an influential eighteenth-century Swedish botanist. Linnaeus, whose father was a priest, dedicated himself to naming and categorizing plants and animals from around the world. His work was seen as a way of fulfilling God's command to have dominion over all creatures and plants on Earth, as stated in Genesis 2:19–20:

Now the Lord God had formed out of the ground all the wild animals and all the birds in the sky. He brought them to the man to see what he would name them; and whatever the man called each living creature, that was its name. So the man gave names to all the livestock, the birds in the sky and all the wild animals.[1]

Beyond the realm of religion, philosopher Jean-Paul Sartre made a similar observation about the power of naming. In his memoir *Les Mots* ('The words'), in which he describes his early experiences of producing text where he named living beings, he recalls that 'to write was … to catch living things in the trap of phrases'.[2]

Names and words often go beyond their literal meanings. They can serve as metaphors, drawing connections between different things or phenomena. Metaphors identify symbolic similarities, linking two concepts together.[3] Language, names, and words carry implicit meanings that can influence us, even when we're not consciously aware of them.[4] That's why the God of the Abrahamitic faiths refuses to be named – to avoid being compared to something or someone else. 'I am who I am' represents the absence of metaphor.

While straightforward expressions can certainly carry meaning within specific contexts, metaphors often prove essential in forging our understanding. Metaphors act as mental harbours, providing a place where novel ideas can dock. They stir emotions, making it easier to engage with and retain a concept, be it negative or positive. Imagery-rich expressions, such as depicting deforestation as 'stripping the lungs of our planet', overconsumption as 'a never-ending wildfire', or sustainable living as 'the recipe for a healthy planet', are far more impactful and memorable than plain observations about excessive tree felling, overconsumption, or the benefits of living more sustainably.

Metaphors serve diverse functions depending on their context and intended use. In fields such as environmental and health communication, the need for clarity is crucial. However, the ambiguity introduced by metaphors can cause obscuring misinterpretations that may lead to damaging decisions. In environmental communication, oxymorons such as 'clean coal technology' and 'green diesel' are obvious examples. In health communication, one striking example is the 'hardwired' brain metaphor, which can convey misleading impressions of genetic determinism, disregarding the substantial scope for learning, transformation, and healing. Another damaging metaphor is the 'hydraulic model' of aggression, often linked with the theories of Sigmund Freud. This metaphor implies that aggression amasses within a person, creating escalating pressure much like a hydraulic system. This pressure must be released to avoid system breakdown. As a result, this model inadvertently promotes occasional violent activities as a healthy way of mitigating future aggressive behaviour. While this metaphor still finds traction in certain circles, it has been largely discredited within the human sciences. Studies show that such occasional violent activities usually have a counterproductive effect, reinforcing aggressive behaviours while undermining societal and psychological strategies designed to manage aggressive impulses.

The picture is different in the world of art, literature, and poetry. In these domains, metaphors are often valued for their capacity to clarify as well as simultaneously offering ambiguity and even obscurity that can leave us in awe. Consider this line, written in 1944 by the Polish poet Czesław Miłosz:

On the day the world ends / A bee circles a clover.[5]

Metaphors undeniably exert a significant influence on us. But it's worth exploring if all metaphors resonate equally with our minds and cultures or if some have a stronger impact. Furthermore, might a metaphor be overly precise? Could a slight mismatch between the symbolic representation and the literal meaning of a metaphor enhance its effect, adding an extra layer of influence? We should also consider whether there are times when it is beneficial to use metaphors that cool our framing of a situation. Conversely, when might it be advantageous to use metaphors that incite feelings of action, conflict, or even anger by heating the frame?

Face-pants, mannies, and a crime against humanity

Some metaphors hold the powerful ability to enrich our thinking and leave profound marks on our societies. This effect is something that many can affirm, particularly if we've been deeply influenced by metaphorical expressions in art, poetry, literature, or theatre, leading to notable transformations in our lives. This captivating realm is ideally experienced through active engagement in creating and admiring fine arts. Simultaneously, an often-overlooked aspect also deserves consideration: the elements that lead to the failure of some metaphors. There exist at least two intertwined limitations that may hinder the power of metaphors to influence individuals and society. The first challenge occurs when metaphors do not resonate with the longstanding genetic history of humanity, and the second arises when they fail to align with the historical and contemporary cultural backdrop of the people and society in question.

The clash of metaphors with humanity's genetically evolved risk intuition becomes clear when we contemplate vaccination. There's something about the concept that doesn't sit well with our gut instincts, which perhaps explains why misconceptions and misinformation about it thrive.[6] Vaccination is quite a puzzling notion: injecting something alien into an otherwise perfectly healthy individual, especially a small child. It's probably no coincidence that this odd 'nature' of vaccination is often reinforced through our language. We describe the process as getting a 'shot'. Suddenly, we're on a battlefield, our bodies under assault, and an armed foe is injecting us with something menacing.[7] Interestingly, despite this rather unsettling imagery of vaccination, it doesn't unite us in opposition to it. In fact, it has quite the opposite effect. The resistance to vaccination, rather than rallying us, fragments us. This phenomenon recalls the theory proposed by social anthropologist Mary Douglas. She theorized that our brains, having evolved to avoid anything that could contaminate us, further honed themselves to differentiate between the 'pure' and the 'impure' among us.[8] It seems we've metaphorically transferred this ability into our feelings towards vaccines. It appears our evolutionary coding has extended this ability, amplifying our capacity to learn and react based on these distinctions.

When we perceive people from an 'out-group' – a group different from ours – as untrustworthy, it prompts a feeling akin to disgust, the kind you'd feel toward rotting food.[9] So, when those who create, regulate, and administer vaccines morph into this 'out-group', suspicion quickly follows: perhaps their organizations might prioritize their profits over our safety. Concerning vaccination, the metaphors we intuitively gravitate towards can deceive us into perceiving the risk of vaccination, creating a persistent worry and resistance. This is despite medical research indicating that the hazards – both individually and collectively – are generally much greater if we decline vaccination compared to if we accept it. The issue here lies in the deceptive metaphor's effectiveness in shaping our perception of vaccination, persistently influencing us.

Conversely, a problem arises when one attempts to construct a metaphor to intensify the problem's framing, but the metaphor fails to adequately mirror the problem's nature, thus lacking conviction. Let's revisit the situation in New Delhi, India, where in 2022 the air quality index frequently surged into the 'hazardous' and 'severe' zones, necessitating the closing of schools. Stirred by this acute crisis, Indian author Suhel Seth took to Twitter to express his despair:

> What is happening with air pollution in Delhi is nothing short of a crime against humanity.[10]

The desperation driving this vivid metaphor is something we can all connect with. As we've already unpacked in this book, air pollution claims millions of lives globally each year. So, it's not that the 'crime against humanity' metaphor is overly dramatic. Nor does it diverge from the age-old, narrative components to which our species respond. It's quite the opposite: it fits snugly into our familiar storylines. It suggests distinct ill-doers – targets for our outrage and blame. This process of personalization and the focus on clear culprits pack a powerful punch in many narratives.

But does the metaphor 'crime against humanity' aptly illustrate the complex issue of urban pollution? Likely not. As we're aware, there isn't a single polluter – we're talking about countless contributors, reaching into the millions. The task of assigning blame, creating a diagnostic framing the problem, is far from straightforward. Is it the oil tycoons, the industrial giants, the car manufacturers, local administrators, motorists, consumers, or an intricate network involving all of them? Further complicating matters, there's no clear prognostic frame that suggests a potential solution. It's not apparent that a set of decisive actions by local or regional authorities would resolve the problem. The metaphor 'crime against humanity' – despite aligning with the harsh reality of air pollution – might require significant narrative restructuring to foster not only a sharp but also a motivational, action-oriented understanding of the problem. The intricate matter of air pollution needs to be translated into a compelling, resonant narrative that effectively galvanizes public sentiment and initiates transformative change.[11]

In the same vein, as metaphors can clash with humanity's genetically evolved adaptations to ancestral society, they run the risk of falling flat when they fail to align with the historical and contemporary cultural backdrop of the people and society. Just look at the countless marketing specialists who spend their days fashioning new word uses, combinations, and phrases, often involving metaphors. Their goal? Not just to boost sales, but also to shatter stereotypes. They constantly chip away, for instance, at ingrained ideas about gender roles in various professions. It's a noble endeavour, like small-scale language labs churning out fresh lexicon. But much like every other field, not all creations that emerge from these linguistic workshops are gems.

What about 'Girlboss' or 'SheEO'? These terms, coined to denote female business leaders, are designed to affirm that leadership isn't bound by gender.[12] Yet, if these neologisms make us wince, it's perhaps because they're out of sync with the spirit of the times, much like the somewhat troubling idea of electing 'The least sexually harassing person of the month' in workplaces. Now, let's consider another metaphor – this one on an entirely different theme.

'Face-pants'. Some regions use this term as a euphemism for face masks. Upon hearing 'face-pants', there's a moment of discomfort, as if we've found ourselves trouserless in a crowd. Our reaction after that moment depends largely on our cultural backdrop. In Japan, the birthplace of the term *kao pantsu*, and many other parts of Asia, this sense of awkward exposure might linger more than it would in many Western countries. This stems from the cultural norm prevailing in various Asian countries that mandate face masks, compared with the situation in many Western countries, where they're mandated only during local or global epidemics. Kazunari Onishi, a Japanese public health professor, maintains that in many contexts, people will be stared at if they don't wear a mask in public.[13] Similarly, South Korean cultural studies scholar Sangmin Kim suggests that in South Korea, face masks communicate respect for others and the desire not to cause harm, extending beyond the specific threat of COVID-19.[14] Research has pointed out several culturally and historically rooted reasons why people in Asian countries are more likely to wear masks than their Western counterparts. It's reasonable then to expect a new metaphor like 'face-pants' to have a higher chance of gaining traction over time in these Asian countries compared to Western ones, where dwindling media interest in COVID-19 also diminishes interest in wearing face masks.

Metaphors as frame thermostats

Yachts and tankers

Just because a metaphor doesn't manage to alter the temperature of an issue perfectly doesn't mean it's devoid of value. Let's ponder all the odd and seemingly pointless things that worm their way into our heads, often outliving the quality memories we'd prefer to retain. I'm talking about those maddeningly bad commercials or ridiculous tunes that have a strange knack of spinning endlessly in our minds, solely because they're bad. Our brains register badness – ugliness, immorality, or falsities – as a potential threat and, therefore, crucial to remember. So, perhaps there's a case to be made for the likes of 'SheEO', 'Girlboss', and 'manny' (a man who works as a nanny).

Metaphors are at their most engaging when they provoke us to wrestle with them emotionally and cognitively. In her book *And Then What? Inside Stories of 21st-Century Diplomacy*, Baroness Catherine Ashton, the European Union's first High Representative for Foreign Affairs and Security Policy, endeavours to explain the intricate dance of international crisis management. This dance involves urgent responses coupled with sustained relationship-building between nations. But how does she compel us to move beyond passive acceptance and engage with her recommendations? How does she get us past the lukewarm response of 'that seems reasonable'? She starts by opening the doors to her experiences in conflict resolution and mediation in nations like Libya, Serbia, Somalia, and Iran, offering insights into the journey to the Iran Nuclear Deal in 2015.[15] Secondly, Ashton offers us metaphoric handrails in the form of yachts and tankers as we navigate the tempestuous seas of various conflict hotspots. Yachts, she suggests, represent the swift and nimble crisis management required for specific issues. On the flip side, tankers conjure up an image of long-term, slow but steady cooperation between nations akin to entities like the United Nations or the European Union. The metaphor cleverly elucidates the need for both strategies in diplomacy.

Next time a reader of Ashton's book needs to contemplate strategies for managing a crisis, they might very well find themselves thinking of yachts and tankers. This wouldn't be due to the metaphors being unerringly accurate, because they're not. Doesn't the term yachts trigger thoughts of lavish indulgence and ostentatious showing off rather than vital efforts to swiftly minimize global risks? And does 'tankers' paint a picture of steadfast, principled cooperation between nations aimed at long-term crisis prevention and management? Tankers may carry chemicals, drinking water, wine, and even citrus juice. But the image they're most readily associated with is likely oil transportation, conjuring images of oil crises, leaking ships, and the ongoing climate change crisis.

These associations are narrow and caricatured and don't capture the full range of current and potential uses of yachts and tankers. But the simplistic images are likely to remain in our collective consciousness until we are exposed to that range. Yet, the aim of metaphors need not be to perfectly mirror the subject at hand, as would be suggested by the 'reality speaks for itself' approach. Nor do they have to send the signals predicted by the 'framing is everything' approach, which posits that framing – in this case, metaphors – can completely manipulate our perception of any given issue.

In contrast, our minds are not so rigid or 'photographic' when processing metaphors. For metaphors to be memorable, they need not align perfectly with the reality they represent. Cognitive research shows that memory techniques often contain peculiarities.[16] For instance, if you need to remember to buy milk, shoe polish, and tomato purée, you could imagine a cow in your hallway polishing its hooves before stomping on tomatoes like one might during grape harvests in winemaking regions.

Additionally, an imperfect metaphor keeps us on our toes, stopping us from conflating it with reality. We can be influenced by what the metaphor illuminates without being misled by its layers and undertones. Ashton could have opted for metaphors closer to global crisis management, such as military analogies. She could have talked about elite units or rapid response forces instead of yachts and replaced tankers with long-term military strategies. But she consciously chose not to. Military metaphors would be closer to global political crisis management than yachts and tankers. However, it could be disastrous if we started conflating military metaphors with diplomacy and relationship-building, where military action hopefully only plays a limited part.

In conclusion, it seems fair to assert that yachts and tankers, partly *because of* their imperfections, meet the criteria for engaging metaphors that capture our attention and contribute to our understanding of Ashton's message.

Cooling with metaphors

The realm of gambling presents a striking example of how metaphors can be used to cool the framing temperature of issues. Market researchers observed significant differences in how various forms of gambling were portrayed by the media. According to one study, traditional gambling activities like lotteries and physical casinos were portrayed in a favourable light, labelled as entertainment. On the contrary, online gambling, particularly in its early days, was framed negatively, associated with regulation, criminal activity, and addiction.

A subsequent study explored the effect of terminology on perceptions of online gambling. Researchers presented participants with articles on the subject, differing only in whether they referred to the activity as 'gambling' or 'gaming'. When 'gaming' was used, attitudes among non-participants significantly improved. Interestingly, active online gamblers favoured retaining the term 'gambling'.[17] One could speculate that non-gamblers were swayed by the positive connotations of 'gaming', whereas gamblers, as early adopters of the activity, found the term 'gaming' somewhat juvenile and less exclusive.

A similar impact of metaphors was discovered concerning the use of cognitive enhancers – synthetic or natural supplements that are claimed to improve cognitive functions, such as memory, motivation, or creativity, in healthy people – in the workplace. A team of neurologists and other professionals surveyed 3,700 participants across the US about their views on cognitive enhancers at work. They experimented with the metaphors 'fuel' and 'steroids', analysing their influence on participants' attitudes. Once again, word choice proved significantly influential. When cognitive enhancers were framed as 'fuel', a more positive response was elicited, while the term 'steroids' resulted in a more negative reaction.[18] The examples of online gambling and cognitive enhancers underscore the power of metaphors in shaping our perspectives, with carefully used metaphors often reducing our reservations and leading to acceptance.

Take prenuptial agreements, for instance, the application of which has been hotly debated and caused raised eyebrows in certain cultures and circles. For those who endorse prenups, the challenge is to smoothen and cool the rough, heated frames around them and thereby encourage more people to consider them. Researchers Lynsey Romo and Noah Czajkowski highlight the benefit of finding metaphors that serve this purpose.[19] They have studied how users of the social media platform Reddit try to make sense of prenups. In some posts, the agreements were likened to 'harbingers of doubt' or 'backup plans' – the exact opposite of the ideal type of marriage and lifelong love. But these posts were met with counter-metaphors that smoothed and cooled the framing. They compared prenuptial agreements to insurance and safety nets, things that in society are not only normalized but also strongly advocated. Following the Reddit threads, the researchers could see how counter-metaphors influenced those who had previously been critical, prompting them to express less-negative comments about prenuptial agreements.

It would be biased to define the metaphor changes as a 'success' just because the Reddit threads seemed to be shifting in a positive direction. On the other hand, it would also be simplistic to see the metaphor changes as something positive as soon as they seem to make any type of difference. Nevertheless, I would consider the Reddit threads a success, due to the deliberative and open conversation that the metaphors sparked. If the Reddit discussion followed the 'reality speaks for itself' approach, the metaphors would mostly be a distraction that obscures the facts about prenuptial agreements and their consequences in society. If the conversation instead followed the 'framing is everything' approach, it would only concern a battle of words with a focus on which side is more influential. Instead, the different sides forced each other to clarify in which respects a particular metaphor reflected reality and where the metaphor did not, posing questions such as: which income groups do you guys have in mind? What changes in gender dynamics do you imagine? Do pre-nuptial agreements statistically lead to longer and happier marriages or the opposite? For some specific cohabiting classes or all? What percentage of divorced people would require prenuptial agreements if they were to marry again?

I think the benefit of the metaphors for prenups was that they opened such a conversation, in which there was also respect for statistical data even when they contradicted the initial beliefs or perceptions of one side or the other. At the same time, the par-ticipants did not ultimately reduce the metaphors to any single fact that revealed which were 'true' or 'false'. After all, when people advocate a particular metaphor, it also depends on how they want to be perceived by others and themselves. The facts that emerged – often in favour of prenups – need to be tested against how the par-ticipants' social environments perceive the issue and how the social norm looks and may change. From the beginning of the twenty-first century, an increasing number of women, at least in the United States, have begun to request prenuptial agreements. Yet, by 2020, only 6 per cent of Americans had written them.[20] Maybe the domi-nant norm still distinguishes between, on the one hand, the warm approach – romance, loyalty, non-calculation – and, on the other, the cold one – crass realism, replaceability, and calculation. Hopefully – dare I say normatively – such a clichéd binarity will eventually shift to a new framing that is in phase with our times and resonates with humanity's age-old need to feel safe and not be betrayed by signifi-cant others.

Social media is one place where framing temperatures are raised and lowered around prenups. Another is music. A significant player in this metaphorical arena has been the rapper Kanye West. Not only is he an outspoken advocate of prenuptial agreements, but he has also used his music to promote them, notably in the 2005 hit 'Gold Digger'. If his objective was to encourage more couples to overcome traditional reservations towards prenuptials, we might expect him to attempt to *lower* the temperature of the prenuptial 'framing', thereby normalizing the act of drafting these contracts. But that is not the approach he takes, as we will see on examining the lyrics of the song:

> If you ain't no punk holla, 'We want prenup'
> We want prenup!', yeah
> It's something that you need to have
> 'Cause when she leave yo' ass she gon' leave with half.[21]

The Reddit discussions above exemplified one strategy for achieving wide-scale approval of a hot-button issue – namely, to cool down its framing temperature. In that case, the goal was to render the contentious topic more agreeable to the majority, to take the edge off, thereby minimizing the propensity for division. But Kanye West's tries to influence people to request prenuptial agreements from their partners in the opposite way – namely by *increasing* the framing heat. Instead of soothing the flames around this issue, West's lyrics fan them. It's a tactic that, on the surface, might seem puzzling or even counterproductive. However, there's a subtle brilliance at play, particularly when the endgame is to galvanize a specific cohort – men, in this case – into demanding prenuptial agreements. West cranks up the temperature of his framing to fever pitch, with the focal point being an issue that finds ancestral resonance – the dread of being tricked, deceived, and betrayed. It's a primal concern, one that strikes a chord with us all, regardless of our gender.

But, as with all potent strategies, there's a potential drawback to the one West uses. The conflict-oriented nature of the song's approach, with its targeted emphasis on women, may have the unintended side effect of further entrenching the dispute surrounding prenuptial agreements. This could mean that, paradoxically, the idea of prenups remains as controversial, as hotly contested, as it was before West's fiery lyrics hit the turntable.

Heating with metaphors

In his song, Kanye West utilizes the tactic of 'frame heating', cautioning affluent men against falling prey to financial manipulation by 'gold diggers'. This tactic draws from the longstanding human instinct to rally and actively combat perceived threats when presented with a situation framed as dangerous, where malevolent forces aim to deceive or harm us. Many heated metaphors have connotations of war. The war on cancer, the war on drugs, and the war on microplastics are just a few of them. For instance, the insidious invisibility of microplastics has influenced several organizations and countries to perceive them as threatening in much the same way that viruses, bacteria, or human enemies can be perceived as threatening. There is much to suggest that war is an effective metaphor for heating up engagement and cooperation. The ability and propensity to mobilize quickly and decisively to fight a common enemy is something we got from our early ancestors who, like we, were genetically adapted to life in small-scale hunter-gatherer societies. Evolutionary anthropologists assume this driver was even with us long before we evolved into humans.[22]

War metaphors can prove effective when the objective mirrors the swift rallying of our group for either an attack or defence against a clearly defined adversary within a limited timeframe. Some noncombat operations, both military and non-military, also exhibit these mobilizing characteristics. For instance, obligatory rallying to shield a community from an impending, foreseeable natural disaster, or immediate and decisive fundraising to aid another country experiencing famine due to a temporary drought, which can be alleviated with prompt international support. The capacity to swiftly raise the heat of a problem framing, facilitating unprecedented collaboration among diverse groups and organizations, was notably demonstrated during the COVID-19 pandemic. The accelerated coordination and creativity in medical innovation and crisis management at municipal, national, and international levels, culminating in the development of vaccines against the disease, showcased the potential of this ancient framing strategy on an almost global scale.

However, it's not necessarily true that martial metaphors are suitable for all kinds of threats. This should be approached with caution on an individual level, for instance, when people frame their personal battle with cancer. Empirical research into the effects of war metaphors on cancer patients revealed that such metaphors often diverted patients from self-restraint and preventive actions that have been proven to enhance recovery prospects.[23]

These findings echo previous criticisms related to framing rape as a 'crisis', as discussed in Chapter 6. The sense of urgency implicit in the words 'war' and 'crisis' is often counterproductive to the necessary calm and sustained efforts required in these situations, both at the individual and societal levels.

Part III

Making meanings move – frame positioning

In the mid-1960s, Pablo Picasso was interviewed for the *Paris Review* magazine. One of the topics was the pioneering mechanical 'giant thinking machines' – early versions of computers and calculators – that had been developed at the time. When Picasso was asked how he perceived such machines, he is said to have replied:

They are useless. They can only give us answers.[1]

Impressive, indeed. At the same time, doesn't the answer seem obvious and even predictable, as one would expect Picasso to respond from an artist's perspective, focusing on artistic production? After all, art is very much about asking and raising new questions that – beyond their aesthetic value – help us see the world from new angles and in a new light. New questions can thus have an intrinsic value and be at least as startling and enlightening as the possible answers that follow. Similarly, there are many examples of how, to improve a specific condition, it may be necessary to reposition the frame to anchor the proposed change with a new meaning that has a higher chance of being accepted by the groups in question. One could thus say that the intrinsic value of creatively identifying new questions and problems – as suggested by Picasso's answer above – is the opposite of the stereotype of the neat and linear processes of modern problem management.

Accordingly, questions, answers, problems, and solutions can be clearly defined, distinguished, kept stable, and placed in a certain order. Similarly, the framing literature, especially covering social change and movements, often presents framing processes in a tidy manner – sometimes too tidy.

Many studies of social movements try to make sense of processes of change by identifying three distinct framing components that leaders of such movements have crafted into a simple and coherent narrative. Such a narrative typically starts with diagnostic framing. It identifies the problem and assigns blame. Next, movement leaders add a prognostic framing. It outlines potential solutions, which could range from political to religious. Finally, they push forward a motivational frame. It's a powerful message rallying people to work towards the change they want to see, making them believe that change is both achievable and beneficial.[2] Although the simplification by the scholars of social movements is admirable and disarming to the reader, the risk of studying certain, more multifaceted cases in this way is one of generating overly distilled versions that obscure rather than clarify the intricate processes these movements follow.

Framing, as orchestrated by key figures like movement leaders or politicians, may indeed have traits of such goal rationality. For example, anything from governmental and civil society organizations to groups in the public may *try* to follow such a well-planned, neat order. But if any 'pattern' can be deciphered, it's usually that framings of problem, solution, and motivations is often much more fluid and can constantly be repositioned. Climate change may lead some groups to active engagement if it is framed as a problem of shortage of climate-mitigating technologies. Such groups are strongly motivated to participate if the solution is framed as a matter of investing and working harder on technological innovation to mitigate climate change but are much less willing to engage if climate change is framed as primarily an issue of socio-economic inequality that needs to be addressed.[3]

In the context of genetically modified crops in food, for instance, the strong ecological and health-related focus among environmental and health groups in favour of regulating or banning genetically modified organisms (GMOs) – arguments that were first presented as the *raison d'être* of the protests – are repositioned into a completely different type of framing. The new positioning may shed full light on ethical aspects, emphasizing instead that GMOs should be regulated or banned because it is the moral and democratic right of people not have to consume GMOs. Additionally, it could be considered the right of farmers not to be locked in to the business models and increased control of the world's food supply by GMO multinationals. This could hold true whether the GMOs are harmful to the environment or to health.[4] Several such alternative frame positionings can undoubtedly be reasonable. The point is rather that framings of what is a solution, a problem, an end, or a means are often fluid and repositioned in the social art of framing.

Frame repositioning is the theme of the following two chapters. It's the property that enables frames to be moved around, between different possible aspects and meanings of a condition or situation, all playing a central part in conflicts, negotiations, and deliberations, and with a big potential for exerting social influence. Two cardinal directions of frame repositioning are covered. First, we'll examine up–down positioning, between the explicit, substantive matter and the implicit, underlying level of an issue. Then we move to sideways positioning, which refers to how we can move frames that cover an issue so that it's given a different meaning, such as between being a matter of what's true or what's morally right, or aesthetically valuable.

8

Up–down positioning: reading on
or between the lines

Whispers from below

'The greatest of follies is to sacrifice health for any other kind of happiness', writes the philosopher Arthur Schopenhauer.[1] The need to prioritize health is not a new concept – although rarely presented so succinctly – and is a universally adopted axiom. In a survey of employees and employers conducted by Deloitte and Workplace Intelligence in the US, UK, Canada, and Australia in 2022, the vast majority (91 per cent) said they had well-being goals, and 75 to 89 per cent of respondents said improving their health and well-being was a top priority for them.[2] But is the truth of our priorities reflected in our actions? The paradoxical popularity of junk food, even among those who have the means to access healthier alternatives, begs the question. The health argument, frequently employed to persuade us to adopt more nutritious and less harmful eating habits, is a straightforward pitch: rational, factual, and relevant. Yet the gap between statistics, the widespread knowledge about nutritious and harmful diets, and the actual eating habits of many is puzzling. What if we repositioned the frame away from health towards a different issue?

In an enlightening study published in the journal *Nature Human Behaviour*, researchers explored an innovative approach. They tested the effectiveness of repositioning the framing of junk food to see if this would influence teenage boys to change their dietary choices. Instead of being warned about health risks, these young men were exposed to the *morally* darker side of the junk food industry. They learned about the greed-driven tactics employed by many of the corporations, and about the systematic efforts to hook consumers on unhealthy food. The exercise continued with a critique of misleading junk food ads, where the boys got to deconstruct and rewrite these persuasive narratives. Strikingly, this approach led to a marked reduction in the consumption of unhealthy food and drinks by 31 per cent more than a control group, who were given conventional material on the benefits of a healthy diet. Evidently, the ethical reframing strategy yielded a stronger impact than the 'eat healthily' approach, compelling us to reconsider the effectiveness of our framing mechanisms.[3]

It's a revelation that topples the 'reality speaks for itself' notion. The reality that a culture perceives to be critical, such as the saliency of health and healthy food, may be masking other significant underlying factors that can be harnessed through strategic framing. To influence how we perceive and respond to issues, framing must align not just with our current culture. Framings must interweave current culture with ancestral life. With this insight, the allure of junk food seems far from paradoxical; it rather exemplifies a disconnect between our ancestral and contemporary lifestyles. Our forebears' proclivity to seize every chance to consume salt, fat, and sugar was a significant survival trait. The sweetness signified food safety and provided energy. Sodium, a mineral found in salt, is essential for normal nerve and muscle functions, yet it was scarce in ancient times. Thus, individuals with a strong predilection for salty foods were motivated to locate these vital resources, enhancing their survival and reproductive prospects. Similarly, fat, being calorically dense, was a much sought-after commodity during lean periods, conferring an evolutionary advantage to those craving fatty foods. However, in today's world, where junk food – laden with fat, sugar, and salt – is plentiful, there is an elevated risk of overconsumption.[4]

What might one of this book's favourite thinkers, Thomas Huxley, have advised in the nineteenth century regarding this mismatch between our ancestral inclinations and modern society?[5] First, he would stress the importance of acknowledging this mismatch.

Up–down positioning

My grandmother's mantra, 'you need what you crave', advocating for the continual indulgence of our innate cravings for sugar, salt, and fat, might have been beneficial during the two world wars she experienced. But in our current world saturated with junk food, it doesn't hold up. On the other hand, Huxley would also caution against 'running away' from these near insatiable cravings. What would 'run away from' mean in this context? It could be exemplified by health authorities and others relying solely on providing the public with standard health warnings. If health authorities and other advocates of healthier eating rely entirely on demonstrating how people's diets are inconsistent with the recommendations of the surface-level 'take care of your body' framing of affluent societies, this would be a form of government 'running away from', by their ignoring or downplaying our deep-seated, million-year-old yearnings for sugar, salt, and fat. It reduces these cravings to recent cultural quirks. It assumes that simply highlighting the health risks of junk food will prompt individuals to prioritize their long-term health.

As to what Huxley would suggest for what he calls 'combating' the cosmic, natural order – which he would in a mismatch such as this one – is difficult to say without knowing his ideological position. If his ideology wouldn't allow for a hard and authoritarian regulation of junk food, he would very likely suggest that health authorities and others experiment with campaigns, policies, and practical arrangements that serve to reposition the junk food frame 'up–down', from the surface level (where factual health information is in focus) down to the latent, deeply social level. A frame repositioning down to the underlying level would have a higher chance of vibrating in correspondence with the ancestral past of the human species. A promising candidate would be people's inherent dislike for deception and betrayal. In the case of the reframing of junk food with teenage boys, the adolescents' visceral reaction to being manipulated was more impactful than the mainstream health-oriented narratives. It aligns more deeply than the now-ubiquitous exhortation to eat healthily.

If we look at history, warnings against deceit and trickery echo down the ages, carrying a strong resonance in our collective consciousness. Timeless wisdom from ancient texts such as the *Epic of Gilgamesh* and the *Tao Te Ching* speaks to this narrative, cautioning against the perils of naivety. This theme is also prevalent in age-old fairy tales, those stories handed down from generation to generation. In essence, by being highly motivated to resist manipulation, people have through the ages ensured their survival and the continuity of generations – not through a myopic focus on selecting a diet that reduces the risk of getting cardiovascular diseases three decades later, but through a fundamental wisdom that harks back to a time when food choices were not a luxury, but a necessity for survival.

Relevant irrelevance

Let's move beyond food and health issues and look at another area of public engagement: protests and strikes pushing for action on climate change. Studies have found that the framing which sparks the most public engagement isn't about how far climate change has advanced and how grave the explicit, surface-level issue – the physical condition – is, which is where the United Nations Intergovernmental Panel on Climate Change (IPCC) mainly places their problem frame. What really captures attention is framing that hinges on the underlying moral level, particularly injustice across generations and the skewing of power. We can see these patterns courtesy of moral psychology and social movement research. It seems we're naturally drawn to social and procedural issues of fairness, honesty, and the avoidance of betrayal more than to substantive ones such as the physical state of the planet. It's almost like we're on guard, ready to spot these moral issues. This instinct is so deeply ingrained that we don't always realize we're acting on it.[6] Feelings of deceit and unfairness, whether they're directed at us or someone else,[7] provoke a kind of righteous anger. Yet, as I've shown across different areas and situations, we often let group loyalty or empathy for others distract us from the original issue. For example, when presented with evidence contradicting the idea that genetically modified crops are harmful to the environment and health or that wind power threatens bird life, we may – out of loyalty with others with whom we share a cultural identity as 'greens' or 'locals' living close to such sites – become more convinced of these risks.[8]

Behavioural economists like Richard Thaler would explain this as a failure to act rationally. This is one of the defining traits of 'Humans' as opposed to 'Econs', according to Thaler and his colleague Cass Sunstein. 'Econs' is their abbreviation for *Homo economicus*, an 'imaginary species' the members of which systematically, with perfect information and without bias, make optimal forecasts and decisions in light of their well-defined, conscious interests – a description that 'thus fits within the usual depiction of human beings offered by economists'.[9] How about us real people, *Homo sapiens*, for whom the authors use the term 'Humans'? Their short answer is that 'Unlike Econs, Humans predictably err', a notion they explain further using words such as 'fallacious', 'biased', 'unrealistic', 'myopic', and 'inert'.[10] Humans are best understood by our failing to be rational is the foundation of the authors' concept of 'nudging'. A nudge is an intervention that 'alters people's [erroneous, biased, irrational] behavior in a predictable way without forbidding any options or significantly changing their economic incentives'.[11]

Indeed, the viewpoint that humans are deeply irrational is logical and helpful if the focus of all humans, and those who study human behaviour, is solely on achieving explicit, substantive, and stable goals. This includes developing a statistically accurate understanding of wind power and the risks and opportunities of GMOs through optimal data analysis. Portraying humans as irrational also holds true, and is supported by sophisticated scientific analyses and rich data, in other areas but – again – only if the sole focus is on optimizing some stipulated, explicit, and highly specific interests, such as the best planning of pension funds or boosting voluntary organ donations. Behavioural economists also conduct valuable studies into many other seemingly advantageous modifications, like enhancing recycling efforts and decreasing car usage. However, labelling humans as irrational seems somewhat disconcerting and oversimplified. It suggests a surrender or a hybrid of the two notions I contest: the belief that 'reality speaks for itself' (or at least *should* do) and the assertion that 'framing is everything'.

Fortunately, we are not confined to perceiving humans as primarily irrational. Evolutionary biologist Robert Trivers offers an alternative in his book *Deceit and Self-Deception: Fooling Yourself the Better to Fool Others.*[12] He proposes that our behaviours are deeply rooted not just in the era of *Homo sapiens'* emergence but also in the even earlier epochs of our more primitive ancestors, who were less reflective than we have become. Evolution has shaped our consciousness to primarily focus on facets that promote survival, reproduction, and offspring care. Trivers and other scientists posit that most of our mental processes operate 'automatically' or 'pre-consciously'. Our capacity for reflective, conscious planning is a more recent development of the human brain, and it is not tied as deeply into our fundamental emotions.

Looking beyond individual cognition, society also possesses partly hidden layers, composed of deeply ingrained social norms that often go unnoticed, much like a fish being unaware of the water it swims in. Let's not forget that it's the norm, and somewhat handy, not to nitpick every aspect of our cultural habits. Sure, some elements may fall short of ideal, raise a few moral eyebrows, or just be flat-out wrong, but most folks will shrug it off, probably because shaking society's core could open a Pandora's box of problems and uncertainties. We often don't press pause to dissect the frameworks upholding our cultural norms. When invited to the home of some new acquaintances, instead of contemplating whether air travel should be strictly rationed, questioning John Lennon's genius, or suggesting that the TV volume be turned off during segments of the marathon pre-game coverage on Super Bowl Sunday, we can choose the path of least resistance.

An intriguing parallel exists between moral and aesthetic dimensions, as shown in the issues mentioned above, and a third dimension – that of knowledge creation. Take, for instance, the reactions to a variety of health and environmental claims. Each assertion, whether it's scientifically substantiated or not, has the potential to be inaccurate. Occasionally, even scientific advice on diet, health, or the environment might require modification. But if we focus merely on the apparent aspects, such as when media highlight the need for re-evaluation of a scientific claim or the debunking of an unscientific one, we risk accepting an oversimplified narrative of 'science in crisis'. This perspective overlooks the deeper truth, less visible but fundamental, that the discovery of erroneous scientific claims is often a sign that the scientific process is functioning as intended. At the heart of this truth is the realization that effective science relies on a continuous, often underrepresented in media, self-examination within the scientific community. This self-correcting process is unique to science.[13] The capacity to position frames between the clear, overt level and the implicit, semi-obscured level presents us with potential risks or opportunities, depending on the lens we choose to apply to the issue at hand.

Obscuring the underlying level

At first glance, it seems sensible to frame an issue by focusing solely on its explicit, visible nature. This feels like the direct, methodical way to address the matter. However, to avoid tricking ourselves and misleading others, we must acknowledge that this approach can hide or overlook underlying factors that often play a huge role in shaping the issue.

We've already discussed this through the case of how best to encourage healthier eating habits. Whereas it's common to focus solely on 'relevant' factors located at the surface level, such as by sharing information about the health effects of a diet, 'irrelevant' but potentially highly influential factors may lurk beneath the surface. In the constant intertwining of evolution and culture, these underlying factors can influence dietary choices as much as health facts. One such factor turned out to be the slick and misleading marketing tactics of the junk food industry and their influence on policies.

A study published in *Nature Human Behaviour* explored dynamics around recycling and financial incentives in Sweden, analysing more than twenty thousand observations from about seventeen million individual decisions. The study examined how increased expectations of financial rewards might affect recycling decisions. Common sense might suggest that the more people are financially rewarded for recycling, the more motivated they'll be to do it. This aligns with the 'reality speaks for itself' approach, emphasizing both the social desirability of recycling and the importance of financial incentives in society. Indeed, both diligent recycling and monetary rewards often lead to social recognition, as you perform an appreciated act and are financially rewarded for it, creating tangible social affirmation.

However, the researchers found that the relationship between financial reward and recycling isn't that straightforward. Instead, it follows an S-shaped curve. As financial rewards for recycling household waste (such as cans) increased, recycling did increase – but only up to a certain point, known as an 'inflection point'. Beyond that, recycling levels fell until reaching another inflection point, where the curve ascended again. One explanation offered by the researchers is that important signalling is going on below, something that – at certain intervals – is distorted by the surface of eco-friendly behaviour and financial incentives. Higher financial rewards can negatively affect the signals recyclers can send to themselves about their underlying motivation for recycling.[14] This motivation often relates to personal credibility and the sacrifices made for prosocial commitments, like investing time and effort with little or no monetary gain. The intrinsic satisfaction of performing good acts is diminished when the reward is increased. As the financial incentives rise further, the external financial motivation takes over, until it reaches a level where people feel their prosocial signal has become too muddied or conflicting. The curve then goes up again, reflecting these complex relationships between motivation, reward, and behaviour.

Another example concerns how to frame the need to support policies to reduce environmental and climate impacts. By framing the issue only around 'relevant' factors, like the latest findings from the IPCC and discussions on climate change solutions, we unintentionally hide a world of 'irrelevant' factors. These include our habit of comparing our behaviours with those of others, organizations, and countries we identify with – what experts call 'descriptive norms' – instead of comparing our impact with the practices needed to lessen environmental harm. This kind of overlooking happens in many other areas too.

Historical international conflicts illustrate that the drive towards peace entails more than just securing or defending a specific territory. It's equally important in peace negotiations to facilitate a new story or a reframing of the situation. This reframing should accommodate the latent social rationality of all involved, ensuring that each party can save face and avoid going home a loser. One such example of this, although only a temporary one, could be seen in the 1978 Camp David Accords, in which Egyptian president Anwar Sadat and Israeli prime minister Menachem Begin, assisted by US president Jimmy Carter, managed to draft a peace treaty between their warring nations. It enabled both Sadat and Begin to declare victory at home – Sadat regained the Sinai Peninsula, while Begin was able to ensure Israel's security.

Another instance was the Good Friday Agreement of 1998, which brought an end to the enduring conflict in Northern Ireland. It permitted both the Protestant and Catholic communities to retain their honour by offering a structure for sharing power and by ensuring the residents of the region the right to determine Northern Ireland's status.

These examples show that successful negotiations and peace agreements involve more than just crafting a new narrative or framing, contrary to what the 'framing is everything' approach suggests. It requires significant changes to the underlying, deeply social conditions, which allow the creation of a convincing and compelling narrative. For peace between nations, this might mean giving minority groups in other countries more autonomy, ensuring strategic interests in the region are met, securing access to vital ports, and so on. More generally, this necessitates addressing the less visible processes shaping the conflict.

Obscuring the surface level

On the flip side, by only focusing the framing of a matter around its *underlying* factors, as we did above, other risks of misleading ourselves and others emerge. Consider again the case of teenage boys consuming unhealthy food. If the factual health-related issue of food is solely pegged to the underlying question of whether various sectors of the food industry are honest or misleading influencers of policies, the focus on the manifest level concerning which food is most unhealthy could get blurred. It may turn out that producers of seemingly healthy foods like carrots and broccoli were the most deceitful in marketing and lobbying, whereas the junk food industry, relying on the irresistible taste of their salty and fatty foods, was only moderately aggressive. Thus, positioning the frame entirely on the underlying level of honesty and deceit may render the surface level of nutrition invisible.

Over the years, I've had conversations with various government agencies and municipalities whose job is to educate and assist citizens in reducing their environmental impact. I've often asked them what markers of success they identify in their enthusiastic and persistent efforts. The responses, surprisingly, have seldom centred around tangible outcomes like a decrease in car usage, an uptick in recycling, a measurable decrease in food waste, or a reduction in air travel. Rather, success is often gauged by the number of citizens attending environmental campaigns, the amount of 'likes' their activities receive on social media, or the frequency of their initiatives being highlighted in the press. Although we hope that this public attention eventually converts into practical actions that diminish environmental impacts, this is far from a guaranteed outcome. This shift in focus from the explicit factual issue – reducing environmental impact – may create a risk of the issue itself becoming obscured by underlying social factors.

On one side of the underlying level, there's the deeply social motivation to get the public's attention as quantified by the citizens' responses, interest levels, and social media likes. On the other side of the underlying level, there is the deeply social motivation to receive positive reinforcement from managers, colleagues, and society for this public action. To prevent self-deception and mutual misunderstanding, it's critical for organizations in all societal realms to consistently assess whether the underlying community factors of connection, affirmation, and appreciation are indeed reinforcing our explicit, substantive goals.

So far, I've delineated the factors involved in vertical frame repositioning. These insights will come in handy in the next chapter, where we discuss another direction in which frames can be repositioned: sideways. The success of these lateral frame movements in influencing people greatly depends on how well these framing positions align with evolutionarily rooted and culturally entwined factors, which are often not entirely visible.

9

Sideways positioning: what *is* the matter?

The supply chain – weak links

Picture the highly advanced logistics and structure of modern globalization, particularly with respect to the extensive variety of goods available. Each product is the result of an intricate supply chain – a series of interconnected processes and activities often spanning multiple countries. This complex yet efficient system involves seamless cooperation between suppliers, manufacturers, distributors, retailers, and transporters, ultimately delivering a product to the customer. Every stage of this supply chain is carefully monitored for efficiency – whether it's the quality of raw materials, timeliness of deliveries, transportation costs, or customer service. The system's optimization is driven by effective logistics management, production enhancements, and data analysis.

The term 'supply chain' is a metaphor, a frame that offers us a glimpse into what customers around the globe don't see in its entirety when they purchase a product. The metaphor of the supply chain, in the benevolent interpretation of the purpose of frames, has been coined to simplify and clarify what's intricate and intangible. However, we also know that the exclusions from any frame – in this case, the invisibility of extensive and messy factors that hugely compromise the living conditions for people working remotely from most customers – might also have more cynical rationales. There can be differing opinions as to whether the sideways positioning of any frame has been deliberately adjusted to conceal certain parts of reality. Yet, I believe answering this question is rarely crucial unless it's necessary for legal proceedings. To understand the function of a framing position, one could ask the ancient question from Roman emperor Cicero: 'Qui bono?', or 'Who benefits?' Who gains from this framing position being known as a 'supply chain' – a functional, well-lubricated, optimizable system marked by win–win collaboration and a shared goal of delivering a good, affordable product to the end consumer? Conversely, it might be even more enlightening to ask: who is less advantaged by the 'supply chain' framing? Michael Gibb convincingly argues that many people involved in the supply chain, especially the workers who are often exploited, become invisible, overshadowed by the material and economic movement.[1] Next to the text in Gibb's informative text is a photo of illegal gold miners in Manicaland, Zimbabwe – eight bare-chested teenage boys labouring in a pit, their bodies half-covered in mud, working in heat and humidity. Despite the hellish conditions, the boys cooperate, exerting great effort to haul rocks and gravel. These conditions are deplorable, reminiscent of slavery, and highlight those marginalized in our conception of the supply chain.

The metaphor of a supply chain is largely focused on the end product, such as our electronics and jewellery, often overlooking the workers, particularly those involved in extracting the raw materials. Since its emergence in the 1980s, the image of a 'chain' has provided a basis for logistics and business strategy to search for weaknesses that lead to suboptimal operations, weak links that reduce the quality, delay delivery, or compromise the level of financial gain for those with the power in that 'chain'. In the twenty-first century, the supply chain metaphor regarding gold has attracted an increasing, parallel curiosity, prompting NGOs, investigative journalists, and researchers to search for these weak links, drawing public attention to the detrimental health effects and harsh working conditions endured by mining workers. This increased public awareness has sparked moral outrage, boycotts, and other forms of 'political consumption',[2] putting pressure on companies and policymakers to revise and ethicize gold's part in the supply chain. This all sounds great to anyone with a heart: the notion of a supply chain, which is now taken for granted, often implies the need to address not only financial and logistical suboptimalities but also of ethical issues, such as the exploitation of workers.

However, the supply chain metaphor poses a conundrum: it suggests that weaker links could be swapped for sturdier ones, much like in a physical chain. Still, it's challenging to imagine frames that offer environmentally friendly and humane alternatives to the prevailing supply chain narrative. We seem stuck within the supply chain frame, only able to perceive and make small adjustments within it, and at the same time tricked *between* frames, unable to envision or build alternative ones. In gold mining, the ethically weak links pertain to exploitative labour causing environmental degradation and human suffering. Can we truly rectify these issues while dealing with the tremendous pressures to deliver enhanced profits, greater production rates, and lower prices? Resolving this intricate issue may require a complete frame repositioning – one that brings the systemic pressures to the fore.

Keeping in mind this general challenge of being stuck within a frame and tricked between that frame and its alternatives, we'll now delve into three inventive ways to reposition a frame that involve moving issues between cultures, what's right and what's beautiful, and what's right and what's true. The examples I've chosen below are varied in a normative sense, referring to cases that might have positive or negative overtones. Sideways positioning, despite its potential for deceitful framing tactics, also holds a remarkable capacity for creativity and providing fresh insights into the multifaceted perspectives and values associated with various issues.

Moving between cultures

The first type of frame repositioning involves generating alignment for a new idea or order by introducing a different framing name, while ensuring that the idea remains anchored and aligned with current cultural conventions. This process amplifies the likelihood of people feeling at home with the new idea, despite its significant variance from prior cultural notions.[3] This can be likened to the practice of introducing a different wine in old, time-honoured bottles, albeit with a new label. It's quite usual for something new to be shaped to fit into an already accepted cultural frame when it's being introduced. Take Christianity as an example. When it arrived in pagan communities, it had to be tweaked to match existing customs, celebrations, and eating habits. Historians and ethnologists have found that, to these communities, keeping their traditions was more important than simply declaring a belief in God. In pre-Christian Scandinavia, around the winter solstice, there was an annual midwinter festival called Yuletide. It lasted more than a week and its purpose was to ensure a good harvest and good hunting for the coming year. It was a time of great feasting, drinking, dancing, and sacrifice to the gods. In the tenth century, Christian missionaries took the pagan Yuletide and adapted it into a Christian celebration. Many of the foods and games enjoyed by the pre-Christian Vikings at Yuletide are similar to those enjoyed at Christmas in Scandinavia today. Indeed, Christmas time is referred to as *Juletid* in modern Swedish.

In promoting international relations, fostering cultural connections, and championing human rights globally, the alignment of new ideas with prevailing culture is essential. Consider democracy – a concept tied to human rights that is often perceived as inherently good by many in the West. However, it may not always align with the dominant cultural framework everywhere.

Western leaders like Joe Biden have launched initiatives, such as the 'Summit for Democracy' to address this. By repositioning this frame, they can align it with cultures outside the Western traditions while maintaining its core content and at the same time show respect for values in non-Western cultures. In some non-Western countries, 'democracy' means following specifically Western (or particularly American) norms. But in Western countries, democracy has a broader, more inclusive meaning. Meanwhile, the term 'pluralism' might mean embracing political and cultural differences beyond American norms, values, and political institutions for many non-Westerners.[4] But for some Western conservatives, 'pluralism' might bring to mind multiculturalism, which they might not appreciate.

Ultimately, how we position a solution to a socio-political issue – be it as a democratic or pluralistic approach – significantly influences its acceptance across different cultures. This is somewhat akin to the dilemma in ensuring certain environmental and health goals are achieved: should we frame the issues at stake as economic ones, or as priceless ones, relying on cultural etiquette or moral decency? In his insightful book *What Money Can't Buy*, Sandel criticizes cases where priceless things are turned into commodities. He is against turning things like blood and organ donation or picking up your child late from kindergarten into monetary issues, by rewarding the former with payments and penalizing the latter with fines. Why? Sandel believes that over time we have created norms and values to deal with these issues. Turning them into economic issues is a moral degradation. Sandel highlights how these issues are framed in contemporary American culture. Framing them in monetary terms would either lead to them being inconsistent with the dominant cultural framework or, at worst, contribute to a change in the dominant cultural framework where all issues, not just these, are reduced to mere dollars and cents.[5]

Sandel's argument is in line with the criticisms of both the political left and social conservatives. They emphasize the need to protect the cultural and moral fabric that holds us together. But Sandel goes one step further. For each issue that he identifies as unsuitable for monetization, he adds another layer: whether monetization would make the issue more efficient. For example, would paying for blood and organ donations lead to more donations and thus save more lives? Working from two different perspectives simultaneously, Sandel's answer to the efficiency question is always that monetization would either not be more efficient or would reduce efficiency compared to non-monetary arrangements. This dual approach allows Sandel to align his argument with both cultural values and to find efficient solutions to real-world problems, such as healthcare. But what happens when cultural values collide – as they undoubtedly do sometimes – with considerations of efficiency? Can we compare and assess these fundamentally different values against each other? We will explore these questions more in the rest of this chapter.

Sideways positioning

Moving between what's right and what's beautiful

Let's dive into a second way to reposition the frame. It's one that sticks out for me as much as the repositioning between traditions and ideals mentioned above. It can be illustrated by looking at the nineteenth-century philosopher Friedrich Nietzsche. Perhaps surprisingly, Nietzsche had an ambivalent view of Socrates, the man many people consider the pioneer of philosophy. According to Nietzsche, Socrates was too fixated on rationality, rigid, and an excessive dreamer, hoping that more knowledge will make us more virtuous, and not – as Nietzsche believed – that chaos, instincts, and the will to power were the core human qualities.[6] Among Nietzsche's gripes with Socrates, one peculiar point stands out: although with great subtlety, Nietzsche criticized Socrates for his physical appearance:

> Socrates was a rabble. One knows, one sees it for oneself, how ugly he was. … The criminalists among us say that the typical criminal is ugly: monster in face, monster in soul.[7]

Though it may sound strange to us, Nietzsche associates Socrates' philosophical reasoning – which Nietzsche saw as decadent, cold, life-denying, full of 'rickety malice' – with Socrates' unfavourable physical appearance. Since Nietzsche was a classical philologist, with particular interest in the Ancient Greeks, this might have been rooted in the notion of *kalos kagathos*, which translates as 'the beautiful and virtuous'.[8] This idea deeply weaves together outward beauty and internal virtue, creating an intricate bond between external and internal qualities. The gods of Greek myths personify this concept, for they were depicted with impeccable physical attractiveness and balanced features. This aesthetic perfection, combined with their potent power and general supremacy, made them worthy of worship, although the ethical conduct of these gods often diverged significantly from what is traditionally perceived as moral in Christianity and other faith traditions.

In today's world, we usually separate what's right from what's beautiful. However, sometimes we try to tie them together or use one to justify the other. For example, the idea of rejecting materialism and embracing a simpler, frugal lifestyle connects ethical and aesthetic ideas. The ethical aspect may include reduced recourse to energy use, a reduction beneficial for the natural environment. The ethical aspect voluntary striving for craving less 'stuff' can also be connected to the notion of reducing our cognitive load. By not accumulating clutter around us, we have a higher chance of developing an inner peace and calm, which in turn might free up more 'affordances' and mental resources to gear towards ethical behaviour, the argument goes. We can see a similar connection in global efforts to protect the environment. Groups such as the World Wildlife Fund and Rainforest Alliance often use beautiful pictures of animals in documenting their work to protect biodiversity. UNESCO uses a similar strategy to protect cultural heritage sites. They say they're protecting the beauty and importance of these places for future generations.

It's interesting to think about how beauty and the need for protection come together. Does it mean we only want to protect what looks good, or that we don't care about protecting ugly animals or places with lots of history? Or could it be that the rarity of something makes us want to protect it, regardless of how it looks? Here it's crucial to note that beauty is just one part of what we consider aesthetic. Even something ugly can have aesthetic value, like the raw power of a crocodile catching its prey, or art depicting a wounded person or an old, lonely house. We can also find aesthetic value in expressions of emotion, the grandeur of nature, humour, drama, cuteness, and the strange or unusual.

We see this same idea in how we think about the best way to live. People who reject materialism and embrace a simple, frugal lifestyle are trying to combine ethical and aesthetic ideas. They think of simplicity, cleanliness, and being free from clutter as beautiful, and they believe these things are good for the environment and make us feel calm. But there's a catch. Even people who've managed to create a clutter-free space can feel uneasy. They may have only a few beautiful and timeless possessions, using these things as a symbol of their social status. Marketers take advantage of this, constantly changing their message to convince us to buy more, telling us that buying these beautiful and ethical items will show others our social standing. 'Eco-fashion' is a telling example of this.[9]

But perhaps beauty can also help us do what's right by inspiring us to imagine a sustainable future, motivating us to work towards it as we deal with the environmental and health problems we face today.[10] For example, research shows that people who initially deny climate change are more likely to accept it if they see a positive vision of a sustainable future, compared to those who just see the hard facts about how quickly our climate is changing.[11]

Far more challenging is the positioning of frames when there is a conflict between ethical and aesthetic values. One – in terms of cultural resonance – particularly unsuccessful attempt to position a moral framing into an aesthetic one was by the German composer Stockhausen. When asked by a journalist about the impact of the 9/11 attacks on him, Stockhausen shockingly remarked, 'So, what happened [in New York] is, of course – now all of you must adjust your brains – the greatest work of art that has ever existed. Minds accomplishing something in one act that we could never dream of in music, that people practise like crazy for ten years, totally fanatically, for one concert, and then dying. ... It is a crime, you know of course, because the people did not agree to it. They did not come to the concert. That is obvious. And nobody had told them: "You could be killed in the process".'[12]

The composer's comments, delivered so shortly after the tragedy, incited widespread outcry, and justifiably so. Yet, part of this dismay might stem from the questionable assumption that a 'great work of art', something with impressive aesthetic qualities, must also be ethically sound, if not beautiful. Stockhausen's concession that 9/11 was a crime may suggest, given a charitable interpretation, that he viewed it as ethically reprehensible. It might comfort some to think that he kept his aesthetic appreciation separate from his ethical judgement. However, it is likely that many will remain irate at the notion that such an appalling act could be assessed on aesthetic grounds.

This controversy broaches murky territory. Many creators of sublime art, possessing immense aesthetic value, have been unequivocally unethical. Some violated the ethical codes of their era, while others, deemed upright then, are seen as detestable now in light of shifting moral standards. Further, should we permit aesthetics and suffering to coexist? If not, we risk denying those living under oppression the ability to perceive beauty and humour in their lives. Yet, it is precisely such art that often leaves a deep impression on us. This manipulation and sometimes conflation of values via frame positioning extend beyond the oscillation between aesthetic and ethical values. Equally common, and often equally problematic, is the repositioning between what's morally right and what's true.

Moving between what's right and what's true

In a world where technology advances at an astonishing pace, often leaving us scrambling to understand, many of us instinctively seek out what we perceive as natural and authentic. We tend to associate these qualities with what is good – ethical, environmentally friendly, and healthy. Naturally, marketers are quick to capitalize on this, branding products as 'natural', 'organic', and 'ecological'. Indeed, in many instances, natural can be good. But assuming it is invariably so leads us into the trap of the naturalistic fallacy, one of the most pervasive and damaging misconceptions.

We touched upon this notion in Chapter 2, albeit indirectly, through Thomas Huxley's ethical philosophy, long before the term was established by George Edward Moore.[13] Huxley warned against the blind imitation of nature. His caution is likely to have stemmed from how some misconstrued Darwin's theories on natural selection, equating what *is* with how resources *should be* distributed in society. Often, this led to a laissez-faire approach and neglect of the vulnerable – a gross misunderstanding of Darwin's own societal views.

The naturalistic fallacy rears its head in today's discussions on environment and health. Terms like 'natural', 'organic', and 'ecological', now protected by laws and labelling systems, enable sellers to demand premium prices. While a natural frame can align with environmental and health values, this alignment isn't inherently guaranteed.[14]

The belief that what is natural is inherently good is problematic. Recall the mismatch between, for instance, our natural craving for consuming salt, fat, and sugar as soon as we have access to them, and the almost limitless supply and availability of these substances in many parts of the world today. Or consider arsenic – a natural substance, yet toxic to humans beyond a certain limit. In contrast, actions like wearing glasses, having our hair cut, or taking advanced medicines are not natural, but this doesn't indicate their goodness or badness. Our awareness of the naturalistic fallacy should also make us problematize the notion by which natural products are automatically assumed to be environmentally sustainable. Certain natural ingredients in cosmetics may lead to overharvesting of natural resources, biodiversity loss, and excessive land, water, and energy use, making it crucial to assess from case to case whether natural or synthetic ingredients are environmentally preferable.[15]

To avoid being tricked by the 'natural is always ethically superior' frame, we need to dig deeper. This works the other way around as well – that is, we should watch out for the reverse loophole, the moralistic fallacy. This refers to assuming that how we feel things *ought to be* somehow leads to how things *are.* I know this sounds cryptic, but it's more common than we're often aware of. Suppose we stand for a society where men and women are provided the same freedoms and conditions to pursue their goals and fulfil their potential. Essentially, we join most modern individuals who advocate gender equality – an expected and highly plausible stance, if you ask me. Does our belief in gender equality necessitate the belief that men and women are uniformly equal in all respects, such as physical strength, empathy, agreeability, and propensity to violence? Although the question may appear unusual, it's not uncommon to perceive a logical progression from 'ought to be' to 'is'. However, if we champion gender equality and wrongly infer that this suggests complete statistical equality between men and women, we might inadvertently cultivate a resistance to knowledge. As I noted in my book *Knowledge Resistance,* the titular phenomenon is 'a relative immunity to evidence and arguments tied to a particular knowledge claim'.[16] This can result in certain knowledge domains, both existing and prospective, being deemed as 'dangerous knowledge'. In the context of gender equality, this would represent a form of 'running away' – as Thomas Huxley would say – from knowledge concerning the lengthy ancestral history of our species. There may be an aversion to confronting any knowledge that could potentially challenge our erroneous assumption that our 'ought to be' position must align with our 'is' position for it to be valid. This misconception could cause us to miss out on crucial insights that could aid in the fight against gender inequality and help us formulate better strategies to promote equality over the long haul.

Disregarding weapons research and development, the idea of dangerous knowledge posing a threat to societal values and moral progress is somewhat outdated – to be blunt, a relic of eras dominated by authoritarian rulers who employed religious dogmas to suppress independent thought. Fortunately, history also illustrates that as we broaden our framings of the needs and living conditions of humans, animals, and nature, we come to increasingly recognize the significance of addressing these needs.

Part IV

Making boundaries bend – frame sizing

On the island of Crete in 1944, in the latter part of the Second World War, a British commando named Patrick Leigh Fermor orchestrated a bold plan with local guerrillas. Their mission was to capture German general Heinrich Kreipe. And so they did. When they had successfully kidnapped the general, they fled with him into the mountains, beginning a trek lasting several days. Fermor recalled in his memoirs an unforgettable moment three days into their journey. As dawn broke over Mount Ida, they found themselves among the rocks, witnessing the peak aglow in the morning light. In that moment, the captured Nazi general Kreipe, taking in the radiant mountain peak, quietly murmured a line of Latin verse:

> Vides ut alta stet nive candidum Soracte...
> (See how Mount Soracte stands gleaming white with deep snowfall...)

The words were part of a Roman ode penned by the poet Horace in the first century BCE. Fermor, recognizing the verse, instinctively completed the line out loud where Kreipe had left off:

> Nec jam sustineant onus Silvae laborantes, geluque Flumina constiterint acuto
> (No longer can the labouring woods bear the weight, and rivers have frozen over with biting cold)

This shared poetic moment was a turning point. From then on, Fermor began caring for Kreipe's injuries and ensuring his safety. Their bond was strong enough to survive the war. The former enemies kept in touch and even made a joint appearance on Greek television. Kreipe, far from bearing a grudge, praised the brave British operation.[1]

It would be naive to think that a shared interest in classical poetry could magically dissolve deep-seated enmity, let alone could have helped to prevent any of the atrocities committed by German officers. My point is an entirely different one – namely, to ponder the following question that the Crete moment raises: how did two adversaries, each entrenched in their own 'us' versus 'them' mindset, manage to resize and reshape their views into a 'you and I' frame? How significant is it that two enemies could recite the same poem, given the hostility they'd displayed against each other's people and themselves?

The straightforward approach of 'reality speaks for itself' doesn't help us understand this, since 'reality' was that the main actors were in the middle of the Second World War, in a situation where an exchange of poetic recitation between enemies seems to be the most extraordinary thing to care about. On the other hand, the 'framing is everything' view would suggest that this isn't strange at all. If it's the case that anything can become a basis for reframing anytime people can find or create common symbolism and meaning anywhere with anyone, then why not poetry? However, if framing is everything in that sense, how come some international, cross-cultural, and cross-ideological initiatives have contributed to an actual widening of a frame, inviting more groups, more issues and ideas to be included, whereas other such initiatives have more or less failed, even leading to deeper enmity, contractions of a frame, and stricter borders?

In the upcoming two chapters, we'll delve deeper into the fourth basic technique of the social art of framing: the ability to resize frames. This technique ties back to the points made at the beginning of the book about our innate tendency to categorize – seeing things in terms of 'us' versus 'them' and associating issues with particular groups. Sizing can manifest in two distinct ways. First, frames can expand to become more inclusive. This bears partial resemblance with what is sometimes called frame bridging.[2] Secondly, frames can contract, becoming more exclusive. This latter phenomenon shares certain traits with the term frame amplification.[3] While expansion often radiates a positive aura due to its inclusivity, and contraction might be seen more negatively because of its exclusivity, this perception is largely dependent on the context.

A personal memory serves as an illustrative example here. A few years before the major Russian invasion of Ukraine in 2022, I found myself among colleagues – both Ukrainian and Russian – at a conference. With the majority not understanding Russian, they chose English as the common language. During the conversation in the evening over a glass of wine, I overheard one of the Russians saying to the others, in a warm and friendly voice: 'You know what? We really belong together! We are like a family, with the same cultural heritage and basic values, don't you think?' The Ukrainians did not follow up on this attempt towards frame expansion, but instead managed to smoothly change the subject.

Conversely, it's essential to recognize that frame contraction isn't inherently negative. At all levels of social life, amid efforts of expansion, networking, and globalization, we still periodically gravitate towards contracting our frames because of the security, clarity, focus, sense of belonging, trust, and predictability it offers. It's common wisdom that less is more, and that a friend to all is a friend to none. Additionally, the value of community, social distinction, and subcultural bonding, as underlined by sociological studies, can't be overlooked.

In essence, to master the art of framing, one needs a comprehensive understanding of the constant interplay of expansion and contraction. The subsequent chapter delves into the age-old roots of social elasticity, and how we can handle gaps and mismatches between these roots when facing situations that call for frame resizing in an advanced, urban, super-connected society. We'll then transition to discussing what is arguably the pinnacle of frame change: blending and reconciling opposing frames from disparate viewpoints into a unified metaframe; doing so is sometimes shown to loosen up rigid stances into a more constructive interaction.

10

Roots to social elasticity

Seven pillars of friendship

To grasp how we can both widen and contract the frames, or circles, of people we connect with and trust, it's essential to examine the foundation of what makes the phenomenon of friendship possible. This understanding must take into account how bonds of friendship, and the level of intimacy and trust we associate with various relationships, can change over time. The anthropologist and evolutionary psychologist Robin Dunbar and his team have spent years studying the fascinating topic of what brings people together. By combining several different methods, such as ethnographic evidence from different communities, cognitive experiments on how many people we can keep track of, measurements of endorphin levels during various types of social interaction, and by analysing digital communication, surveys, and questionnaires about people's friendships, Dunbar and his team have identified and explained the mechanisms of what he labels the seven 'pillars' of friendship, which are: sharing the same language, place of origin, educational background, hobbies, interests, worldview, and sense of humour. The more of these pillars we have in common, the more likely we are to show kindness towards each other. This applies as much to family as to friends, according to Dunbar.[1]

How does the initial example in this part of the book – the unexpected friendship formed between two enemy combatants reciting a Horatian ode – align with Dunbar's seven pillars of friendship?

At first glance, it doesn't seem to neatly fit any of these pillars. But somehow, this shared, pleasant, high-brow activity did turn the two enemies into lifelong friends. Perhaps we need to see the pillars in a more flexible light. Germans and Anglo-Saxon societies shared an admiration for and identification with Roman culture. That said, not every German or British person could recite ancient texts. In this case, the shared knowledge of the Horatian ode was a connection point for Kreipe and Leigh Fermor, and a point of exclusion for the less-educated soldiers. And beyond just being educated, knowing this specific poem in the original Latin language marked them as culturally distinct, even among their highly educated peers. Sociological insights into the immense social energy involved in cultural and aesthetic distinction[2] are relevant for explaining this sudden, excluding frame contraction, where only the most highly educated and refined officers – from either camp – were welcome. This sense of camaraderie is something many of us have experienced, like finding someone who knows the lyrics to the same obscure rock song as we do. It's easy to see how the Horatian ode had such a transformative effect.

But there's an enigma left: why, according to Dunbar, should friendship between former strangers involve an inclination to act kindlier and more unselfishly towards each other than towards people outside the friendship? After all, this special loyalty somewhat resembles the tendency people have to act selflessly towards their own family members. Isn't blood thicker than water, after all? Evolutionary science says that by helping our family, we're also helping our own genes survive and propagate since we share more genes with our family than with our friends, something referred to as 'kin selection'.[3] In 2022, Robin Dunbar generously let me interview him about this and other topics. He invited me to revisit the seven pillars of friendship from the viewpoint of our prehistoric ancestors. Back then, who would have been most likely to share my language, beliefs, interests, and sense of humour? Who would have grown up nearby and therefore been more likely to be loyal and kind towards me? The answer is probably a relative. Being related, whether first, second or third cousins, means that we share more of each other's

158

genes than people who are genetically distant from us. The latter are people who, in ancestral societies, were likely to be more different from us in terms of Dunbar's pillars.

In today's urban, advanced societies, people move, let alone communicate, over much greater distances. They move between places and often belong to several communities and groups at the same time. As a result, they adopt parts of Dunbar's pillars from different social contexts. There are now far greater opportunities to build community and form intimate, highly emotional friendships with people and groups who are genetically distant from us. The pillars thus have immense potential for people to expand their frames of who they experience and interact with as 'us'. Later in this chapter, we will explore this potential and show how it includes opportunities to develop what might be called 'pseudo-kin'.

With the seven pillars of friendship in mind, we are equipped with a unique toolset to strategically expand our frame, or circle, of 'us' and envelop more people within our shared frame of reference. Let's explore this using the healthcare industry as an example. Often, research highlights that reluctance and anxiety in the face of medical procedures are rooted in a view of medical experts, pharmaceutical companies, and public health authorities as outsiders – as 'them' rather than 'us'. This scepticism is particularly pronounced concerning vaccination programs, where the perceived outsider status of healthcare professionals fuels public apprehension. But what if we could bring down these walls of suspicion? Encouragingly, research has shown that when vaccinations are given by familiar local nurses or doctors, resistance decreases.[4]

The goal here is to illuminate the common ground between 'experts' and the 'lay public'. The seven pillars concept is not just a bridge for healthcare professionals and the public, it also holds potential to address divisions along racial and ethnic lines. Many believe that race and ethnicity are the prime catalysts for prejudice and stereotypes, an assumption strengthened by the unfortunate pervasiveness of racism worldwide. And, yes, psychological studies provide ample evidence of both explicit and implicit biases against individuals from different races and ethnicities.

However, if we zoom out and look at our lengthy evolutionary journey, it's clear that racial differences are a recent phenomenon. Science suggests that while *Homo sapiens* has been around for about three hundred thousand years,[5] distinct races within *Homo sapiens* are thought to have begun to emerge only a few tens of thousands of years ago as a results of mutations that helped our ancestors adapt to the different geographical regions to which they began to migrate.[6] But more important for making assumptions about how deeply our tendency to care about racial differences – explicitly or through implicit biases – is to consider the extent to which such a tendency would have made a difference in the lives of our ancestors, even as racial differences began to emerge. We know that ancestral hunter-gatherers travelled on foot, residential moves further than forty miles would have been very rare. It was therefore highly unlikely that an individual would encounter a person of a different skin colour for most of our history. This was most obvious during the long period when there were no racial differences, but also for much of the time when there were. Since it was extremely unlikely that one would encounter someone with different racial characteristics from oneself, it is also extremely unlikely that a racial recognition system would have evolved that would have given Homo sapiens a special and distinct propensity for racial categorization that would have been genetically inherited and deeply ingrained in those of us living today.[7]

How, then, can implicit and explicit racial categorization, often in the form of racial prejudice and racism, and all their associated injustices, be so prevalent in contemporary societies?

On the basis of the above argument, supported by a wealth of experimental data, the psychologist Robert Kurzban and his colleagues argue that the racial categorization we all do, explicitly and implicitly, is best understood as a by-product of something much more fundamental, namely our tendency to engage in what we call in this book 'frame texturing': categorizing people into 'us' and 'them', and making quick normative assumptions about 'us' and 'them' in order to track alliances, decide whom to trust, and so on. In a highly segregated, unequal, and racially biased society, race serves as a proxy for who is 'us' or 'them'. The reason that racial categorization can be used as a proxy in our society is because of the stark differences in socio-economic status, education, and self-identity between different racial or ethnic groups that have been created in society and are reproduced by our continued racial stereotyping and categorization.[8] On the other hand, it also means that as we succeed in eliminating some of these racial inequalities, race becomes an increasingly unreliable proxy for shaping assumptions about people and groups. This understanding offers a hopeful direction for the substantial changes needed to combat the destructive effects of racism.

Indeed, there is some evidence that a little effort at the individual level might go some way to reminding us to reduce social categorization based on superficial differences such as skin colour. Our amygdala, the brain's fear centre, can be trained to react differently to an image of someone of a different race, particularly if we see the person as an individual rather than a racial stereotype. For example, studies have shown that when people of different skin colours are shown holding a vegetable, viewers begin to perceive the person primarily as someone who likes the vegetable, rather than as a person with a particular skin colour. This simple shared preference, however insignificant it may seem, can help to narrow the racial divide.[9]

Similarly, Kurzban has shown in a series of experiments that less than four minutes of social interaction or exposure to a social scenario in which people belonged to different groups – where race was irrelevant to the formation, interaction, and goals of the group – significantly reduced participants' tendency to categorize people by race.[10]

Of course, we shouldn't oversimplify these findings by believing that simple tweaks and quick fixes will suffice to reduce frame sizing based on racial categorization, a concern that researchers have highlighted in follow-up studies.[11] At the same time, it's not overly optimistic to assume that these findings get along well with Dunbar's seven pillars of friendship. If we can reduce the likelihood that race will continue to be a proxy for these pillars – for example, where we live in a city, what hobbies we have, and our educational background – we'll have come a long way in providing opportunities for frame expansions that ignore racial categories and stereotypes.

Kin and pseudo-kin

When we uncover the common ground that binds us within the seven pillars of friendship, we gain the power to widen our communal lens. This raises a question: what role does the number of people in the groups we form play in the function and success of those groups? This field of research was founded by the same anthropologist and evolutionary psychologist who – together with colleagues – has studied the pillars of friendship: Robin Dunbar. Dunbar has identified what he claims are distinct 'circles of friendship' through extensive empirical studies and calculations. He argues that these distinct circles are governed by how our brains have evolved.

Let's break it down. Our innermost circle includes around five of our closest friends. These are the people we talk to every week, the ones who know us best. Next, we have our best friends, around fifteen people we share deep bonds with, the ones we turn to when we need support. Further out, we have fifty good friends. We may not see them every day, but we know they're there for us when we need them. Then, there's a circle of about 150 people, also known as 'Dunbar's number'. This is the cognitive limit on the number of stable social relationships that an individual can maintain. Historically, this number has been important in structuring human social groups. Beyond that, we have acquaintances (around 500), people we know by name (1,500), and faces we recognize (around 5,000). These are the people we're aware of but don't have a personal connection with.

Dunbar's concept of friendship circles can help us foster more cohesive communities. Consider a workgroup of 30 people, which falls between Dunbar's circles of 15 and 50. You could expand this group to 50 or divide it into two groups of 15. Interestingly, groups have been unconsciously formed around Dunbar's circles long before his research, as seen in military companies typically containing 120 to 180 people.

Roots to social elasticity

Pairing Dunbar's circles with human susceptibility to framing, metaphors, and symbols of social bonding, it becomes possible to construct arrangements where people feel like they're part of a tribe, even without being blood relatives. This concept, known as 'pseudo-kinship', can help non-relations form bonds as strong as familial ones. Examples of pseudo-kinship abound. Monastic and religious communities refer to each other as brothers and sisters, creating a familial sense of connection. Organizations often label their members 'team players', comparing them to being part of a sports team, a social unit that shares some of the group spirit of the family unit. We refer to the natural world as 'Mother Nature', a shared mother figure, and to our homeland as our 'motherland' or 'fatherland'. In times of crisis, we label our comrades as brothers and sisters in arms. These metaphors aim to widen our sense of 'us' and promote group interests over individual ones. In extreme situations, like warfare, this mindset can lead to the willingness to make the ultimate sacrifice, a commitment usually reserved for protecting close family.

In the twenty-first century, we've seen new forms of pseudo-kin groups and networks emerge, particularly among those outside the 'typical' bell curve. Members of these groups include, for example, people with autism, learning difficulties, and other forms of neurodiversity. The goal of these pseudo-kinships is to shift the perspective from 'abnormal and sick' to 'normal and healthy'. Ideally, nurturing these pseudo-kinships can help build communities that value the unique contributions of everyone. This could promote greater tolerance, pluralism, and inclusivity, making all groups feel valued and integral.

But, thinking about the social energy generated by both the seven pillars of friendship and pseudo-kinship strategies, we're left with two important questions. First, what factors make some attempts at frame expansion more successful and long lasting than others? Second, can we distinguish between different frame-expanding strategies in a normative sense, deciding which are good and which are bad? Intriguingly, these two questions – one about results and the other about judgement – overlap more than we researchers usually acknowledge.

Successful and failed frame sizing

> Hey, now I suggest we all sing 'We Shall Overcome' together in this
> room ... Yes, we should, because it doesn't benefit any of us who are
> humanists, who defend your right to be here [in Sweden] ... So let's do
> it now![12]

It's 1992 in a school assembly hall nestled in the heart of Rinkeby, an
immigrant-rich suburb on the outskirts of Stockholm. Immigrants
from all over the globe are gathered here, joined by Birgit Friggebo, the
Swedish minister for immigration. The motive behind this meeting
isn't a pleasant one. It's spurred by a string of horrifying hate crimes,
culminating in the chilling murders of immigrants at the hands of a
criminal infamously known as 'the laser man' for his bizarre weapon
of choice. Understandably, the Rinkeby residents are terrified and
indignant, demanding immediate action against racism from the
politicians present. In a somewhat off-kilter attempt to lighten the
mood, Minister Friggebo begins to sing 'We Shall Overcome'. Not a
single person in the room joins in, and her bid to inspire unity only
stokes the crowd's annoyance.

Yet, we've learned earlier in this book about the powerful effect
that community-building strategies can have. Tools such as metaphors, shared symbols, stories, poetry, and music can indeed foster
a sense of kinship between strangers, even enemies, as we saw in
the case of the Second World War British commander and Nazi general forming a lifelong bond over reciting a Horatian ode. Singing
well-known songs together can powerfully unite people, transcending religious, cultural, and military boundaries. Another real-world
example took place during the First World War. On a Christmas Eve,
the carol 'Stille Nacht' ('Silent Night') helped initiated spontaneous
ceasefires along parts of the Western Front, fostering a short-lived
peace and bond among German, British, and French soldiers.[13]

Robin Dunbar argues that activities like singing, dancing, feasting, and emotional storytelling developed as means for large human
groups to stimulate social bonding through the release of endor-
phins. Before these practices evolved, the only methods for fostering
group bonding were direct physical interactions such as grooming,

caressing, and hugging, which for practical reasons were only feasible in small groups. Interestingly, group singing can lead to higher endorphin levels and stronger bonding intensity in larger groups compared to smaller ones. Research indicates that the endorphin levels, and consequently, the intensity of group bonding, are notably higher in a two-hundred-member choir than when the same choir is broken down into ten separate sub-choirs.[14]

The concept of frame expansion might seem boundless in its potential, and according to the 'framing is everything' approach, these strategies can indeed be numerous. However, it's important to understand that there are limits. The research by Dunbar and others shows that there are restrictions on how large each circle of friends can be, as humans aren't infinitely adaptable to every cultural construct. Expanding community frames beyond these limits can weaken emotional bonds. Historical instances of totalitarian regimes trying to reposition familial loyalties into political loyalties, by assigning collective ownership of children to the community, serve as a grim reminder.[15]

While it might be possible to quickly strengthen bonding by 'moving people' from an outer to an inner circle of friends, the distinct social demands of each circle imply that flexibility and mobility depend on certain conditions for stable bonding. An illustration of these limits can be found in Minister Friggebo's well-intentioned mishap. The success or failure of attempts to rapidly strengthen group bonds is determined by deep-rooted factors and conditions that we've explored in this book. One such factor, explored in Part I, is the *texture* – ranging from smooth to rough – that groups use to frame each other, often related to their power dynamics. For example, politicians can't expect working-class groups subjected to violent racism to readily tune in to a song about peace and unity without visible political action by those in power against the violence.

Although the Minister may have intended for her singing initiative to quickly cool down the temperature of the situation, we remember from Part II that hasty changes in *frame temperature* may not effectively tackle deep-rooted issues in the long run. Moreover, as discussed in Part III, for successful inclusion and community building to be achieved through *frame positioning*, there needs to be some level of agreement on where the different groups 'position' their problem frame – how they define the main problem. For example, if the citizens of Rinkeby think the politicians' primary focus is on stopping individual violent racist incidents, while the residents themselves are more concerned with broader issues of segregation and marginalization, this divergence in perspective makes it difficult to establish a sense of unity quickly, even if there is agreement on the need to stop violent racists.

In summary, broadening a problem's framing is a feasible approach, but is dependent on several conditions. Aspiring to expand frames can be risky. Sometimes, the key to effectively addressing an issue lies in narrowing the problem frame. For example, let's revisit the transformation of Amsterdam's traffic from a car-centric environment to a haven for cyclists, at least as perceived by tourists. During the 1970s and early 1980s, a pressing concern was the high number of traffic accidents affecting Amsterdam's residents of all ages. Yet this broad problem framing, despite its alarming nature, seemed too generalized to create a significant cultural impact. It wasn't until the issue was narrowed down to the specific vulnerability of children on bicycles that enough urgency and social momentum were generated. This specific framing aligned with the universal experience of either being a parent or having been a child. When the protesters were invited to Prime Minister Joop den Uyl and his wife's home, it was possible for the protesters to frame the couple as parents (they had several children), including giving them a gramophone record with the protest song 'Stop the Child Murder', a gift the couple accepted.[16]

Having dissected some of the factors that influence successful community sizing, it's time to delve into the ethical considerations. Can we, aside from ideological disparities, differentiate between morally right and wrong ways to reshape our social frames?

Moral and immoral frame resizing

Exploring how we resize our social circles can be quite the ethical tightrope walk. You've probably noticed, for example, that it's easier to feel emotionally connected to your friends and family than to total strangers. However, as the moral philosopher Peter Singer has pointed out, our 'moral circles' have steadily grown over the centuries. Our empathy has broadened to include not just other humans, but animals, and even certain parts of nature.

Our brains are wired for learning and adapting to new environments, which gives us the ability to expand these circles even further. We also have the capacity to question the status quo and drive change. It's thanks to these traits that social movements for causes like civil rights, women's rights, children's rights, and animal welfare have been so successful. But we still have a lot of work to do. In the future, people might look back on our era and judge us for the way we treat animals today, and for turning a blind eye to the needs of those who are far away from us.

So, how do we know if it's morally right to expand our social circles in a particular situation? It's tempting to just stick to our own beliefs. If you were a follower of Lenin, you might think that he and his comrades did the right thing when they expanded their community to bring about the Russian Revolution. But if you're not a fan of Lenin, you might not agree. Similarly, if you consider yourself part of the far right, you might believe it justifiable to try to convince the working class to join your movement based on traditional values and religion. However, there are some universal rules that can help us figure out if an attempt to expand social boundaries has a chance of gaining ancestral, and by extension cultural, resonance on all sides. The first rule is that expanding a community should make life better, or at least not worse, for everyone involved. But as experiments in behavioural economics and economic anthropology have shown in cultures around the world,[17] it's not enough simply to ensure that no one is worse off, or even that everyone benefits. The benefits should also not be distributed in a way that's perceived as highly unequal – our second rule. If one group gets a lot more out of the deal than another, people from the other group will start to feel like they're being taken advantage of, even if their own situation has improved. Sometimes, when people and groups are faced with what they perceive to be excessively unequal deals, the ancestral 'whispers from below' (introduced in Chapter 8) tell them to reject the deal altogether, even if it leaves them worse off than those who accepted the deal.[18]

We can use these two universal rules – that no one should be made worse off and that benefits should not be distributed too unequally – to look at different attempts to expand social circles. If a powerful country takes over a smaller one and forces it to become part of its community, it's likely that neither of these rules will be followed. The big country might justify this by saying that they share a culture and history with the small country and should be together.

But this doesn't fully answer our question about which expansions of boundaries are morally right or wrong, acceptable or unacceptable. Take a young person working in terrible conditions in a gold mine for very little pay. They might have chosen to work in the mine and might be better off than if they were jobless, but the huge gap between their income and the mine owners' wealth could make the situation seem unfair.

To successfully build different 'we' frameworks that last, we need to understand how friendships work, how timing matters, how social circles work, and what fairness means. We also see that groups and networks can grow larger than our principles might suggest, and that they can sometimes do well even without regular or personal interactions. This doesn't mean Dunbar was wrong, but it does raise questions about other ways humans might be able to expand their social circles. We'll dig into these strategies in our next chapter.

11

Metaframing: from difference
to higher sameness

Look out and up!

In my early twenties, I, along with a few friends, decided to host a small dinner party. We were aiming for a quaint gathering – nothing extravagant. The venue was my friend's kitchen, which had just enough space for ten of us. Each of us was given the task of inviting a few guests. The unexpected twist came once we'd all finished extending our invitations. We realized, to my great unease, that our guest list was a potential recipe for disaster. One friend had invited a fiercely passionate left-wing activist, while another had invited a staunchly conservative woman who was an active member of a Swedish right-wing party.

The dinner proceeded pleasantly for some time, with several chats humming along in parallel. Our two ideological pundits engaged in hushed exchanges, a murmur that began to amplify as they, known for their fondness for a drink, indulged a bit too generously. It was inevitable that their cordial chit-chat, beginning to sound a lot like a political debate, would spiral into a tone-dampening squabble. And sure enough, their voices ascended, growing progressively more heated and confrontational in that slurred, alcohol-fuelled way. However, the tension and contention weren't aimed at each other. Instead, they aimed their verbal darts at the rest of us attending the dinner. With fluid ease, they alternated who commanded the room when speaking to us:

How about you guys? Why aren't you involved in anything that actually matters? There must be something you believe in? Or are you not
passionate about anything beyond shopping and TV? You're fucking
egotists, damn it! Come on, let's get out of here!

And so, our politically charged duo departed, likely bound for a
local tavern where their pendulum of conversation would continue
to oscillate between stark agreement and absolute disbelief at the
other's perspective. Meanwhile, back at our humble kitchen table,
an odd silence filled their space. It took us a few minutes to recover
to save the evening from the ghost of their heated debate.

Such self-important assholes, ruining the whole God-damn evening.
So glad they left! Cheers to that!

As dusk gave way to the indigo night, a wave of honesty washed
over the remaining guests. Some started to admit that the fiery face-
off between our two fervent thinkers, although disruptive, had provided a kind of unrefined amusement – a surprising plot twist to our
evening. Among the lingering aftershocks of the dispute, one guest
chimed in:

And weren't they right, after all? That all of us should do something
important?

Courage in metaframing

The story of our two youthful politicians, decades on, no longer
shines solely because of their selfless devotion to grander causes.
What truly captivates me is their embodiment of an idea reflecting
Elie Wiesel's insight that the true antithesis of love is not hatred
but indifference. They exhibited how divergent beliefs and actions
can converge at a more encompassing meta-level. As that dinner
party showcased, the conservative woman and her newfound friend,
the leftist man stepped beyond their distinct ideologies, if momen-
tarily, and crafted a shared realm, a metaframe where contrasting
perspectives could peacefully coexist. This high-level understanding
emphasizes the need to pledge ourselves to causes that go beyond
our personal gains. This dedication, be it political, humanitarian,

or associational, is critical for the advancement of democracy, the upliftment of humanity, and the betterment of our world. Creating this metaframe demands considerable intellectual prowess, the ability to navigate and embrace abstract thinking. This is not an easy task. It necessitates cognitive effort and, even more notably, social courage. The chasms of ideology are frequently deepened by divergent cultural identities and group affiliations, often resulting in separate community frames, where the frame of 'us' feels smooth and 'them' rough.

Social psychologists have conducted a plethora of experiments to gauge individuals' willingness to interact with and learn from the 'other side' in the so-called 'Culture War'. They tested on hot-button issues like gun control, abortion, same-sex marriage, and marijuana legalization. The question was whether people would be open to listening and understanding the opposing side's arguments. Participants were incentivized with the opportunity to enter a free lottery in exchange for listening to both opposing viewpoints and confirming beliefs. Yet, surprisingly, two-thirds on both ends of the spectrum chose to engage in a monotonous task rather than participate in a knowledge exchange.[1]

This result suggests that many people, liberals and conservatives alike, would rather avoid confronting opposing views. Anger is another common characteristic of what I described earlier as 'affective polarization'[2] among groups with differing ideologies. Research on radical social movements indicates that anger is unsurprisingly the primary motivator in their mobilization and struggle. Yet, another factor, pointed out by the political philosopher Hannah Arendt and others, plays a pivotal role within both the reactionary right and revolutionary left: a refusal to self-examine.[3] This refusal is evident across diverse examples, from conflict zones to stereotypes that insist on fundamental differences between us and people from other ethnicities.[4]

But let's reconsider the term 'refusal'. It perhaps fails to encapsulate the profound challenge of self-questioning. Studies on overconfidence,[5] confirmation bias,[6] and self-deception[7] illustrate that it isn't simply a matter of choosing to question ourselves. This difficulty

171

stems from the fact that an unwavering belief in one's moral superiority has likely benefited our survival throughout human evolution.

When psychoanalyst Josh Cohen advocates for 'vigilant self-suspicion', he distinguishes between genuine political anger and 'manufactured anger'.[8] He attributes the former to figures like Audre Lorde, the renowned Black feminist activist and theorist. Lorde, in her 1981 piece 'The uses of anger', admits, 'I have tried to learn my anger's usefulness to me, as well as its limitations'.[9] Meanwhile, Cohen connects 'manufactured anger' with populist leaders and dictators.[10]

However, the lack of self-critical reflection isn't something that just 'happens' automatically or unconsciously. Some conflicts between polarized groups are so deeply entrenched that it's reasonable to assume conscious tactics are at play. Bear in mind the longstanding conflict between LGBTQ+ rights and Christian groups in the United States, a tug of war over issues like establishing LGBTQ+ student groups, the inclusion of sexual orientation in harassment policies, and inclusive comprehensive sexuality education in schools. Researchers have noticed that Christian groups doggedly adhere to their 'morality politics' framing, while LGBTQ+ rights groups staunchly maintain their 'identity politics' framing. Breaking such impasses through dedicated efforts at metaframing, which involves (self-)critical frame reflection, undoubtedly introduces new uncertainties within and between groups – a risk that groups in conflict are often reluctant to take.[11] However, there is often much to be gained from bringing polarized positions to the meta-level. This approach provides a new understanding among conflictual groups, not only of the positions and their foundations but also of the confirmation biases that are likely to be present.

Yet, there's often much to gain from opening oneself to critical frame reflection. To counteract confirmation bias and foster intellectual humility, cognitive science researchers have developed exercises. One such activity is the Wason four-card selection task,[12] in which individuals attempt the task solo before collaborating in a group. Studies have demonstrated that a group is around four times more likely to solve the task than an individual. The hope is that, having experienced this difference first hand, participants will become more aware of their own confirmation bias and make a conscious effort to compensate for it through intellectual and epistemic humility.[13]

While these exercises are admirable, we have seen throughout this book that the propensity for confirmation bias is so deeply ingrained at both the individual and group levels that it demands continuous challenge from others. If people and groups can be assisted, the likelihood of self-critical frame reflection increases considerably.

The first step in metaframing is to search for common ground, to find similarities across opposing frames. This involves combining distinct perspectives on what's true, right, or beautiful into a unified frame where dynamics and tensions are still allowed to avoid stagnation. The core idea is to dive beneath apparent conflicts to find shared, underlying traits, and then elevate these to form the basis of an expanded metaframe. Examples that immediately come to mind in the aesthetic realm include the emergence of jazz, fusion cuisine, yoga, renaissance art, and Mozarabic chant. These are just a few of the types of aesthetic expression that emerged from bridging previous divergent – sometimes opposing – aesthetic norms and practices into a shared cultural space.

Metaframing between truth-seeking traditions

Scientific disciplines sometimes operate like insular tribes, often sidelining or misrepresenting other disciplines due to perceived competition. Sociologist Thomas Gieryn coined the term 'boundary work' to describe the demarcation processes between disciplines and between science and other forms of knowledge generation. Many researchers have used Gieryn's term to study how various organizations delineate boundaries between 'us' and 'them', 'relevant' and 'irrelevant', 'scientific' and 'unscientific', and so on.[14] This research aligns well with our discussion on framing. However, in this section I want to focus on processes that, while defining the boundaries of truth-seeking traditions, also pinpoint areas where different traditions can conflict or enrich each other. Achieving collaboration is undoubtedly challenging, but it is essential for generating not just new but also novel knowledge and insights.[15]

In certain places there are mechanisms in place that occasionally help to stimulate knowledge exchange between compartmentalized disciplinary silos, sometimes even to the point of integrative, knowledge synthesis. Such mechanisms of metaframing may stem from visionary individuals, chance encounters, or intentional strategies by research foundations promoting interdisciplinary collaboration. This type of collaboration has become increasingly vital as we grapple with complex issues like climate change, public health, and the intricacies of artificial intelligence. Hence, we see the emergence of interdisciplinary fields like behavioural economics, biochemistry, cognitive science, evolutionary feminism, and environmental sociology. These fields underscore that knowledge boundaries are mutable, and breakthroughs often emerge where established domains intersect. Beyond this, metaframing extends to collaborations between academia and non-academic organizations, known as transdisciplinarity.

One instance of transdisciplinarity took place in Leeds, UK, a few years ago. A church played host to a science festival, inviting attendees to share family heirlooms and stories tied to technology. This initiative, 'Equipping Christian Leadership in the Age of Science', aimed to position science as a divine marvel, not an antagonist. UK church leaders and scientists have begun to collaborate, enriching public policy discussions with a scientifically informed religious perspective, especially on subjects like artificial intelligence.[16] Partnerships like these underpin common themes between science and faith: awe, uncertainty, and a recognition of our humble place in the universe. They also resonate with moral foundations, like the sacredness and purity of nature, that are often overlooked in conventional scientific dialogue.[17] A similar project in Cornwall, 'Life on the Edge', showcases lectures by scientist-Christians on topics like oceanography and marine ecosystems.[18]

What's truly promising about such efforts towards metaframing is the spotlight on role models, individuals at the intersection of faith and science. People like Gregor Mendel, the father of genetics;

Metaframing: from difference to higher sameness

Georges Lemaître, the Big Bang theory pioneer; Kenneth R. Miller, a Catholic biologist challenging creationism; the Pakistani physicist and practising Muslim Ghulam Murtaze, who has often spoken in media about the harmony between his scientific work and faith; or Nobel Peace Prize recipient John T. Houghton, a devout Christian and pivotal figure in climate science, have historically bridged the divide between faith and science, fostering deeper understanding and trust.

Let's also consider a fascinating collaboration between scientists and another breed of creative explorers: fiction writers. For decades, scientists have turned to fiction, notably science fiction, for inspiration and perspective in framing their research questions. In the twenty-first century, this cross-pollination has taken on a more direct, tangible form. In 2015, something curious unfolded in the medieval German city of Tübingen, now a stronghold of the Greens political party and a hotbed of progressive academia. The German Ministry of Defence reached out to the university with a proposal to collaborate – not on advanced mathematical models, AI algorithms, or intelligence studies, but on a project that would require the insight of literary scholars. The project was named Cassandra, after the Trojan priestess from Greek mythology who had the gift of foresight but was doomed never to be believed. Leading the project, Jörgen Wertheimer, a celebrated literary scholar, acknowledged the remarkable sensory acuity of great writers. Fiction has a way of capturing societal moods, trends, and conflicts that politicians either overlook or choose to ignore. So, the strategy of Wertheimer and his team was to reach out to literary critics and writers in regions of the world of particular interest to them – think Morocco, Algeria, Israel, France, and Egypt. Working alongside the Ministry of Defence, the literary scholars developed 'emotional maps' of crisis regions.[19]

This idea of metaframing – integrating divergent approaches to uncover a more profound, shared understanding at the meta-level – seems to require a starting point of humble acknowledgement of one's own limitations and a genuine respect for the other party's perspective. Interestingly, this process may be smoother when the perspectives involved are culturally distant, like science and religion or science and fiction. It's almost as if the greater the ideological chasm, the more we're forced to recognize our mutual insufficiencies and respect the value of the 'other'.

Metaframing of what's morally right

Let's shift from a focus on metaframing aimed at better truth-seeking to metaframing for better assessing how to assess what's morally right and wrong. In a way this ties in with our politically opposed friends at the dinner party who metaframed their different ideologies into the moral imperative contending that we should be involved and engaged in issues that matter beyond our individual comfort and well-being.

Since the late 1700s one of the most transformative metaframings for prescribing our ethical responsibilities to people, animals, and nature has been the utilitarian principle. Existing in several varieties, it contends that we ought to prioritize striving towards maximizing the amount of happiness (or satisfaction of basic preferences) and minimizing the amount of suffering in the world, regardless of who the moral objects are – that is, what group of people, animal, or even plant we're talking about, given the organism in question has the capacity to sense pleasure or pain.

To be sure, ethical components that crudely resemble parts of utilitarian thought have been present in human societies for thousands of years, appearing in different forms across religious doctrines and philosophical texts.[20] Understanding and crafting utilitarian ideas might seem simple in theory, but applying them consistently in practice proves difficult amid the broader social tensions. These strains arise from strong loyalty bonds within family and friendship groups, the observed lack of reciprocation of beneficial actions between in-groups and out-groups, and the risk to one's social and political standing. It's therefore hardly surprising that few, if any, utilitarian aspects found in ancient religious and philosophical doctrines have been consistently followed in practice.

Despite these obstacles, dedicated efforts across political, social, and environmental spheres have made it possible to apply the utilitarian principle at least partly in certain areas, resulting in reduced suffering and greater fulfilment of needs. The originator and popularizer of the specific utilitarian doctrine of maximizing the total amount of happiness and minimizing the total amount of suffering was the British philosopher Jeremy Bentham.[21] Descriptions of Bentham from his time, the late eighteenth and early nineteenth centuries, paint him as a rather disagreeable person, reputedly aloof and devoid of emotional attachment to others. For example, the eminent nineteenth-century thinker William Hazlitt, who knew Bentham personally, wrote:

> He [Bentham] has lived for the last forty years in a house in Westminster, overlooking the Park, like an anchoret in his cell, reducing law to a system, and the mind of man to a machine. He scarcely ever goes out, and sees very little company. The favoured few, who have the privilege of the entrée, are always admitted one by one. He does not like to have witnesses to his conversation. He talks a great deal, and listens to nothing but facts. When anyone calls upon him, he invites them to take a turn round his garden with him.[22]

Perhaps Bentham's likely neurodivergence was a prerequisite for him to become completely immersed in a rational and almost mathematical principle that became his mission: the belief that the only reasonable moral goal is to minimize suffering and maximize happiness, regardless of whom it may concern. Driven by his beliefs, Bentham ardently championed the abolition of slavery, equal rights for men and women, the decriminalization of homosexuality, and the protection of children and animals. Remarkably fresh thinking, we might contend, considering that he advanced these ideas as early as the eighteenth century.

However, the utilitarian metaframe has often failed, and still often fails, to generate the cultural and political alignment in the struggle to expand the inclusion of different 'categories' of people, animals, and plants. John Stewart Mill, another utilitarian thinker, expanded upon the metaframework originated by Bentham, aiming to grow cultural acceptance for including more individuals in the principle of minimized suffering and maximized happiness or 'preference satisfaction'. This philosophy led him to advocate for women's full membership in society, such as their right to vote. However, Mill quickly recognized the futility of only arguing from a utilitarian standpoint that allowing women to vote would boost happiness for them and society at large in the long run, outweighing any potential discomfort to men or women. Instead, Mill had to move down to the level of rule-based, deontological ethics, more specifically the long-accepted maxim of justice, which Mill called 'the oldest of our constitutional maxims'. The maxim of justice held that all tax-payers should have voting rights. Since women contributed to the household economically, even if not working outside the home, Mill considered them as taxpayers. This rationale also led him to recommend the replacement of the word 'man' with 'person' in civil rights legislation.[23] Mill's determined efforts, mainly around 1866 and 1867, were a precursor to the eventual extension of voting rights to women on equal terms with men in the UK, although it took several more decades and the robust support of the Suffragette movement to achieve this goal.

From these impressions of the complexities of expanding the moral circle, three main observations stand out. First, the enduring nature of societal norms that favour men's dominance over women is striking. Across various eras and nearly all cultures, this male-centric view persists. As highlighted by evolutionary psychologist Anne Campbell, men historically inclined to dominate or have multiple women partners often had more descendants.[24] Genetic data indicates we have 67 per cent more female than male ancestors,[25] suggesting that while some men had multiple female partners, many had none. This male competition over female partners could account for the reluctance to grant women more rights. The resistance to female suffrage epitomizes this, though there were varied reasons, such as the stance of the Women's National Anti-Suffrage League in 1908 that women should avoid the contentious world of politics to maintain their innate pacifism.[26]

Our second observation ventures beyond gender and warrants further expansion. It concerns the intricate task of advancing the utilitarian perspective that outcomes, be they in terms of satisfaction or suffering, outweigh intentions. Morally, empathy seems the most accessible base for many. It drives us to protect those we emotionally resonate with, especially close relatives. But empathy has boundaries, primarily rooted in safeguarding our immediate kin. As societies grew more diverse, a formalized moral basis emerged, rooted in rules and laws. This framework accommodated the growing numbers of competing factions. Historically, such ethics, like the Ten Commandments, were established to regulate interactions between different groups, with clear repercussions for non-compliance, both societal and divine.[27]

This rule-based approach, which focuses on deeds rather than non-actions, is more intuitive than utilitarian ethics, which view actions and non-actions equally and is only concerned with their consequences as measured in amounts of happiness and suffering. Traits that emerged early in evolution can be expected to be more deeply rooted in us, and be more intuitive to us, than traits and reasoning that developed more recently.[28] The historical dominance of empathy and rule-based morals, which have shaped our social norms for millennia over the relatively recent emergence of systematic utilitarian thinking, seems to tell us something. It's perhaps no coincidence that it took someone who might today be identified as being neurodivergent, Jeremy Bentham, to be the first to deeply explore the principles of utilitarianism, a benevolent but socially unconventional and highly counterintuitive ethos.[29] Furthermore, Bentham has been credited with being the originator of the term 'international', showcasing his propensity for expansive thinking.

To shed additional light on how moral reasoning approaches differ in terms of their intuitiveness, and thus how deeply they are rooted in us, we can look beyond the history books and into our brains. Neuropsychological research experiments, particularly those involving moral dilemmas, have produced some fascinating findings.

As it turns out, research experiments, especially on moral dilemmas, have provided intriguing insights here. Take 'the trolley problem', a thought experiment devised by English philosopher Philippa Foot.[30] Here's the essence of the problem: in the first scenario, you're standing next to a set of points on a tram track. Five people are tied to the tracks ahead. If you flip the switch, the oncoming tram will divert to a side track, where one person is tied. Do you change its course, thereby choosing to save the five over the one? Studies reveal that most people would. In the second scenario, you're on a footbridge above a track where five people are tied up. An oncoming tram will hit and kill them. You recognize that a fat man happens to be standing close to you, leaning casually over the low rail of the footbridge. All that could stop the tram from running over and killing the five people would be if you were to push the man onto the tracks, something you know would kill him. The man's size in the most common version of the story is not for humour but to ensure the reader understands he can halt the tram.[31]

In the results of these psychological experiments, conducted in hundreds of different varieties and involving people from different age groups, ethnicities, with different levels of education, different political ideologies, and so forth, one pattern stands out: even though the choice in the two hypothetical scenarios is the same – whether to sacrifice one person to save five – most study participants in the first scenario say that they would flip the switch, which would lead to the loss of one life while saving five, whereas most in the second scenario say that they wouldn't push the man off the footbridge to save the five people on the track.[32] We should note that this result holds true even if the respondents learn that neither action in the two scenarios would have any legal repercussions. What do these consistent findings tell us about people's ethical intuition and reasoning? They reveal that people, on average, are inclined to subscribe to a classical rule-based ethics – here, thou shall not kill. In addition, people spontaneously perceive a huge ethical difference between killing and letting die. The former is considered fundamentally worse than the latter. Finally, people's tendency to empathize may be influenced by the fact that the big man on the footbridge in the thought experiment is standing very close to the respondents, so they would have to touch him directly and physically to make him fall onto the track.

We find ourselves looking at two distinct research results, both pointing in the same direction. One explores the long history of humankind, while the other reveals that, regardless of vast cultural differences, various respondents have consistently expressed the same moral preference in a statistically significant way. However, it's essential to recognize that responses in surveys or interviews might not accurately reflect what people genuinely think or believe. Instead, such answers often serve as a window into the image people wish to portray to themselves or to researchers. Understanding this can be as vital as the responses themselves.

Digging deeper into how individuals grapple with moral dilemmas, neuropsychologist Joshua Greene has studied the brain's activity during thought experiments involving the two stages of the trolley problem. He's also compared the brain responses when people reason using rule-based logic versus utilitarian principles. At a first glance, one might expect the brain activity to appear similar in these two scenarios, as both present a moral quandary and force a decision that could mean life or death for six people. Surprisingly, the opposite of what one might expect holds true. Greene and his team uncovered significant distinctions. When participants grappled with the choice of whether to pull the points switch, their dorsolateral prefrontal cortex often showed increased activity. This area, a later evolutionary development in the prefrontal cortex, aids in complex, reflective decisions. Its heightened activity indicates cognitive control, helping manage emotional urges. In moral choices, the dorsolateral prefrontal cortex becomes especially active to prioritize rationality over intense emotional reactions, like empathy, and to think about long-term outcomes. Conversely, when participants encountered the footbridge dilemma, which required pushing someone directly onto the tracks, the ventromedial prefrontal cortex became more active. This older part of the prefrontal cortex supports swift, instinctual decisions. When it's active, it suggests personal moral judgements, especially when deciding on actions that could harm those nearby. Such decisions also weigh up the societal implications – whether the community will view the choice as commendable or reprehensible.[33]

Neuropsychological studies show how different regions in our brains, particularly in the prefrontal cortex, are activated according to distinct patterns depending on what options we have to deal with specific moral dilemmas. This suggests a clear link between the likely challenges that humanity has faced throughout our long history and the genetic adaptations of the human brain to cope with these challenges. This link helps us understand the challenges and opportunities for expanding or contracting society's moral frames. Our challenge extends beyond determining who is under our moral care, whether men, women, children, or animals at different stages. We must also define our moral duty. Is it merely to avoid causing harm? Should we actively shield those in our care from harm? Or should we boost their prospects for happiness and well-being? A significant ethical hurdle is the utilitarian belief that passive behaviour, or not acting out of malice, can be as condemnable as active harm. This is highlighted by the notion that indifference, not hatred, is love's true opposite.

Doing good for earthly reasons

The literature particularly on social change and movements often oversimplifies the framing process, making framing straightforward and goal-oriented. In the introduction to Part III, we learned about the three main components that social movement leaders use to create a clear and coherent narrative. First, diagnostic framing is used to identify the issue and assign blame. Then prognostic framing suggests potential solutions, which may be political, religious, or other. Lastly, motivational framing delivers a compelling message that encourages action and instils belief in the possibility and benefits of change.

A crucial element in the motivational frame, according to movement scholars that study framing, is addressing the 'free-rider' problem. This issue, borrowed from economics and rational choice theory, concerns how leaders of social movements must articulate why investing time and effort in actively participating is worthwhile.[34] Although framing scholars are probably deeply knowledgeable about the messiness of framing processes, the distinctly separated framing factors may tempt the reader to think of 'framers' – be it movement leaders, politicians, or public intellectuals – as mainly consciously strategic and only driven by the explicit cause of the movement.

Framing, as orchestrated by key figures like movement leaders or politicians, may to be sure have traits of such goal rationality. But often, the unfolding events reveal far less straightforward social processes with changes in both means and goals along with impact of personal motivations that may deviate from the collective cause. To truly grasp these intricate dynamics, we need to move beyond a linear, textbook understanding of framing. This means embracing a broader perspective that includes but transcends, linking present cultural behaviours to the deep-rooted genetic inclinations of humanity. Some framing techniques are universally effective, while others align only with specific cultural contexts. To illuminate this, the book has included, but also transcended, the standard social sciences, by drawing from diverse disciplines, such as behavioural economics and evolutionary psychology, creating a comprehensive 'metaframe' of understanding.

Now, I must confess that this book, too, might appear to present an overly tidy picture of framing processes, albeit differently from previous literature on the subject. I've neatly divided framing into three categories: what's seen as true or false, morally right or wrong, and aesthetically valuable or not. This distinction has been completely deliberate, though, as part of the attempts to help us recognize where logical fallacies might sneak into the framing process – tricks we all could fall for if we're not careful. For example, research shows that men have been more likely to use physical violence than women across cultures and history. This is a claim about what's true or false. But those who wish to engage in the art of framing unscrupulously may fallaciously draw moral conclusions from this truth claim, by contending that men's aggression, since it seems 'natural', should be tolerated or even encouraged. This mistake, called the naturalistic fallacy, confuses a factual frame with a moral one. Still, my breakdown of frames into those covering claims of truth, morality, and aesthetics, respectively, also serves a bigger purpose: to illustrate how these and other elements interplay, often subconsciously, in shaping dominant narratives, many times without falling into logical fallacies, but nevertheless played out in the multifaceted and crooked ways that signify social life.

One lesson from all this should be that societal outcomes that most people may agree are good aren't just about direct efforts towards achieving them. Instead, such outcomes are much more likely influenced by various factors, sometimes to the extent that they fall into the category of doing good for the wrong reasons. Here are some examples that were introduced earlier.

Although political and economic authorities, along with the rest of us, might, in principle, share some moral concerns, we all often divert our attention to other, more earthly goals and interests, many of them plausible. This diversion can be highly problematic, of course, but not always, and not entirely. The diverted focus need not only be an obstacle but can also provide some hope, aided by – along with other resources – good skills in the art of framing. History has proven that the expansion of our moral understanding has rarely been a direct path driven solely by moral awakening or insight. Other factors have usually been part of the mix. Take the case of Amsterdam in the 1970s and 1980s, where I have directed the focus of my book, as well as media attention at the time, on the urgent issue of child mortality in traffic accidents. This specific focus resonated strongly with the local culture and greatly contributed to political and cultural acceptance of increasing space for bicycles while decreasing space for cars. At the same time, societal change is a multifaceted process, often influenced by factors that may not be immediately apparent. For example, in Amsterdam's case, we should investigate whether the success of the social cycling movement was coincidentally contemporaneous with the oil crises and significant uncertainty over oil availability for fuel and heating at the time.

This type of intricacy also extends to entirely different cases and sectors. One is the increasing inclusion of women in the workforce globally in the post-war period and beyond. It might be easy to attribute this solely to women's emancipation, propelled by moral pleas and widespread protests against female suppression. However, in-depth social history studies reveal a more nuanced picture. The need for labour during this time, not least in the Nordic countries, played a pivotal role. Women's entry into the labour market was not just a moral imperative but a result of a complex interaction between labour needs, understanding of gender equality, and practical political measures to ease women's integration into the workforce.[35] In essence, widening the moral circle requires recognizing that societal transformations are neither simple nor linear; rather, they're woven from intricate and sometimes invisible threads.

Let's revisit, in some depth, a set of opportunities and challenges concerning agreeing on what width society's and its members' moral circle should be, and what this inclusion ought to mean in terms of our responsibility for the well-being of people, animals, nature, and future generations.

First, consider the topic of animal welfare. It's easy to believe that throughout history, only a handful of compassionate individuals stood up against the mistreatment of animals, urging others to recognize the cruelty in how livestock were treated. However, the advocacy against animal cruelty has evolved over centuries, often presented as a means to achieve broader objectives. One notable example is Immanuel Kant, a leading philosopher in Western thought. While Kant strongly opposed animal cruelty, his reasoning wasn't based on the animals' welfare. Instead, he believed cruelty towards animals cultivated a tendency for humans to be cruel and violent towards one another:

> We have duties towards the animals because thus we cultivate the corresponding duties towards human beings. ... If he is not to stifle his human feelings, he must practice kindness towards animals, for he who is cruel to animals becomes hard also in his dealings with men [whereas] tender feelings towards dumb animals develop humane feelings towards mankind.[36]

Kant's notion of our 'indirect duty' to animals, which focuses solely on fostering harmonious between people, has left a lasting impact. For example, nearly a century after Kant, the French Animal Protection Society underscored the significance of preventing children from mistreating animals, mirroring his sentiments.

> If ... the child indulges in acts of cruelty [to animals], care must be taken to prevent such habits from developing. If nothing is done the

danger will be that, having spent his tender years tormenting animals, his first subordinates, he will go on to spend the rest of his life bullying anyone who is put under his command. [The behaviour will be the same], the only thing that will change will be the victims.[37]

Moral progress concerning animal cruelty in Western culture has been a gradual process, resonating quietly through the decades and centuries. Traditional views, rooted in biblical beliefs of human dominion over animals, left society unprepared to consider humans and animals within the same utilitarian framework. Though there was recognition that animals, like humans, had the capacity to suffer and a strong interest in avoiding suffering, this perspective took time to develop and find cultural acceptance.

Another series of arguments that added momentum to the social norm against animal cruelty was economic in nature. The emerging field of veterinary science revealed that stressed and tormented animals produced tough and poor-quality meat, making it harder to sell. Additionally, veterinarians showed that deplorable living conditions for animals increased the risk of spreading diseases. These revelations motivated powerful groups controlling meat production to prioritize animal welfare, not for the animals' sake, but for economic reasons. This broadened framing of arguments led to a normalization of practices against animal cruelty, allowing the intrinsic value of not harming animals to be expressed, at least verbally.

Despite progress, much work remains to create better lives for animals. Controversies are profound, and significant conflicts of interest persist. Even within groups dedicated to animal welfare and rights, there are deep disagreements. The utilitarian question about the future direction of protein production asks whether meat consumption brings more happiness than suffering. Some utilitarians, known for advocating animal liberation and anti-speciesism, argue that being human doesn't grant our pleasures or pains higher moral value than other species. Others suggest that fewer cattle would be born and experience potential happiness if we didn't consume their meat, milk, and skin. From this perspective, the moral recommendation is to continue raising cattle for human consumption but, crucially, to ensure a high quality of life for the animals. This includes measures like letting calves stay with their mothers, providing ample space, and minimizing stress, particularly before slaughter.[38]

Most of us with at least half a heart – carnivores included – advocate for reducing animal suffering in the protein industry. However, the approach of breeding healthy animals only to slaughter them for food doesn't align with any strong moral principles, including utilitarianism. Findings since the 1960s in environmental, health, and social sciences emphasize that our approach must be holistic, merging various objectives for a sustainable future. The term 'sustainable development', introduced in the 1980s, represents a profound shift in our understanding. Its foundational principle is to address the needs of the present without jeopardizing those of future generations.[39] Drawing inspiration from utilitarianism, sustainable development highlights the intertwined nature of ecological, social, and economic needs.

Given this, the global protein production industry's aim for increased happiness and preference satisfaction can't settle with breeding more cattle, even if treated well. To truly uphold the sustainable development principle, we must consider an intricate web of factors. This includes addressing greenhouse gas emissions, land and water usage, eutrophication, and biodiversity loss resulting from protein production and consumption.

A comprehensive study in the journal *Nature* revealed the environmental impacts of various diets in the UK. It demonstrated that meat-based diets have the most significant environmental footprint, varying with the type and quantity of meat. Diets relying on fish proteins have the second-highest environmental impact. On the other hand, vegetarian diets have considerably lower impacts, and purely plant-based diets leave the smallest environmental footprint.[40]

It is interesting to witness the implicit story of frame expansion and integration of all good things that seem to be part of the reality of organizations in the political, market-oriented but also civil society sphere. In the early modern period, much like today, the emphasis was on making progress, albeit with different ideals and approaches. To achieve progress during early modernity, compartmentalization, specialization, and the division of responsibilities were advocated.[41]

Issues affecting physical health, mental health, culture, and nature, such as environmental pollution, were best understood and managed as isolated problem areas handled by separate organizations, entities, and experts.

However, starting roughly in the mid-twentieth century, partly with the development of systems theory, there has been a growing recognition that life is an interconnected whole; this realization has spurred efforts to integrate different aspects. Issues such as physical and mental health, the relationship between health and the environment, nature and culture, quality of life, equality, economics, and morality are now seen as intertwined. Sustainable development has indeed been a milestone in this holistic thinking, even if many argue that sustainable development still places disproportionate emphasis on economic sustainability at the expense of the ecological and social pillars.

All good and well – a food example

This approach of frame expansion is often welcome and constructive. Let me in some depth discuss a specific example that I've studied closely, namely the Nordic Nutrition Recommendations. They are revised periodically by collaborating nutrition experts from the Nordic countries, including Sweden, Norway, Denmark, Finland, and Iceland, with one such revision of occurring between 2022 and 2023.[42] This update introduced a requirement to consider not only the nutritional content but also the distinct needs of various population groups, including women, men, the young, and the elderly. Furthermore, there was a new emphasis on incorporating environmental factors. The recommendations now had to highlight diets that were both nutritionally optimal and environmentally sound, considering factors like climate impact and biodiversity. Developed transparently, these guidelines were open to suggestions from the public, food corporations, and NGOs, although they were not to be mandates. To achieve this comprehensive approach, experts in the environmental impact of food joined the traditionally nutrition-focused panel from different countries. From my perspective, this was a commendable demonstration of broadened thinking. The process and its outcome were intricate, but not overwhelmingly so. Among the many insights, three challenges that these experts shared with me stood out. These challenges, or dilemmas, are valuable to understand as we attempt to merge and balance multiple positive objectives within an expanded frame.

The first challenge was striking a balance: integrating various 'good things' without compromising the credibility of their knowledge assertions. In a series of in-depth interviews I conducted in 2022 with experts involved in shaping the Nordic Nutrition Recommendations for 2023, the participants candidly acknowledged their stronger competence, as individuals and as a team, in health over environmental aspects: 'We don't aim to equate environmental considerations with nutritional facts', noted one of the nutrition experts who sat on the committee. However, this person also recognized the importance of upholding a substantial environmental standard to ensure their primary nutrition-based recommendations remained reputable: 'We don't want to affect that credibility [on the nutrition side] by doing the environment a bit carelessly'.

The second challenge involved creating an open consultation process incorporating suggestions and critiques from the public, food companies, and NGOs without succumbing to special interests. The challenge was to establish legitimacy for hearing various perspectives without being unduly influenced by them. One of the experts addressed this by affirming their independent stance: 'we never had any intention that the food industry or the Finnish vegan association should influence the recommendations'.

The third challenge they highlighted was navigating the cultural and sectoral variations in food production and diet across different countries. Such differences could be perceived as 'special interests' unique to each nation. For instance, Norwegian experts, backed by their country's robust fishing industry and traditions, might be inclined to stress the health and environmental advantages of fish and aquaculture. Similarly, Swedish representatives could highlight the virtues of their 'organic' beef production, drawing attention to their pastures' role in promoting biodiversity. To address this, they viewed these national nuances as valuable insights, allowing them to bring diverse expertise to the table and enrich the overall nutritional recommendations. As one of the interviewees put it, 'that's the advantage of our experts coming from different countries; so, hopefully, it will be balanced in the end'.

The challenge of aligning health and environmental considerations in food recommendations reveals unavoidable challenges involved in processes that serve to expand frames, no matter how benevolent. Frame expansion has dilemmas, trade-offs, negotiations, and compromises. This should be something we should all keep in mind in order not to be tricked into simplistically assuming that various positive and desirable goals can seamlessness merge into a harmonious whole.

From incomplete to renewed metaframing ahead

Beyond the Nordic Nutrition Recommendations, where such trade-offs and compromises have arguably been handled very constructively, there are other cases where many of those involved have fallen for the trick mentioned above. That's usually a result of being caught in a 'reality speaks for itself' mindset, assuming that substantive, explicit goals – better overall health, environment, and prosperity – can, or should, make people overlook or accept the underlying social tensions, such as increases in social inequality. This has been apparent in partially failed attempts at a globally expanded, liberal democratic framing. Fired up by their leaders, many groups of people have found, despite a general increase in prosperity, significant deviations from the age-old human demand for reciprocity and fairness – moral elements which go against increases in inequality – as well as the demand for keeping some cultural expressions sacred.

For instance, in the early 1990s, the notion of 'the end of history', championed by political scientist Francis Fukuyama, suggested that the fall of the Berlin Wall, along with several other signs of progress, indicated that liberal democracy had triumphed. Though Fukuyama's thesis is often mischaracterized, it arguably was steeped too much in superficial problem-solving. It was subsequently challenged by works like Samuel Huntington's 'Clash of Civilizations', which argued that the notion of the end of history had overlooked several underlying social concerns and resentments. However, as we have argued in this book, reality itself, such as a lack of resources, thinly framed by individual concerns and resentments, is hardly enough to cause large-scale clashes and change. Rather, such clashes and change occur, for better or worse, when political leaders and representatives of different groups and social movements employ thick framing strategies. These strategies include texturing, tempering, positioning, and sizing to construct and reinforce a simplified image of this reality.

When these framing processes are designed to exploit people's vulnerability, framing can make people more likely to accept, advocate, and even engage in violent acts. These acts are destructive for all parties, especially the most vulnerable. On the other hand, as we have seen throughout this book, framing processes, particularly those of social movements with environmental and health agendas, can be immensely powerful in bringing about peaceful social change. These changes reduce suffering, increase happiness for humans and non-human animals, and reduce damage to ecosystems.

As all of us continue to explore and be engaged in the social art of framing, one key lesson is that if efforts towards frame resizing are to succeed, we need to make use of the hereditary screws and glues that have always been necessary in order for frames to capture human reality in meaningful ways. Some frames seem to be almost infinitely expandable. I'm thinking, for instance, about a specific body of scholarly work that began to emerge in the late 2000s. These publications aspire to provide society with moral direction, focusing on taking into account the pains, pleasures, and interests not just of a dozen future generations, but. also of generations of sentient and intelligent creatures hundreds of thousands, perhaps millions of years into the future. This hyper-utilitarian strand of thought is called 'long-termism'. Frames have new ideas are always surfacing, including how we should consider the needs of life forms that won't exist for hundreds of thousands of years. These ideas should remain part of our ongoing discussions about the future path of society.

Just like nature assesses new mutations for their usefulness, we must carefully evaluate any new thoughts about society's moral direction.

Meanwhile, there are, fortunately, many opportunities within far closer reach in time and space to be created or discovered. There, substantive goals of increased, basic well-being among humans (possibly coupled with artificial intelligence) as well as non-human animals and the rest of living nature, can be made to converge with other interests, some of them not primarily moral in nature. We might have to accept that our goals, especially for those of us with limited power, can only be reached if we can persuade those with more power that our concerns align with what they find valuable. This could be our way to make the most use of our skills in the art of framing, which this book has hopefully helped to strengthen.

12

Questions, answers, and discussion

Does framing merely clarify and obscure, or can it also enlighten and deceive?

Framing sometimes has the characteristics of being simply true or false. This can happen in at least two ways. One is in situations where there exists a dichotomy in the real world that a dichotomous framing is or isn't aligned with (or adjusted to).

In the area of consumption, it is common to divide various products and services into eco-friendly and eco-unfriendly. This binary framing is, strictly speaking, most often false, since even so-called eco-friendly products and services can have negative environmental impacts. Thus, to correct framings in this area it is necessary to visualize the spectrum of impact levels that the product or service has. How this reframing should look, and what supplementary information would be needed given the goal of steering producers and consumers towards the options with the lowest negative impact, is a second, separate step. That second step would likely need to include decisions about how consumers should be helped to navigate between the principle of eco-efficient consumption and the separate, more comprehensive principle of reducing one's total material resource use such that it helps reduce environmental harm.[1]

Another way in which framing can be true or false is in situations where there is or isn't a real-world dichotomy to which a dichotomous framing can correspond in any respect. For example, there are researchers in behavioural genetics who argue that the common,

193

dominant dichotomous framing in psychiatry has no counterpart in the real world. Behavioural genetics professor Robert Plomin, for instance, criticizes what he sees as the erroneous framing of psychological traits into binary categories, framing one category of people as *being* mentally ill and the other category as *being* mentally healthy. Plomin's point is not primarily about what framing of psychological variation is morally right or wrong. His focus is instead on what type of framing would be true or false. Drawing from extensive research, he asserts that what we term mental illness or disorders are merely extreme manifestations of genes present in all of us to varying degrees. If he's correct, the genetic predisposition to these conditions differs *quantitatively* – in degree – and not *qualitatively* – in kind or essence – from the norm.[2] And again, if this is true, it should be part of the knowledge background when framings and categorizations of mental disorders are to be reassessed. Still, as we've learned throughout this book, as with other truth claims, this one can't be logically translated into how mental disorders *should* be reframed, as such a normative assessment must consider a wide range of societal and ethical considerations, in order not to be subject to the naturalistic fallacy.

Framing frequently simplifies or complicates aspects of reality either to clarify or obscure it. Determining whether a frame clarifies or obscures requires nuanced examination based on several factors, including context and the individuals involved. The term 'esoteric' has evolved to denote vague, abstract arguments detached from reality. Historically, Plato and his peers used it to refer to advanced discussions intended for a scholarly audience. Translating these complex discourses into more accessible exoteric terms was necessary to avoid muddying the waters for the general populace.

Truth and clarity aren't the sole objectives in human communication. Art, for instance, leverages framing to evoke deep emotions, transcending mere factual correctness. Framing functions both at an overt level and a more subtle, perhaps pictorial, layer, influencing perception and interpretation. Consider the tale of the boy who cried wolf: while possibly fictional, it imparts a vital lesson on trust and cooperation. Today, however, we face a surge in factually accurate yet misleading narratives that subliminally convey incorrect or exaggerated conclusions, often seen in manipulated climate change discussions that zoom in on specific, decontextualized periods to refute broader established trends.[3]

In conclusion, understanding framing demands mastery over mechanisms that shape our perception of reality, requiring a depth of insight beyond distinguishing truth from falsehood. It is a vital tool in navigating the complex social dynamics of communication.

How is the 'irrelevant' relevant in framing?

When this book asserts that 'the irrelevant is relevant', it challenges the commonplace belief that 'reality speaks for itself'. Most people, myself included, often find the latter approach reasonable, viewing it either as true or as a guideline for how individuals and groups should operate. However, extensive research contradicts this perspective, highlighting many cases where reality doesn't seem to speak for itself. A primary example of this is the 'framing effect', whereby our perception of the central issue shifts as we consider the seemingly 'irrelevant' details surrounding it.

Think again about the area of sustainable consumption. Studies have shown that a significant proportion of us feel that buying some 'environmentally friendly' products *in addition to* conventional goods makes us more environmentally sound than if we hadn't purchased the additional products. In reality, it is irrelevant, of course, whether the added goods are 'environmentally friendly' or not. The environmental impact increases regardless.[4] Another notable factor is the presentation of an option as the 'default'. Studies show that individuals are more inclined to opt for energy-efficient domestic solutions when they are the default choice, even if the price remains constant in other presentations.[5]

The clearest and most comprehensive way to understand the relevance of the seemingly 'irrelevant' is through observing how our perceptions and actions are shaped by the behaviour of others around us. Naturally, when it concerns those in our immediate circles or the groups we belong to, such influence might be considered relevant.

However, consider celebrities. Their professed actions, especially on matters like environment and health, significantly sway public perception and behaviour. Take celebrity-endorsed campaigns advocating reduced meat consumption. These have undeniably impacted people's perceptions and habits, even if these celebrities don't profess to have more expertise on health and the environment than the average person.[6]

It's striking how the endorsement of a statement – on topics such as the looming threat to biodiversity, or the adoption of an action like avoiding certain products – by someone we admire, expert or not, can compel us to emulate them. This influence often surpasses that of raw facts, challenging the belief that 'reality speaks for itself'. It underscores the principle that the seemingly 'irrelevant' matters.

I highlight 'irrelevant' in quotation marks for two primary reasons. Firstly, these seemingly 'irrelevant' factors profoundly influence our perceptions and reactions. Secondly, even if deemed irrelevant to the primary issue, from a broader viewpoint – namely the social context – these factors become paramount. These influences serve as social cues that we instinctively react to. Our response to these cues signifies various things: our alignment with mainstream thought, our stance on environmental issues, reflected perhaps by our 'green' purchases, and our affinity with influential figures with whom we share a perceived bond. To illustrate, psychological research in the 1950s recognized a 'para-social interaction' where individuals 'interact' with celebrities via mass media. This highlighted the powerful influence celebrities have over their audiences. Researchers at the time demonstrated that para-social interaction could significantly influence people's lifestyles and values. They saw this interaction as exclusively 'one-sided, nondialectical, ... and not open to mutual development'.[7] In today's social media age, there is far more actual interaction between celebrities and their followers. This increased interaction is likely to increase the influence of celebrities on their followers. Whether we're discussing mass media in the 1950s or today's more multifaceted media landscape, the wide reach and influence of celebrities on the general public is only one example of how 'irrelevant' factors are, in fact, highly pertinent from a social perspective. This is in line with a notion that has underpinned several parts of this book, namely that 'the "irrelevant" is relevant'.

What does it mean when we say framing needs ancestral resonance?

Much existing social science research on effective framings emphasizes cultural resonance, meaning the frame aligns with the prevailing norms of a particular culture, thus facilitating its acceptance. Yet, this explanation presents a circular argument – presupposing that successful framing necessarily resonates with existing cultural norms, thereby excluding the potential for change. It raises critical questions such as: why do certain norms prevail over others in a culture? Does a framing always have to vibrate in correspondence with the *existing* norms to be successful? How can societies evolve if frames must always align with the current culture?

I argue that for a framing to have a long-lasting impact, it must have 'ancestral resonance'. This term refers to a reflection corresponding with the deeply ingrained memories and experiences from humanity's extensive history, including the innate predispositions encoded in our genes. Ancestral resonance leverages not only recent cultural history but also the ancient lessons vital for problem-solving and fostering cooperation embedded in our genetic makeup.

A pertinent example is the modern Western emphasis on healthy living and diet. While health-framed nutritional information might resonate with some due to current cultural norms, it falls short for others, especially groups where health insights do not foster group cohesion. Among teenage boys, a more profound connection was achieved by exposing them to the deceitful practices of junk food producers, a strategy that tapped into a deeper, ancestral predisposition towards moral vigilance and social cooperation.

Thus, framing strategies grounded in what Oliver Scott Curry describes as 'human moral molecules' – elements shaped over humankind's history to aid in social navigation, highlight untrustworthiness, and occasionally foster self-serving deception – hold great promise.[8] Such strategies, with an ancestral resonance, potentially harbour a profound, inherent power to influence and foster deep engagement.

Can framing properties – texture, temperature, position, size – change independently of the others?

In this book, we have explored the four framing properties and techniques – texturing, tempering, positioning, and sizing – individually, dedicating separate sections to each. This approach was essential to achieve the book's goal of delving deep into the intricacies of how and why framing occurs and understanding its variable impacts on society. These techniques share ancestral roots embedded in human genetic 'memory'. This memory, encompassing the entire range of human inherited variations, continually resurrects through common cultural elements, even among cultures that have never interacted, as well as our ability to mould and navigate the unique culture we find ourselves in, which can significantly differ from others.

In real-world scenarios, alterations in one framing property seldom occur without the influence of others. To illustrate, consider introducing a special tax on certain products – meat, for instance. For society to accept this, the 'frame' might need repositioning from the product being seen as a staple to a luxury. This could also entail a retexturing of its perception from a healthy choice to a potential sustainability and health hazard, aligning it with products that have a history of extra taxation such as alcohol, cigarettes, and sugar. Successful implementation of this kind of tax demands concerted efforts from policymakers, civil society, and experts in various fields, facilitating farmers to adapt to new production norms.

I have endeavoured to portray the interconnected nature of these properties, revisiting examples throughout the book to offer a richer understanding of each case. As readers, when you find yourself pondering the deep-seated or transforming issues in your personal life, organizational involvements, or broader societal discussions, I urge you to utilize all four framing techniques to give you a detailed and enlightening view of the realities you are exploring.

Questions, answers, and discussion

How can we assert control over the framing around us?

While it is generally not possible to control all the frames that surround us, we do have an increasing ability to understand and influence the dominant narratives present in our daily lives, community groups, and organizational activities. Becoming aware of these prevailing frames involves a deep level of reflection and understanding, a process that is admittedly not straightforward. Humans have a natural propensity to adhere to the established norms, often without giving them a second thought. To truly grasp the framework we exist within, it is necessary to engage in or encounter comparative analysis.

Emile Durkheim, a renowned sociologist of the late nineteenth century, elucidated a method to recognize and understand a dominant cultural frame, albeit using the different terminology of 'collective consciousness'. According to him, witnessing individuals or groups deviating from the accepted norms to a degree that incites anger, mockery, or shock in the general populace is an incredibly useful way of identifying the prevalent frame.[9] This essentially enables an individual to attain 'frame awareness', where one recognizes and analyses how certain actions oppose the established norms, a process referred to as 'reflection within a frame'.

Today, identifying the dominant cultural frame is theoretically simpler than in Durkheim's era. This is not necessarily because more individuals are challenging the frame, but because contemporary media, cinema, literature, and the cosmopolitan nature of modern cities expose us to a plethora of perspectives, showcasing the variability in adherence to different cultural norms.

Moreover, this exposure facilitates the understanding that alternative frames exist which are equally valid and functional, hence debunking any notions of these frames being 'strange'. Consequently, we find ourselves oscillating between different frames, a critical stance allowing us to appreciate both the merits and demerits of various perspectives, an approach referred to as 'reflection between frames'.[10] This nuanced approach fosters a more inclusive and empathetic viewpoint, creating fertile ground for understanding and collaboration in a diverse society. In the groups and organizations we participate in, there is a broad understanding that dominant frameworks and expectations can coexist with differing perspectives without dismissing them as strange or irrelevant. This understanding fosters an environment where, in many collaborative contexts, it is perfectly acceptable to propose principled discussions that scrutinize both the prevailing framework and potential alternatives openly.

Such discussions might explore various critical points of uncertainty, such as understanding the decision-making process in our organization, evaluating whether all group members have equal opportunities to influence decisions, and handling divergent opinions. It is essential to delineate clear guidelines regarding what can be shared outside of group discussions, and to identify which norms are immutable and which can be debated and altered. By making these things clear, group members can achieve a better understanding and possibly amalgamate elements from diverse frameworks into a unified structure.

Engaging in principled discussions like these offer three primary benefits. First, they elucidate the underlying implicit order, reducing the chances of unnecessary confusion, misunderstandings, and mismatched expectations. Secondly, exchanging experiences and knowledge about different frameworks allows us to learn from past collaborations and to sidestep previous pitfalls. Finally, when conducted with openness, clarity, and a genuine curiosity towards the experiences of others, these discussions can bolster both the communal bond and each member's sense of agency, validation, and belonging in the group.

Such a thoughtful approach to discussions not only strengthens the group's cohesion but also enhances individual members' sense of value and involvement, cultivating a rich ground for synergized and harmonious collaborations. However, there exists a broader scope of framework reflection, opening even greater opportunities for controlling and redefining societal issues and challenges. This is particularly pertinent in instances where we encounter challenges, choices, and conflicts involving groups and individuals grounded in fundamentally diverse frames – stemming from disparate ideological, cultural, and identity-based foundations.

At times, particularly when advocates of distinct frames interpret the perspectives of others superficially, escalating conflicts, this is referred to as controversy.[11] It is common for individuals, groups, or organizations to be embroiled in disputes spanning divergent frames without necessarily viewing each other's stance as adverse. One universal characteristic of inter-framework challenges is that mere facts are insufficient to resolve them. Indeed, adding more facts, even accurate ones, could potentially exacerbate divisions unless coupled with a reconfiguration of the issue at hand.

To illustrate, attempts to emphasize the heightened health risks associated with avoiding a specific vaccine compared to receiving it often intensify the staunch anti-vaccinationists' opposition while bolstering the advocates' support. Similar dynamics have been observed in other areas such as climate debates, where an influx of facts without accompanying social reframing strategies deepens divisions.

Overcoming such inter-frame disputes frequently demands a more holistic approach termed 'reflection above frames'. Generally, this entails deliberating among various potential frame positions (as explored in Part III), culminating in the formation of a metaframe (discussed in Chapter 11), where adversaries and their respective frames can find common ground in a superior, unified frame.

Implementing this strategy can be concrete and practical, assuming parties are willing to embrace open-minded thinking. Consider the issue of school meals in a multicultural setting, characterized by diverging preferences on the type of meat served. Arriving at a consensus through debate seems futile given the fundamental value differences and the unlikelihood of individuals altering their views based on facts or assessments from distinct cultural groups – as research on resolving controversies indicates. A more inventive and transformative solution could be to sidestep the controversy altogether by offering only vegetarian or vegan meals, thereby ensuring a protein-rich diet without privileging any cultural group. Similar principles apply in the pursuit of sustainability, health, and societal well-being.

Rather than focusing on how to make traditional forms of transportation more eco-friendly – a topic prompting diverse responses from transport researchers and policymakers – the discourse has elevated to address the central concern: enhancing accessibility to various essential aspects of life, such as nature, work, and community engagement.

Perhaps the deepest way we can influence each other is through an approach that doesn't cling to fixed goals. This way, we allow our values to bloom not just in dogged pursuits but subtly, in the questions we ask, the paths we forge, and in the spontaneous moments that genuinely reflect what we hold dear.

Notes

Introduction

1 Renate Van Der Zee, 'How Amsterdam became the bicycle capital of the world', *Guardian*, 5 May 2015, sec. Cities, www.theguardian.com/cities/2015/may/05/amsterdam-bicycle-capital-world-transport-cycling-kin dermoord.

2 George Gaskell, Katrin Hohl, and Monica M. Gerber, 'Do closed survey questions overestimate public perceptions of food risks?', *Journal of Risk Research* 20, no. 8 (August 2017): 1038–1052.

3 cf. Matthias Lehner et al., 'Living smaller: acceptance, effects and structural factors in the EU', *Buildings and Cities* 5, no. 1 (June 2024): 215–230, https://doi.org/10.5334/bc.438.

4 Kenneth Cukier, Viktor Mayer-Schönberger, and Francis de Véricourt, *Framers: Human Advantage in an Age of Technology and Turmoil* (London: Penguin, 2021), 15.

5 James N. Druckman and Toby Bolsen, 'Framing, motivated reasoning, and opinions about emergent technologies', *Journal of Communication* 61, no. 4 (August 2011): 659–688, https://doi.org/10.1111/j.1460-2466.2011.01562.x; Sheila Jasanoff and Marybeth Long Martello, eds, *Earthly Politics: Local and Global in Environmental Governance*, Politics, Science, and the Environment (Cambridge, MA: MIT Press, 2004).

6 Kai Kupferschmidt, 'Can skeptical parents be persuaded to vaccinate?', *Science*, 27 April 2017, www.sciencemag.org/news/2017/04/can-skeptical-parents-be-persuaded-vaccinate.

7 Mikael Klintman, *Human Sciences and Human Interests: Integrating the Social, Economic, and Evolutionary Sciences* (London: Routledge, 2018).

8 Kevin B. Murch and Daniel C. Krawczyk, 'A neuroimaging investigation of attribute framing and individual differences', *Social Cognitive and Affective Neuroscience* 9, no. 10 (October 2014): 1464–1471, https://doi.org/10.1093/scan/nst140.

9 Christy Spivey, Tara L. Brown, and Maureen R. Courtney, 'Using behavioral economics to promote advanced directives for end of life care: a

national study on message framing', *Health Psychology and Behavioral Medicine* 8, no. 1 (December 2020): 501–525, https://doi.org/10.1080/21 642850.2020.1823227; Charles Collet *et al.*, 'Combining Economics and psychology: does CO_2 framing strengthen pro-environmental behaviors?', *Ecological Economics* 214 (December 2023), https://doi.org/10.1016/j. ecolecon.2023.107984.

10 Geoffrey Fisher *et al.*, 'Price promotions, beneficiary framing, and mental accounting', *Quantitative Marketing and Economics* 21, no. 2 (June 2023): 147–181, https://doi.org/10.1007/s11129-023-09261-0.

11 Lukas Fesenfeld, Lukas Rudolph, and Thomas Bernauer, 'Policy framing, design and feedback can increase public support for costly food waste regulation', *Nature Food* 3, no. 3 (March 2022): 227–235, https://doi.org/10.1038/s43016-022-00460-8.

12 Matt Guardino, *Framing Inequality: News Media, Public Opinion, and the Neoliberal Turn in U.S. Public Policy* (New York: Oxford University Press, 2019).

13 Erving Goffman, *Frame Analysis: An Essay on the Organization of Experience* (Boston, MA: Northeastern University Press, 1974); cf. Thomas F. Gieryn, *Cultural Boundaries of Science: Credibility on the Line* (Chicago, IL: University of Chicago Press, 1999); Michèle Lamont, *The Dignity of Working Men: Morality and the Boundaries of Race, Class, and Immigration* (Cambridge, MA: Harvard University Press, 2009).

14 Roberto Franzosi and Stefania Vicari, 'What's in a text? Answers from frame analysis and rhetoric for measuring meaning systems and argumentative structures', *Rhetorica: A Journal of the History of Rhetoric* 36, no. 4 (October 2018): 393–429.

15 Stevie N. Berberick, *Reframing Sex: Unlearning the Gender Binary with Trans Masculine YouTube Vloggers* (Lanham, MD: Lexington Books, 2020).

16 The sociologist Ervin Goffman (in *Frame Analysis*, p. 21) defined the frame metaphor by using another metaphor: 'schemata of interpretation' that enable people 'to locate, perceive, identify, and label'. The psychologists Amos Tversky and Daniel Kahneman, who were mainly interested in individual decision-making, preferred to conceive of frames as 'the decision-maker's conception of the acts, outcomes, and contingencies associated with a particular choice' (A. Tversky and D. Kahneman, 'The framing of decisions and the psychology of choice', *Science* 211, no. 4481 (January 1981): 453). Still, they recognized the significance of the social context by maintaining that the adopted frame is to some extent controlled by the habits, norms, and the decision-maker's personal characteristics along with the problem formulation. The term 'frame' can also be tweaked towards an analytical focus on how social power games take place through our use of language and discourses. In this sense, 'frame' and 'discourse' can sometimes be used interchangeably. The sociologist Michel Foucault defined discourse in numerous ways in his books, including as a regulated practice where cultural and value structures produce particular statements and utterances, for instance concerning what types of sexual rules are prescribed in society; see

Michel Foucault, *The History of Sexuality*, vol. 1: *An Introduction*, reissue edn (New York: Vintage, 1978).

17 Martin Rein and Donald Schön, 'Reframing policy discourse', in *The Argumentative Turn in Policy Analysis and Planning*, ed. Frank Fischer and John Forester (Durham, NC: Duke University Press, 1993), 145–166.

18 Other definitions that account for both the automatic and strategic dimensions of framing include media and communication scholar Todd Gitlin's definition of media frames, described as 'persistent patterns of cognition, interpretation, and presentation, involving selection, emphasis, and exclusion, through which symbol-handlers routinely organise discourse, whether verbal or visual' Gitlin, *The Whole World Is Watching: Mass Media in the Making and Unmaking of the New Left* (Berkeley, CA: University of California Press, 1980), 7.

19 Linsey McGoey, *Unknowers: How Strategic Ignorance Rules the World* (London: Zed Books, 2019).

20 A company specializing in nature tourism might, when they describe their efforts to minimize environmental harm, proffer detailed descriptions of how they ensure their tourists don't drop litter or feed the animals. Although this is all very well, it is a very narrow framing of environmental concern that may serve to obscure wider or alternative sustainability aspects, such as what fuels the company uses for cooking and transportation, if fires are lit, and whether the company has eco-based limits to how many tourists they invite to pristine sites in nature.

21 Committee on the Science of Science Communication: A Research Agenda, Division of Behavioral and Social Sciences and Education, and National Academies of Sciences, Engineering, and Medicine, *Communicating Science Effectively: A Research Agenda* (Washington, DC: National Academies Press, 2017).

22 Tversky and Kahneman, 'The framing of decisions'.

23 Richard H. Thaler and Prof. Cass R. Sunstein, *Nudge: The Final Edition* (New York: Penguin, 2021).

24 R. D. Benford and D. A. Snow, 'Framing processes and social movements: an overview and assessment', *Annual Review of Sociology* 26 (2000): 611–639.

25 For framing in literary criticism, see, e.g., Gerard Genette and Richard Macksey, *Paratexts: Thresholds of Interpretation*, trans. Jane E. Lewin (Cambridge: Cambridge University Press, 1997).

26 Goffman, *Frame Analysis*.

27 Isabela Fairclough and Irina Diana Mădroane, 'An argumentative approach to "framing". Framing, deliberation and action in an environmental conflict', *Co-Herencia* 17, no. 32 (June 2020): 119–158, https://doi.org/10.17230/co-herencia.17.32.5; A. Carvalho, 'Media(ted) discourse and society: rethinking the framework of critical discourse analysis', *Journalism Studies* 9, no. 2 (2008): 161–177, https://doi.org/10.1080/14616700701848162.

28 See, e.g., Jean Baudrillard, *The Intelligence of Evil: Or, The Lucidity Pact*, trans. Chris Turner (London and New York: Bloomsbury Academic, 2013.

29 Framing shares fundamental similarities with sister concepts, such as discourses, boundaries, schemata, scripts, and narratives. These concepts are

concerned with constructing, organising, and communicating meaning in social contexts, showing how individuals and groups make sense of the world by selectively emphasising, structuring, and interpreting information. Each concept influences perception and behaviour by providing cognitive and communicative tools to help people navigate complex social realities. Whether through the broader cultural frameworks of discourse, the cognitive patterns of schemata and scripts, or the coherent and causal flow of narratives, they all activate particular mental models and structures. In this way, framing and related concepts help to organise reality, enabling individuals and societies to filter information, understand relationships, and guide their actions. Framing, discourses, schemata, scripts, and narratives also demonstrate the power of selective attention – what is included or excluded, what aspects are emphasised, and how specific interpretations are given priority over others. This selective structuring shapes how events, issues and social phenomena are understood and responded to.

30 Franzosi and Vicari, 'What's in a text?'

31 It is important to note that terms such as discourses, boundaries, schemata, scripts, and narratives, in addition to their many overlaps with framing, also have certain distinct applications. They can be found in various intellectual traditions that cannot be entirely subsumed under the umbrella of framing. In this book, I argue that framing has certain characteristics that the other concepts do not embody in quite the same way. First, framing has been established in an even wider range of disciplines – from neuroscience to cultural studies – and is more embedded in everyday language than these other concepts. Second, framing is more pluralistic regarding the epistemological and ontological positions it accommodates. For example, while the analysis of discourse and boundary work is typically rooted in social constructivist traditions, framing analysis is found not only in social constructivist approaches but also in critical realist and positivist traditions – something that becomes clear when one considers the disciplinary breadth of framing research. Moreover, framing is not limited to text, language, words, or images. It extends to the physical arrangements of our societies and the social structures to which even non-human primates are susceptible. Although theories of discourse and narrative sometimes go beyond words and text, for instance through 'multi-modal discourse analysis', framing analysis, more often than the other types of analysis, captures interactions between organisms and encompasses areas beyond human language – whether spoken or unspoken – including non-human forms of organization and arrangement. To do full justice to all the concepts is far beyond the scope of this book. Nevertheless, I believe that framing and framing analysis have immense potential to both enrich and be enriched by interpretive approaches rooted in their sister concepts (see e.g., Merlijn van Hulst et al., 'Discourse, framing and narrative: three ways of doing critical, interpretive policy analysis', *Critical Policy Studies* (April 2024).

Notes

1 Perspectives on framing

1 Christian Wienberg, 'Danish artist takes museum's money and runs, calls it artwork', *Bloomberg UK*, 27 September 2021, www.bloomberg.com/news/articles/2021-09-27/danish-artist-takes-museum-s-money-and-runs-calls-it-artwork.

2 Aristotle, *Rhetoric* (Mineola, NY: Dover Publications, 2004); Jamie Dow, *Passions and Persuasion in Aristotle's Rhetoric* (Oxford: Oxford University Press, 2015), https://doi.org/10.1093/acprof:oso/9780198716266.001.0001.

3 I view both 'reality speaks for itself' and 'framing is everything' as ideal types. These notions arise from our common ways of interpreting and engaging with the world and our experiences. More aptly, they fit into the realm of folk epistemology, folk sociology, and folk psychology rather than any formal stance within these disciplines. Recognizing them as ideal types means we regard them as heuristic tools – analytical constructs that spotlight specific thought patterns. According to Max Weber, 'an ideal type is formed by the one-sided *accentuation* of one or more points of view' according to which '*concrete individual* phenomena ... are arranged into a unified analytical construct' (quoted in Sung Ho Kim, 'Max Webber', *The Stanford Encyclopedia of Philosophy*, winter 2022 edn, ed. Edward N. Zalta and Uri Nodelman, last updated 21 September 2022, https://plato.stanford.edu/archives/win2022/entries/weber/).

On the one hand, 'reality speaks for itself' emphasizes the 'core' or the inherent truth of a situation, suggesting we can genuinely understand it. This approach holds that deeper knowledge about an issue can determine our actions towards it. For instance, understanding the facts about climate change might lead to actions to mitigate its effects. This perspective intertwines a realist worldview with a moral utilitarian viewpoint. However, it can be criticized for its potential to fall into the naturalistic fallacy. It operates under the assumption that humans are 'problem-rational', meaning we're driven to find and optimize solutions to challenges, be they health, environment, or societal issues, both individually and collectively. This viewpoint parallels what I've previously termed the 'Apollonian model'.

On the other hand, the 'framing is everything' perspective posits that our understanding of any subject is shaped by cognitive and cultural framing. While it's a mainstream idea in neuroscience and neuropsychology that our perception of reality is filtered and selective, this approach takes it further. Some proponents might argue there's no core reality, only frames – a perspective that falls under ontological constructivism. Even if some concede that an independent reality exists, they might argue that our understanding is bound only by the cultural frames we find meaningful. This stance aligns with the 'blank slate' view, suggesting humans possess limitless adaptability. In our daily lives, we sometimes act as though framing is paramount. For example, we might value presentation, marketing, and personal contacts over the actual substance of a situation. This perspective can be associated with constructivist, hermeneutic, or postmodern viewpoints.

Notes

4 Lydia Catling, 'Are you feline alright? Elderly couple thank daughter for buying them "gorgeous" pate that they enjoyed on baked bread – only to discover they'd eaten CAT FOOD by mistake', *Daily Mail*, 25 May 2021, www.dailymail.co.uk/news/article-9615025/Elderly-couple-thank-daughter-buying-gorgeous-patediscover-theyd-eaten-cat-food.html.

5 Sergio Edú-Valsania, Ana Laguía, and Juan A. Moriano, 'Burnout: A Review of Theory and Measurement', *International Journal of Environmental Research and Public Health* 19, no. 3 (February 2022): 1780, https://doi.org/10.3390/ijerph19031780; Jill Lepore, 'Burnout: modern affliction or human condition?', *New Yorker*, 17 May 2021, www.newyorker.com/magazine/2021/05/24/burnout-modern-affliction-or-human-condition; Duncan Rozario, 'Burnout, resilience and moral injury: how the wicked problems of health care defy solutions, yet require innovative strategies in the modern era', *Canadian Journal Of Surgery / Journal canadien de chirurgie* 62, no. 4 (August 2019): E6–E8.

6 Lepore, 'Burnout'.

7 Van Gogh Museum, 'Vincent van Gogh: The Letters', Letter 290, Vincent van Gogh to Theo van Gogh, 3 December 1882, 21:5, page 14, www.vangoghletters.org/vg/letters/let290/letter.html#translation.

8 My depiction of a thin, functional frame layer bear similarities with what Erwin Goffman in *Frame Analysis* calls 'primary framework'.

9 Corinne Ramey and Bob Tita, 'The summer of plastic-straw bans: how we got there', *Wall Street Journal*, 7 August 2018, sec. US, www.wsj.com/articles/the-summer-of-plastic-straw-bans-how-we-got-there-1533634200.

10 My depiction of a thick frame bears similarities with what Erwin Goffman in *Frame Analysis* calls 'secondary framework'.

11 Daniel Kahneman, Olivier Sibony, and Cass R. Sunstein, *Noise: A Flaw in Human Judgment* (New York: Little, Brown Spark, 2021).

12 Adam Burgess, '"Nudging" healthy lifestyles: the UK experiments with the behavioural alternative to regulation and the market', *European Journal of Risk Regulation* 3, no. 1 (2012): 3–16; Antonj. M. Dijker, Robm. A. Nelissen, and Mandym. N. Stijnen, 'Framing posthumous organ donation in terms of reciprocity: what are the emotional consequences?', *Basic and Applied Social Psychology* 35, no. 3 (2013): 256–264.

13 George Lakoff, *The ALL NEW Don't Think of an Elephant! Know Your Values and Frame the Debate*, 2nd revised edn (White River Junction, VT: Chelsea Green Publishing, 2014).

14 In Chapter 11 of this book I discuss metaframes, although it means something different here from how it's used in Lakoff's book.

15 Mark Alfano, Marc Cheong, and Oliver Scott Curry, 'Moral universals: a machine-reading analysis of 256 societies', *Heliyon* 10, no. 6 (March 2024): 1–13, https://doi.org/10.1016/j.heliyon.2024.e25940.

16 John Bargh, *Before You Know It: The Unconscious Reasons We Do What We Do* (New York: Penguin, 2017); Ran R. Hassin, ed., *The New Unconscious*, Oxford Series in Social Cognition and Social Neuroscience (Oxford: Oxford University Press, 2007).

Notes

17 Francine Russo, 'Like humans, apes are susceptible to spin', *Scientific American*, 1 July 2015, https://doi.org/10.1038/scientificamericanmind 0715-12.

18 Susanne Shultz, Christopher Opie, and Quentin D. Atkinson, 'Stepwise evolution of stable sociality in primates', *Nature* 479, no. 7372 (November 2011): 219–222, https://doi.org/10.1038/nature10601.

19 Oliver Scott Curry, Daniel A. Mullins, and Harvey Whitehouse, 'Is it good to cooperate? Testing the theory of morality-as-cooperation in 60 societies', *Current Anthropology* 60, no. 1 (February 2019): 47–69, https://doi.org/10.1086/701478.

20 Oliver Scott Curry *et al.*, 'Moral molecules: morality as a combinatorial system', *Review of Philosophy and Psychology* 13 (August 2021): 1041, https://doi.org/10.1007/s13164-021-00540-x.

21 Scott Curry *et al.*, 'Moral molecules', 1041.

22 Similar notions of a limited number of forms of cooperation can also be found in scholarship that, in contrast to the bottom-up identification of evolutionary types of morality, has been developed by analysing society at the macro level. For example, Boltanski and Thévenot have identified seven orders of worth: market, industrial, civic, domestic, inspired, fame, and – more recently – green. These orders of worth are used by individuals as a basis for framing their actions, justifying them, and making judgements in social contexts. It is worth noting that, for instance, the 'domestic' order of worth might correspond to Curry's 'family values', the 'civic' order to 'group loyalty' and 'fairness', and the 'market' order to 'reciprocity' and 'property rights'. See Luc Boltanski and Laurent Thévenot, *On Justification: Economies of Worth* (Princeton, NJ: Princeton University Press, 2006).

Part I: Making bad seem good – and other frame texturing

1 Abba Kungshamn, 'Kalles i Tokyo' (video), YouTube, 2 April 2012, www.youtube.com/watch?v=SOPPYENlpqY; Kalles Kaviar, 'Kalles Kaviar i Los Angeles' (video), YouTube, 14 April 2014, www.youtube.com/watch?v=HMyfZydK-4s.

2 Harry F. Harlow and Robert R. Zimmermann, 'Affectional responses in the infant monkey', *Science* 130, no. 3373 (1959): 421–432.

3 Neil J. Smelser, *Theory of Collective Behavior* (New Orleans, LA: Quid Pro Books, 2011).

4 John D. McCarthy and Mayer N. Zald, 'Resource mobilization and social movements: a partial theory', *American Journal of Sociology* 82, no. 6 (May 1977): 1212–1241, https://doi.org/10.1086/226464.

2 Why is our frame smooth and theirs so often rough?

1 cf. 'fast thinking' as analysed by Daniel Kahneman, *Thinking, Fast and Slow*, reprint edn (New York: Farrar, Straus and Giroux, 2011).

2 Robert M. Sapolsky, *Behave: The Biology of Humans at Our Best and Worst*, illustrated edn (New York: Penguin, 2017).

Notes

3 Daniel Nettle and Robin Dunbar, 'Social markers and the evolution of recip-rocal exchange', *Current Anthropology* 38, no. 1 (February 1997), https://doi.org/10.1086/204588; Robin Dunbar, *Friends: Understanding the Power of Our Most Important Relationships* (London: Hachette UK, 2021).

4 Robert Kurzban, John Tooby, and Leda Cosmides, 'Can race be erased? Coalitional computation and social categorization', *Proceedings of the National Academy of Sciences of the United States of America* 98, no. 26 (December 2001): 15387–15392, https://doi.org/10.1073/pnas.251541498; William Graham Sumner, *Folkways* (Charleston, SC: CreateSpace Independent Publishing Platform, [1906] 2008), ebook, www.gutenberg.org/cache/epub/24253/pg24253-images.html; Henri Tajfel, *Human Groups and Social Categories: Studies in Social Psychology* (Cambridge: Cambridge University Press, 1981).

5 Jillian J. Jordan *et al.*, 'Why do we hate hypocrites? Evidence for a theory of false signaling', *Psychological Science* 28, no. 3 (March 2017): 356–368, https://doi.org/10.1177/0956797616685771.

6 Thomas Huxley, *Evolution and Ethics, and Other Essays* (Urbana, IL: Project Gutenberg, [1893] 2001), ebook, www.gutenberg.org/cache/epub/2940/pg2940-images.html, pp. 81–83.

7 Sapolsky, *Behave*.

8 Steven A. LeBlanc, with Katherine E. Register, *Constant Battles: The Myth of the Peaceful, Noble Savage*, 1st edn (New York: St. Martin's Press, 2003); Jan-Willem van Prooijen, *The Psychology of Conspiracy Theories*, 1st edn (New York: Routledge, 2018).

9 Frank W. Marlowe, 'Hunter-gatherers and human evolution', *Evolutionary Anthropology: Issues, News, and Reviews* 14, no. 2 (2005): 54–67, https://doi.org/10.1002/evan.20046.

10 Justin H. Park, 'Evolutionary perspectives on intergroup prejudice: impli-cations for promoting tolerance', in *Applied Evolutionary Psychology*, ed. S. Craig Roberts (New York: Oxford University Press, 2011), pp. 186–200, https://doi.org/10.1093/acprof:oso/9780199586073.003.0012.

11 Jan-Willem van Prooijen, 'Suspicion makes us human', *Aeon*, 4 November 2019, https://aeon.co/essays/how-conspiracy-theories-evolved-from-our-drive-for-survival.

12 See Benford and Snow, 'Framing processes and social movements'.

13 Emily N. Lasko *et al.*, 'Neural mechanisms of intergroup exclusion and retal-iatory aggression', *Social Neuroscience* 17, no. 4 (August 2022): 339–351, https://doi.org/10.1080/17470919.2022.2086617.

14 Shiri Lev-Ari and Boaz Keysar, 'Why don't we believe non-native speak-ers? The influence of accent on credibility', *Journal of Experimental Social Psychology* 46, no. 6 (January 2010): 1093–1096, https://doi.org/10.1016/j.jesp.2010.05.025.

15 Consumer Freedom, 'Synthetic Meat Spelling Commercial Bee: 60 Sec' (video), YouTube, 29 January 2020, www.youtube.com/watch?v=zTtI4Vexw4k.

16 Bertram F. Malle, Joshua M. Knobe, and Sarah E. Nelson, 'Actor–observer asymmetries in explanations of behavior: new answers to an old question',

Notes

Journal of Personality and Social Psychology 93, no. 4 (2007): 491–514, https://doi.org/10.1037/0022-3514.93.4.491.

17 *Philosophy Bites*, 'Overdoing democracy' (podcast), 23 July 2018, https://philosophybites.libsyn.com/robert-b-talisse-on-overdoing-democracy.

18 Claudia Denke *et al.*, 'Lying and the subsequent desire for toothpaste: activity in the somatosensory cortex predicts embodiment of the moral-purity metaphor', *Cerebral Cortex* 26, no. 2 (February 2016): 477–484, https://doi.org/10.1093/cercor/bhu170; Sapolsky, *Behave*.

19 Harriet Over, 'Recognising our common humanity might not be enough to prevent hatred', *Psyche*, 2 September 2020, https://psyche.co/ideas/recognising-our-common-humanity-might-not-be-enough-to-prevent-hatred.

20 Bargh, *Before You Know It*.

21 D. J. Witherspoon *et al.*, 'Genetic similarities within and between human populations', *Genetics* 176, no. 1 (May 2007): 351–359, https://doi.org/10.1534/genetics.106.067355.

22 Audrey Smedley and Brian D. Smedley, 'Race as biology is fiction, racism as a social problem is real: anthropological and historical perspectives on the social construction of race', *American Psychologist* 60, no. 1 (January 2005): 16–26, https://doi.org/10.1037/0003-066X.60.1.16.

23 Such assumptions of essential differences may have played a role in the distinct framing textures that Americans applied to their two worst enemy groups after the Second World War: the Nazis and the Japanese. Historians have demonstrated that people of the same race as the majority in the Axis countries – Germany, Italy, and Japan – were treated very differently in the United States during and after the war. The US government implemented policies that aimed to curtail the rights and freedoms of Japanese Americans, including their forced relocation to internment camps. In contrast, German Americans did not face such treatment and were generally not regarded with suspicion or hostility. Even after the war, Japanese Americans continued to face discrimination, while German Americans were more readily reintegrated into mainstream society. The fact that the Nazis were racially and culturally closer to white Americans than the Japanese made it easier for Americans to empathize with individuals from Nazi Germany compared to those from Japan (see Institute for Research of Expelled Germans, 'Comparing the American internment of Japanese-, German-, and Italian-Americans during World War II', 2004 https://expelledgermans.org/germaninternment.htm). However, it is important to note that race alone does not fully explain the differential treatment of these groups. Race was always a significant factor in the US, often triggering stereotypes related to economic status, citizenship, cultural preferences, and character traits.

24 Florence E. Enock and Harriet Over, 'Animalistic slurs increase harm by changing perceptions of social desirability', *Royal Society Open Science* 10, no. 7 (July 2023): 230203, https://doi.org/10.1098/rsos.230203; Florence E. Enock, Steven P. Tipper, and Harriet Over, 'Intergroup preference, not dehumanization, explains social biases in emotion attribution', *Cognition* 216 (November 2021): 104865, https://doi.org/10.1016/j.cognition.2021.104865.

211

25 Over, 'Recognising our common humanity might not be enough to prevent hatred'.

26 Guardian News, 'Greta Thunberg to world leaders: "How dare you? You have stolen my dreams and my childhood"' (video), YouTube, 23 September 2019, www.youtube.com/watch?v=TMrtLsQbaok.

27 Corrina A. Tucker, 'Food practices of environmentally conscientious New Zealanders', *Environmental Sociology* 5, no. 1 (January 2019): 82–92, https://doi.org/10.1080/23251042.2018.1495038.

28 Ryan L. Boyd, Kate G. Blackburn, and James W. Pennebaker, 'The narrative arc: revealing core narrative structures through text analysis', *Science Advances* 6, no. 32 (August 2020): eaba2196, https://doi.org/10.1126/sciadv.aba2196; Gustav Freytag, *Technique of the Drama: An Exposition of Dramatic Composition and Art.*, trans. Elias J. MacEwan, 7th edn (Chicago, IL: Scott, Foresman, 1900).

3 Sanctifying sinners and sinnifying saints

1 Richard Godwin, 'The vegan halo: how plant-based products are transforming British brands', *Guardian*, 3 September 2019, sec. Life and style, www.theguardian.com/lifeandstyle/2019/sep/03/the-vegan-halo-how-plant-based-products-are-transforming-british-brands.

2 Elle Hunt, 'From tofu lamb chops to vegan steak bakes: the 1,000-year history of fake meat', *Guardian*, 12 January 2020, sec. Life and style, www.theguardian.com/lifeandstyle/2020/jan/12/mock-lamb-chops-vegan-steak-bakes-history-fake-meat.

3 Chas Newkey-Burden, 'More fast-food chains are offering plant-based food – but should vegans be celebrating?', *Guardian*, 7 January 2020, sec. Life and style, www.theguardian.com/lifeandstyle/shortcuts/2020/jan/07/more-fast-food-chains-are-offering-plant-based-food-but-should-vegans-be-celebrating.

4 George Reynolds, 'Why do people hate vegans?' (podcast), *Curio*, November 2019, https://curio.io/stories/65WmkxLZrrl659rgIwmbnV.

5 For a detailed discussion of different effects of subtle, less obviously costly prosocial behaviour with high-cost displays to a higher number of people concerning food sharing in subsistence economies, see Rebecca Bliege Bird, Elspeth Ready, and Eleanor A. Power, 'The Social Significance of Subtle Signals', *Nature Human Behaviour* 2, no. 7 (February 2018): 452–457, https://doi.org/10.1038/s41562-018-0298-3.

6 Tadeg Quillien, 'Evolution of conditional and unconditional commitment', *Journal of Theoretical Biology* 492 (May 2020): 110204, https://doi.org/10.1016/j.jtbi.2020.110204.

7 Tadeg Quillien, 'Is virtue signalling a vice?', *Aeon*, 4 April 2022, https://aeon.co/essays/why-virtue-signalling-is-not-just-a-vice-but-an-evolved-tool.

8 Kyle A. Thomas *et al.*, 'The psychology of coordination and common knowledge', *Journal of Personality and Social Psychology* 107, no. 4 (2014): 657–676, https://doi.org/10.1037/a0037037.

Notes

9 Kenneth B. Clark and Mamie P. Clark, 'Emotional factors in racial identification and preference in negro children', *Journal of Negro Education* 19,
no. 3 (1950): 341–350, https://doi.org/10.2307/2966491.

10 E. J. R. David, ed., *Internalized Oppression: The Psychology of Marginalized
Groups* (New York: Springer, 2013).

11 Margaret Mead, *Coming of Age in Samoa: A Psychological Study of Primitive
Youth for Western Civilisation* (New York: William Morrow Paperbacks,
1928); Derek Freeman, 'Margaret Mead's "Coming of Age in Samoa" and
Boasian culturalism', *Politics and the Life Sciences* 19, no. 1 (March 2000):
101–103.

12 Adam Smith, *The Theory of Moral Sentiments*, 2nd edn (London: A. Millar,
1761), https://books.google.se/books?id=bZhZAAAAcAAJ.

13 Jean-Jacques Rousseau, *Discourse on the Origin of Inequality* (Mineola, NY:
Dover Publications, [1755] 2004), 27.

14 Eric Alden Smith and Brian F. Codding, 'Ecological variation and institutionalized inequality in hunter-gatherer societies', *Proceedings of the National
Academy of Sciences* 118, no. 13 (March 2021): e2016134118, https://doi.
org/10.1073/pnas.2016134118.

15 Scott Curry *et al.*, 'Moral molecules'.

16 Dominic D. P. Johnson and Monica Duffy Toft, 'Grounds for war: the evolution of territorial conflict', *International Security* 38, no. 3 (January 2014):
7–38, https://doi.org/10.1162/ISEC_a_00149; Herbert Gintis, 'The evolution
of private property', *Journal of Economic Behavior and Organization* 64, no.
1 (September 2007): 1–16, https://doi.org/10.1016/j.jebo.2006.02.002.

17 Steven Pinker, *The Better Angels of Our Nature: Why Violence Has
Declined* (New York: Viking Adult, 2011); N. Hess *et al.*, 'Interpersonal
aggression among Aka hunter-gatherers of the Central African Republic',
Human Nature 21, no. 3 (2010): 330–354; LeBlanc, with Register, *Constant
Battles*; Dominic D. P. Johnson and James H. Fowler, 'The evolution of
overconfidence', *Nature* 477, no. 7364 (September 2011): 317–320, https://
doi.org/10.1038/nature10384.

18 LeBlanc, with Register, *Constant Battles*.

19 Salil D. Benegal and Lyle A. Scruggs, 'Correcting misinformation about
climate change: the impact of partisanship in an experimental setting',
Climatic Change 148, no. 1 (May 2018): 61–80, https://doi.org/10.1007/
s10584-018-2192-4.

4 The allure of rough

1 Kahneman, *Thinking, Fast and Slow*.

2 Steven D. Hales, *The Myth of Luck: Philosophy, Fate, and Fortune* (New
York: Bloomsbury Academic, 2020).

3 J. R. Keene *et al.*, 'The biological roots of political extremism: negativity
bias, political ideology, and preferences for political news', *Politics and the
Life Sciences* 36, no. 2 (2017): 37–48, https://doi.org/10.1017/pls.2017.16.

4 Marcial Losada and Emily Heaphy, 'The role of positivity and connectivity in the performance of business teams: a nonlinear dynamics model',

American Behavioral Scientist 47, no. 6 (February 2004): 740–765, https://doi.org/10.1177/0002764203260208.

5 Soroush Vosoughi, Deb Roy, and Sinan Aral, 'The spread of true and false news online', *Science* 359, no. 6380 (March 2018): 1146–1151, https://doi.org/10.1126/science.aap9559.

6 Oliver Sacks, *Musicophilia: Tales of Music and the Brain*, 1st edn (New York: Knopf, 2007), 43.

7 Julian Watkins, *The 100 Greatest Advertisements 1852–1958: Who Wrote Them and What They Did*, 2nd revised edn (New York: Dover Publications, 2012).

8 Colin Schultz, 'Shackleton probably never took out an ad seeking men for a hazardous journey', *Smithsonian Magazine*, 10 September 2013, www.smithsonianmag.com/smart-news/shackleton-probably-never-took-out-an-ad-seeking-men-for-a-hazardous-journey-5552379.

9 Janet Shibley Hyde, 'Gender similarities and differences', *Annual Review of Psychology* 65, no. 1 (2014): 373–398, https://doi.org/10.1146/annurev-psych-010213-115057.

10 Bobbi J. Carothers and Harry T. Reis, 'Men and women are from Earth: examining the latent structure of gender', *Journal of Personality and Social Psychology* 104, no. 2 (2013): 385–407, https://doi.org/10.1037/a0030437.

11 Kim Bhasin, 'The rise of the \$2.5 billion ugly-shoe empire', *Bloomberg UK*, 3 February 2022, www.bloomberg.com/news/features/2022-02-03/how-uggs-hoka-and-tevas-helped-build-deckers-2-5-billion-ugly-shoe-empire.

12 Ludovica Cesareo, Claudia Townsend, and Eugene Pavlov, 'Hideous but worth it: distinctive ugliness as a signal of luxury', *Journal of the Academy of Marketing Science* 51, no. 3 (2023): 636–657.

13 Frederick D. Lipman, *Whistleblowers: Incentives, Disincentives, and Protection Strategies*, 1st edn (Hoboken, NJ: Wiley, 2011).

14 James Panero, 'Radical un-chic', *New Criterion*, December 2007, https://newcriterion.com/article/radical-un-chic.

15 Rajiv Khurana, 'Reducing P.A.A.P. – people apathy towards air pollution', *Outlook Planet*, 9 December 2022, https://planet.outlookindia.com/opinions/reducing-p-a-a-p-people-apathy-towards-air-pollution-news-413960.

16 Cass Sunstein, interviewed in Amanda Marcotte, 'Cass Sunstein on "How Change Happens": hope that a better society is possible', *Salon*, 27 April 2019, www.salon.com/2019/04/27/cass-sunstein-on-how-change-happens-hope-that-a-better-society-is-possible.

Part II: Making hot what's not – and other frame tempering

1 Vivian B. Mann, Jerrilynn Denise Dodds, and Thomas F. Glick, eds, *Convivencia: Jews, Muslims, and Christians in Medieval Spain*, 1st edn (New York: George Braziller, 1992).

2 Pinker, *The Better Angels of Our Nature*; Hans Rosling, Anna Rosling Rönnlund, and Ola Rosling, *Factfulness: Ten Reasons We're Wrong About the World – and Why Things Are Better Than You Think* (New York: Flatiron Books, 2018).

3 Jamie Dow, 'How can emotion-arousal provide proof?', in *Passions and Persuasion in Aristotle's Rhetoric*, pp. 94–106, https://doi.org/10.1093/acprof :oso/9780198716266.003.0007.

4 Shanto Iyengar *et al.*, 'The origins and consequences of affective polarization in the United States', *Annual Review of Political Science* 22, no. 1 (May 2019): 129–146, https://doi.org/10.1146/annurev-polisci-051117-073034; Andres Reiljan and Alexander Ryan, 'Ideological tripolarization, partisan tribalism and institutional trust: the foundations of affective polarization in the Swedish multiparty system', *Scandinavian Political Studies* 44, no. 2 (2021): 195–219, https://doi.org/10.1111/1467-9477.12194.

5 Emma A. Renström, Hanna Bäck, and Royce Carroll, 'Protecting the ingroup? Authoritarianism, immigration attitudes, and affective polarization', *Frontiers in Political Science* 4 (July 2022): 919236, https://doi.org/10.3389/fpos. 2022.919236.

6 Jeremy A. Frimer, Linda J. Skitka, and Matt Motyl, 'Liberals and conservatives are similarly motivated to avoid exposure to one another's opinions', *Journal of Experimental Social Psychology* 72 (September 2017): 1–12, https://doi. org/10.1016/j.jesp.2017.04.003.

5 Temperament tricks

1 Bradley Campbell and Jason Manning, *The Rise of Victimhood Culture: Microaggressions, Safe Spaces, and the New Culture Wars*, 1st edn (New York: Palgrave Macmillan, 2018).

2 Samuel Bowles, Eric Alden Smith, and Monique Borgerhoff Mulder, 'The emergence and persistence of inequality in premodern societies', *Current Anthropology* 51, no. 1 (February 2010): 7–17.

3 *The Economist*, 'The link between polygamy and war', 19 December 2017, www.economist.com/news/christmas-specials/21732695-plural-marriage-bred-inequality-begets-violence-link-between-polygamy-and-war.

4 Dominic Johnson, *God Is Watching You: How the Fear of God Makes Us Human* (Oxford: Oxford University Press, 2016).

5 Dov Cohen *et al.*, 'Insult, aggression, and the southern culture of honor: an "experimental ethnography"', *Journal of Personality and Social Psychology* 70, no. 5 (May 1996): 945–960, https://doi.org/10.1037/0022-3514.70.5.945.

6 Greg Lukianoff and Jonathan Haidt, *The Coddling of the American Mind: How Good Intentions and Bad Ideas Are Setting Up a Generation for Failure* (New York: Penguin, 2018).

7 William Samuelson and Richard Zeckhauser, 'Status quo bias in decision making', *Journal of Risk and Uncertainty* 1, no. 1 (March 1988): 7–59, https:// doi.org/10.1007/BF00055564.

8 Karina Fonseca Azevedo and Suzana Herculano Houzel, 'Metabolic constraint imposes tradeoff between body size and number of brain neurons in human evolution', *Proceedings of the National Academy of Sciences of the United States of America* 109, no. 45 (2012): 18571–18576; Alex R. DeCasien, Scott A. Williams, and James P. Higham, 'Primate brain size is

predicted by diet but not sociality', *Nature Ecology and Evolution* 1, no. 5 (March 2017): 112, https://doi.org/10.1038/s41559-017-0112.

9 Robin I. M. Dunbar and Susanne Shultz, 'Four errors and a fallacy: pitfalls for the unwary in comparative brain analyses', *Biological Reviews* 98, no. 4 (2023): 1278–1309, https://doi.org/10.1111/brv.12953.

10 Clive Gable, John Gowlett, and Robin Dunbar, *Thinking Big: How the Evolution of Social Life Shaped the Human Mind*, 1st edn (New York: Thames and Hudson, 2014).

11 Roy F. Baumeister, *The Cultural Animal* (Oxford: Oxford University Press, 2005); Mark R. Leary *et al.*, 'Calibrating the sociometer: the relationship between interpersonal appraisals and the state self-esteem', *Journal of Personality and Social Psychology* 74, no. 5 (May 1998): 1290–1299, https://doi.org/10.1037/0022-3514.74.5.1290.

12 Klintman, *Human Sciences and Human Interests*.

13 Kazuo Ishiguro, *The Remains of the Day* (London: Faber & Faber, 1989), 33.

14 *The Economist*, 'The news events that most engrossed audiences in 2018', 18 December 2018, www.economist.com/graphic-detail/2018/12/18/the-news-events-that-most-engrossed-audiences-in-2018.

15 Ruth Oldenziel *et al.*, *Cycling Cities: The European Experience. Hundred Years Policy and Practice* (Eindhoven: Foundation for the History of Technology, 2016).

16 Malcolm J. Wardlaw, 'History, risk, infrastructure: perspectives on bicycling in the Netherlands and the UK', *Journal of Transport and Health* 1, no. 4 (December 2014): 243–250, https://doi.org/10.1016/j.jth.2014.09.015.

17 Stephen M. Walt, 'Morality is the enemy of peace', *Foreign Policy*, 13 June 2024, https://foreignpolicy.com/2024/06/13/gaza-ukraine-ceasefire-war-peace-morality/.

18 Fonseca Azevedo and Herculano Houzel, 'Metabolic constraint'; DeCasien, Williams, and Higham, 'Primate brain size is predicted by diet but not sociality'.

19 Thomas C. Schelling, 'The life you save may be your own', in *Problems of Public Expenditure Analysis*, ed. Samuel B. Chase (Washington, DC: Brookings Institution, 1968), reprinted in T. C. Schelling, *Choice and Consequence* (Cambridge, MA: Harvard University Press, 1984), pp. 113–146.

20 Eleonora Pilastro, 'Record-breaking donations raise almost £62m for Ukraine in a week', *Guinness World Records*, 12 May 2022, www.guinnessworldrecords.com/news/2022/5/record-breaking-donations-raise-almost-62m-for-ukraine-in-a-week-703573.

21 Graham F. Medley and Anna Vassall, 'When an emerging disease becomes endemic', *Science* 357, no. 6347 (July 2017): 156–158, https://doi.org/10.1126/science.aam8333.

22 Maria Luisa Lima and José Manuel Sobral, 'Threat and oblivion: interpreting the silence over the Spanish flu (1918–19)', in *Societies Under Threat: A Pluri-Disciplinary Approach*, ed. Denise Jodelet, Jorge Vala, and Ewa Drozda-Senkowska (Cham: Springer International Publishing, 2020), pp. 187–199, https://doi.org/10.1007/978-3-030-39315-1_15.

Notes

23 Robert M. Sapolsky, *Why Zebras Don't Get Ulcers*, 3rd edn (New York: Holt Paperbacks, 2004).

24 Nils Ferlin, 'Not even' (Sw. 'Inte ens en gr. liten fågel'), first published in 1938 in his book *Googles: Dikter*. Stockholm: Albert Bonniers förlag. Translated into English by J. M. Nosworthy, retrieved from https://lyricstranslate.com/en/inte-ens-en-gr%C3%A5-liten-f%C3%A5gel-not-even.html-0. The poem is included with written permission from the copyright holder of Nils Ferlin, 18 April 2024.

25 Friedrich Nietzsche, *Ecce Homo: How One Becomes What One Is*, reissue edn (Oxford: Oxford University Press, [1908] 2009).

26 Albert Camus, *The Myth of Sisyphus and Other Essays* (New York: Vintage Books, [1942] 2018).

27 Jon Kabat-Zinn, *Full Catastrophe Living: Using the Wisdom of Your Body and Mind to Face Stress, Pain, and Illness*, revised edn (New York: Bantam, 2013).

28 Jeff Wilson, *Mindful America: The Mutual Transformation of Buddhist Meditation and American Culture*, 1st edn (New York: Oxford University Press, 2014).

29 Julieta Galante *et al.*, 'A mindfulness-based intervention to increase resilience to stress in university students (the Mindful Student Study): a pragmatic randomised controlled trial', *Lancet Public Health* 3, no. 2 (February 2018): e72–e81, https://doi.org/10/gfww8d; Yi-Yuan Tang, Britta K. Hölzel, and Michael I. Posner, 'The neuroscience of mindfulness meditation', *Nature Reviews Neuroscience* 16, no. 4 (April 2015): 213–225, https://doi.org/10.1038/nrn3916.

30 See, e.g., Aldous Huxley, *The Perennial Philosophy: An Interpretation of the Great Mystics, East and West* (New York: Harper Collins, 1945).

31 Elie Wiesel, *The Gates of the Forest* (New York: Knopf Doubleday Publishing Group, 1966).

32 Karine Sergerie, Caroline Chochol, and Jorge L. Armony, 'The role of the amygdala in emotional processing: a quantitative meta-analysis of functional neuroimaging studies', *Neuroscience and Biobehavioral Reviews* 32, no. 4 (January 2008): 811–830, https://doi.org/10.1016/j.neubiorev.2007.12.002.

33 John Stuart Mill, *Utilitarianism*, ed. George Sher, 2nd edn (Indianapolis, IN: Hackett, 2002); Peter Singer, *Life You Can Save* (London: Picador, 2009).

34 Rebecca Solnit, 'We can't afford to be climate doomers', *Guardian*, 26 July 2023, sec. Opinion, www.theguardian.com/commentisfree/2023/jul/26/we-cant-afford-to-be-climate-doomers.

35 Magnus Boström, *The Social Life of Unsustainable Mass Consumption* (Lanham, MD: Lexington Books, 2023).

36 Cara Buckley, 'Man is rescued by stranger on subway tracks', *New York Times*, 3 January 2007, sec. New York, www.nytimes.com/2007/01/03/nyregion/03life.html.

37 Boyer, *Minds Make Societies*.

38 Ernst Fehr and Simon Gächter, 'Altruistic punishment in humans', *Nature* 415, no. 6868 (2002): 137–140.

Notes

6 How timing is of the essence

1 William A. Gamson and Andre Modigliani, 'Media discourse and public opinion on nuclear power: a constructionist approach', *American Journal of Sociology* 95, no. 1 (1989): 1–37.

2 Jörgen Larsson, Simon Matti, and Jonas Nässén, 'Public support for aviation policy measures in Sweden', *Climate Policy* 20, no. 10 (January 2020): 1305–1321, https://doi.org/10.1080/14693062.2020.1759499.

3 N. Stern, *Why Are We Waiting? The Logic, Urgency, and Promise of Tackling Climate Change* (Cambridge, MA: MIT Press, 2015), https://doi.org/10.7551/mitpress/10408.001.0001.

4 OECD, *Understanding and Applying the Precautionary Principle in the Energy Transition* (Paris: OECD, 2023), https://doi.org/10.1787/5b14362c-en.

5 Maxime Gignon et al., 'the precautionary principle: is it safe', *European Journal of Health Law* 20, no. 3 (January 2013): 261–270, https://doi.org/10.1163/15718093-12341272.

6 Matthias Gross and Linsey McGoey, eds, *Routledge International Handbook of Ignorance Studies*, 2nd edn (Abingdon and New York: Routledge, 2022).

7 Huxley, 'Evolution and ethics'.

8 Stephen Buranyi, 'The plastic backlash: what's behind our sudden rage – and will it make a difference?', *Guardian*, 13 November 2018, sec. Environment, www.theguardian.com/environment/2018/nov/13/the-plastic-backlash-whats-behind-our-sudden-rage-and-will-it-make-a-difference.

9 Buranyi, 'the plastic backlash'.

10 Scott Curry et al., 'Moral molecules'; cf. Jonathan Haidt, *The Righteous Mind: Why Good People Are Divided by Politics and Religion* (New York: Knopf Doubleday Publishing Group, 2012).

11 WHO, 'Ambient (outdoor) air pollution', fact sheet, 19 December 2022, Geneva: World Health Organization, www.who.int/news-room/fact-sheets/detail/ambient-(outdoor)-air-quality-and-health.

12 WHO, 'Household air pollution', fact sheet, 22 November 2022, Geneva: World Health Organization, www.who.int/news-room/fact-sheets/detail/household-air-pollution-and-health.

13 Anil Markandya and Paul Wilkinson, 'Electricity generation and health', *Lancet* 370, no. 9591 (September 2007): 979–990, https://doi.org/10.1016/S0140-6736(07)61253-7.

14 *The Economist*, 'Who is keeping coal alive?', 4 June 2023, www.economist.com/finance-and-economics/2023/06/04/who-is-keeping-coal-alive.

15 Yannick Barthe, Mark Elam, and Göran Sundqvist, 'Technological fix or divisible object of collective concern? Histories of conflict over the geological disposal of nuclear waste in Sweden and France', *Science as Culture* 29, no. 2 (January 2020): 196–218, https://doi.org/10.1080/09505431.2019.1645108.

16 K. C. Cole, 'Why you didn't see it coming', *Nautilus*, 8 October 2015, https://nautil.us/why-you-didnt-see-it-coming-235651/.

17 Lea Fünfschilling and Bernhard Truffer, 'The structuration of socio-technical regimes – conceptual foundations from institutional theory',

Research Policy 43, no. 4 (May 2014): 772–791, http://doi.org/10.1016/j. respol.2013.10.010.

18 cf. Magnus Boström and Rolf Lidskog, *Environmental Sociology and Social Transformation*, 1st edn (Abingdon and New York: Routledge, 2024).

19 P. K. Harikrishnan, Prem Prakash Dewani, and Abhishek Behl, 'Scarcity promotions and consumer aggressions: a theoretical framework', *Journal of Global Marketing* 35, no. 4 (August 2022): 306–323, https://doi.org/10.1080 /08911762.2021.2009609.

20 Jihye Park and Wenhan Li, '"I got it FIRST": antecedents of competitive consumption of a new product', *Journal of Retailing and Consumer Services* 73 (July 2023), https://doi.org/10.1016/j.jretconser.2023.103367.

21 Kenneth G. Brown, *Influence: Mastering Life's Most Powerful Skill*, The Great Courses (Chantilly, VA: The Teaching Company, 2013), audiobook, www.audible.com/pd/Influence-Audiobook/B00FPTSNYQ?action_code=AS SGB1490801190000H&share_location=pdp.

22 Cesareo, Townsend, and Pavlov, 'Hideous but worth it'; Andrea Baldin and Trine Bille, 'The avant-garde consumers: a new perspective on quality evaluations of performing arts', *Poetics* 97 (April 2023): 101771, https://doi. org/10.1016/j.poetic.2023.101771.

23 *The Economist*, 'Retirement has become much longer across the rich world', 27 March 2023, www.economist.com/graphic-detail/2023/03/27/ retirement-has-become-much-longer-across-the-rich-world.

24 Eda Sevinin, Didem Danış, and Deniz Sert, 'Double displacement of refugees in the context of the 2023 Turkey-Syria earthquake', *International Migration* 61, no. 4 (2023): 341–344, https://doi.org/10.1111/imig.13171.

25 James C. Davies, 'Toward a theory of revolution', *American Sociological Review* 27, no. 1 (1962): 5–19, https://doi.org/10.2307/2089714.

26 Russo, 'Like humans, apes are susceptible to spin'.

27 SpecialisternaHumor, 'Simon Gärdenfors | UPPVIGLING | Standup-special (HELA SHOWEN) 4K' (video), YouTube, 18 September 2022, www.youtube. com/watch?v=qNyw_040Au4.

28 Jamie R. Abrams, 'The #MeToo movement: an invitation for feminist critique of rape crisis framing', *University of Richmond Law Review* 52, no. 4 (2022): 749–794.

29 C. Wright Mills, *The Sociological Imagination*, 40th anniversary edn (Oxford: Oxford University Press, 2000).

30 Abrams, 'The #MeToo movement'.

31 Katharine Lee *et al.*, 'Perspectives of UK adolescents on the youth climate strikes', *Nature Climate Change* 12, no. 6 (June 2022): 529, https://doi. org/10.1038/s41558-022-01361-1.

32 Leon Festinger, *A Theory of Cognitive Dissonance*, 1st edn (Stanford, CA: Stanford University Press, 1957).

33 Karin Bradley and Ola Persson, 'Community repair in the circular economy – fixing more than stuff', *Local Environment* 27, no. 10–11 (November 2022): 1321–1337, https://doi.org/10.1080/13549839.2022.2041580.

34 Sahra Svensson-Hoglund *et al.*, 'Barriers, enablers and market governance: a review of the policy landscape for repair of consumer electronics in the

EU and the U.S.', *Journal of Cleaner Production* 288 (March 2021): 125488, https://doi.org/10.1016/j.jclepro.2020.125488.

7 Metaphors as frame thermostats

1 Genesis 2:19–20 (New International Version).
2 Jean-Paul Sartre, *The Words: The Autobiography of Jean-Paul Sartre*, trans. Bernard Frechtman, 1st edn (New York: George Braziller, 1964), 182.
3 George Lakoff and Mark Johnson, *Metaphors We Live By* (Chicago, IL: University of Chicago Press, 2003).
4 Bargh, *Before You Know It*.
5 Czesław Miłosz, 'A song on the end of the world', *The Collected Poems 1931–1987* (New York: Ecco, 1990).
6 Sahil Loomba *et al.*, 'Measuring the impact of COVID-19 vaccine misinformation on vaccination intent in the UK and USA', *Nature Human Behaviour* 5, no. 3 (March 2021): 337–348, https://doi.org/10.1038/s41562-021-01056-1.
7 Mikael Klintman, 'Apollonian and Dionysian trust in vaccination', in *Vaccine Hesitancy in the Nordic Countries: Trust and Distrust During the COVID-19 Pandemic*, ed. Lars Borin *et al.* (London: Routledge, 2024), pp. 21–34.
8 Mary Douglas, *Purity and Danger: An Analysis of the Concepts of Pollution and Taboo* (London: Routledge & Kegan Paul, 1978).
9 S. Schnall *et al.*, 'Disgust as embodied moral judgment', *Personality and Social Psychology Bulletin* 34, no. 8 (May 2008): 1096–1109, https://doi.org/10.1177/0146167208317771; Daniel P. Skarlicki *et al.*, 'Does injustice affect your sense of taste and smell? The mediating role of moral disgust', *Journal of Experimental Social Psychology* 49, no. 5 (2013): 852–859.
10 *Reuters*, 'Delhi's air branded "hazardous", spurs calls to close schools', 3 November 2022, sec. India, www.reuters.com/world/india/delhis-air-crime-against-humanity-spurs-calls-close-schools-2022-11-03.
11 For more about diagnostic, prognostic, and motivational framing, see Benford and Snow, 'Framing processes and social movements'.
12 Stav Atir, 'Girlboss? Highlighting versus downplaying gender through language', *Trends in Cognitive Sciences* 26, no. 8 (June 2022): 623–625, https://doi.org/10.1016/j.tics.2022.05.001.
13 Kazunari Onishi, *The Dignity of Masks* (Tokyo: Gentosha, 2022).
14 John Yoon and Hikari Hida, 'Asia is loosening rules on masks. Here's why people still wear them', *New York Times*, 1 February 2023, sec. World, www.nytimes.com/2023/02/01/world/asia/covid-masks-asia.html.
15 The nuclear deal, officially called the Joint Comprehensive Plan of Action, was subsequently suspended in May 2018 following the withdrawal of the United States.
16 Kevin Horsley, *Unlimited Memory: How to Use Advanced Learning Strategies to Learn Faster, Remember More and Be More Productive* (Grainger, IN: TCK Publishing, 2016).

Notes

17 Ashlee Humphreys and Kathryn A. Latour, 'Framing the game: assessing the impact of cultural representations on consumer perceptions of legitimacy', *Journal of Consumer Research* 40, no. 4 (2013): 773, https://doi.org/10.1086/672358.

18 Erin C. Conrad, Stacey Humphries, and Anjan Chatterjee, 'Attitudes toward cognitive enhancement: the role of metaphor and context', *AJOB Neuroscience* 10, no. 1 (January 2019): 35–47, https://doi.org/10.1080/21507740.2019.1595771.

19 Lynsey K. Romo and Noah Czajkowski, 'An examination of Redditors' metaphorical sensemaking of prenuptial agreements', *Journal of Family and Economic Issues* 43, no. 1 (March 2022): 1–14, https://doi.org/10.1007/s10834-021-09765-5.

20 Romo and Czajkowski, 'An examination of Redditors' metaphorical sensemaking of prenuptial agreements'.

21 Kanye West, 'Gold Digger', feat. Jamie Foxx (New York: Roc-A-Fella Records, 2005).

22 Cort A. Pedersen, 'Biological aspects of social bonding and the roots of human violence', *Annals of the New York Academy of Sciences* 1036, no. 1 (December 2004): 106.

23 David J. Hauser and Norbert Schwarz, 'The war on prevention: bellicose cancer metaphors hurt (some) prevention intentions', *Personality and Social Psychology Bulletin* 41, no. 1 (January 2015): 66–77, https://doi.org/10/f6r9qj.

Part III: Making meanings move – frame positioning

1 Quote Investigator, 'Computers are useless. They can only give you answers', 5 November 2011, https://quoteinvestigator.com/2011/11/05/computers-useless/.

2 See Robert M. Entman, 'Framing: toward clarification of a fractured paradigm', *Journal of Communication* 43, no. 4 (1993): 51–58, https://doi.org/10.1111/j.1460-2466.1993.tb01304.x, where he seeks to clarify what framing is: 'Frames, then, define problems – determine what a causal agent is doing with what costs and benefits, usually measured in terms of common cultural values; diagnose causes – identify the forces creating the problem; make moral judgments – evaluate causal agents and their effects; and suggest remedies – offer and justify treatments for the problems and predict their likely effects.'

3 Dan M. Kahan *et al.*, 'Geoengineering and climate change polarization: testing a two-channel model of science communication', *Annals of the American Academy of Political and Social Science* 658, no. 1 (March 2015): 192–222.

4 David Zilberman, Tim G. Holland, and Itai Trilnick, 'Agricultural GMOs – what we know and where scientists disagree', *Sustainability* 10, no. 5 (May 2018): 1514, https://doi.org/10.3390/su10051514; cf. Linda Soneryd and Göran Sundqvist, *Science and Democracy: A Science and Technology Studies Approach*, 1st edn (Bristol: Bristol University Press, 2023).

8 Up–down positioning: reading on or between the lines

1 Arthur Schopenhauer, *Parerga and Paralipomena: A Collection of Philosophical Essays* (New York: Cosimo, [1851] 2007), 23.
2 Jen Fisher and Paul H. Silverglate, 'The C-suite's role in well-being', *Deloitte Insights*, 22 June 2022, www2.deloitte.com/us/en/insights/topics/leadership/employee-wellness-in-the-corporate-workplace.html.
3 Christopher J. Bryan, David S. Yeager, and Cintia P. Hinojosa, 'A values-alignment intervention protects adolescents from the effects of food marketing', *Nature Human Behaviour* 3, no. 6 (June 2019): 596–603, https://doi.org/10.1038/s41562-019-0586-6.
4 John R Krebs, 'The gourmet ape: evolution and human food preferences', *American Journal of Clinical Nutrition* 90, no. 3 (September 2009): 707S–711S, https://doi.org/10.3945/ajcn.2009.27462B.
5 Huxley, 'Evolution and ethics'.
6 Johan Jansson and Ellen Dorrepaal, 'Personal norms for dealing with climate change: results from a survey using moral foundations theory', *Sustainable Development* 23, no. 6 (2015): 381–395; Scott Curry *et al.*, 'Moral molecules'.
7 Robert Boyd *et al.*, 'The evolution of altruistic punishment', *Proceedings of the National Academy of Sciences* 100, no. 6 (March 2003): 3531–3535.
8 Mikael Klintman, *Knowledge Resistance: How We Avoid Insight from Others* (Manchester: Manchester University Press, 2019).
9 Thaler and Sunstein, *Nudge*, 9–10.
10 Thaler and Sunstein, *Nudge*, 9–10.
11 Thaler and Sunstein, *Nudge*, 8.
12 Robert Trivers, *Deceit and Self-Deception: Fooling Yourself the Better to Fool Others* (New York: Penguin, 2011).
13 Yotam Ophir and Kathleen Hall Jamieson, 'The effects of media narratives about failures and discoveries in science on beliefs about and support for science', *Public Understanding of Science* 30, no. 8 (November 2021): 1008–1023, https://doi.org/10.1177/09636625211012630.
14 Conny E. Wollbrant, Mikael Knutsson, and Peter Martinsson, 'Extrinsic rewards and crowding-out of prosocial behaviour', *Nature Human Behaviour* 6, no. 6 (March 2022): 774–781, https://doi.org/10.1038/s41562-022-01293-y.

9 Sideways positioning: what *is* the matter?

1 Michael Gibb, 'Weak links', *Aeon*, 11 September 2020, https://aeon.co/essays/what-the-supply-chain-metaphor-obscures-about-global-justice.
2 Magnus Boström and Mikael Klintman, 'Mass consumption and political consumerism', in *The Oxford Handbook of Political Consumerism*, ed. Magnus Boström, Michele Micheletti, and Peter Oosterveer (Oxford: Oxford University Press, 2019), pp. 855–876. https://doi.org/10.1093/oxfordhb/9780190629038.013.53.
3 Goffman, *Frame Analysis*; David A. Snow *et al.*, 'Frame alignment processes, micromobilization, and movement participation', *American Sociological Review* 51, no. 4 (1986): 464–481, https://doi.org/10.2307/2095581; Michiel

Notes

De Vydt and Pauline Ketelaars, 'Linking consensus to action: does frame alignment amongst sympathizers lead to protest participation?', *Social Movement Studies* 20, no. 4 (July 2021): 439–458, https://doi.org/10.1080/1 4742837.2020.1770071; J. L. Johnson, '"Meet them where they are": attentional processes in social movement listening', *Symbolic Interaction* 44, no. 4 (2021): 728–747, https://doi.org/10.1002/symb.535.

4 Catherine E. Herrold, 'When promoting democracy, less is more', *Foreign Policy*, 8 December 2021, https://foreignpolicy.com/2021/12/08/biden-demo cracy-summit-pluralism-promotion-ngos/.

5 Michael J. Sandel, *What Money Can't Buy: The Moral Limits of Markets*, reprint edn (New York: Farrar, Straus and Giroux, 2013).

6 Friedrich Nietzsche, *Twilight of the Idols and the Anti-Christ: Or How to Philosophize with a Hammer*, ed. Michael Tanner, trans. R. J. Hollingdale, reissue edn (London: Penguin Classics, [1889] 1990).

7 Nietzsche, *Twilight of the Idols and the Anti-Christ*, 40.

8 Werner Jaeger, *Paideia: The Ideals of Greek Culture*, volume I: *Archaic Greece: The Mind of Athens*, trans. Gilbert Highet, 2nd edn (New York: Oxford University Press, 1939).

9 Clare D'Souza, 'Marketing challenges for an eco-fashion brand: a case study', *Fashion Theory: The Journal of Dress, Body and Culture* 19, no. 1 (February 2015): 67–82, https://doi.org/10.2752/175174115X14113933306824.

10 cf. Åsa Svenfelt, Noha Baraka Wadha, and Vishal Parekh, 'Sustainable consumption futures: according to whom?', *Sustainability: Science, Practice, and Policy* 20, no. 1 (December 2024), https://doi.org/10.1080/15487733.202 4.2341495.

11 Kahan *et al.*, 'Geoengineering and climate change polarization'.

12 Karl-Heinz Stockhausen, 'Huuuh! Das Pressegespräch am 16. September 2001 im Senatszimmer des Hotel Atlantic in Hamburg: Press conference with Stockhausen', *MusikTexte*, 2002, 76–77, author's translation, https:// silo.tips/download/huuuh-das-pressegesprch-am-16-september-2001-im-sen atszimmer-des-hotel-atlantic.

13 George Edward Moore, *Principia Ethica* (Buffalo, NY: Prometheus Books, 1903).

14 David Sloan Wilson, Eric Dietrich, and Anne B. Clark, 'On the inappropriate use of the naturalistic fallacy in evolutionary psychology', *Biology and Philosophy* 18, no. 5 (November 2003): 669–681, https://doi.org/10.1023/A: 1026380825208.

15 European Business and Biodiversity Campaign, 'Fact Sheet: Biodiversity in the Cosmetics Sector', 2020, chrome-extension://efaidnbmnnnibpca-jpcglclefindmkaj/file:///Users/socmkl/Downloads/Fact%20Sheet%20 Cosmetics_en.pdf.

16 Klintman, *Knowledge Resistance*, 323.

Part IV: Making boundaries bend – frame sizing

1 Patrick Leigh Fermor and Roderick Bailey, *Abducting a General: The Kreipe Operation in Crete* (New York: New York Review of Books, 2015);

Theodore Ziolkowski, 'Uses and abuses of Horace: his reception since 1935 in Germany and Anglo-America', *International Journal of the Classical Tradition* 12, no. 2 (2005): 183–215.

2 Frame bridging has been described as the process by which new issues are added to current ones, such as when the issue of asylum is bridged with working conditions, racism, and housing; see Pierre Monforte, 'The cognitive dimension of social movements' Europeanization processes. The case of the protests against "Fortress Europe"', *Perspectives on European Politics and Society* 15, no. 1 (January 2014): 120–137.

3 Frame amplification refers to a discourse where several frames are reduced to fewer or only one highly focussed issue; see Snow *et al.*, 'Frame alignment processes'.

10 Roots to social elasticity

1 Dunbar, *Friends*.

2 Pierre Bourdieu, *Distinction: A Social Critique of the Judgement of Taste*, trans. Richard Nice (Cambridge, MA: Harvard University Press, 1987).

3 W. D. Hamilton, 'The genetical evolution of social behaviour. I', *Journal of Theoretical Biology* 7, no. 1 (July 1964): 1–16, https://doi.org/10.1016/0022-5193(64)90038-4; Geoff Wild, Vonica J. Flear, and Graham J. Thompson, 'A kin-selection model of fairness in heterogeneous populations', *Journal of Theoretical Biology* 565 (May 2023): 111469, https://doi.org/10.1016/j.jtbi.2023.111469.

4 Devon Greyson and Julie A. Bettinger, 'How do mothers' vaccine attitudes change over time?', *SSM – Qualitative Research in Health* 2 (December 2022): 100060, https://doi.org/10.1016/j.ssmqr.2022.100060.

5 Aurélien Mounier and Marta Mirazón Lahr, 'Deciphering African late middle Pleistocene hominin diversity and the origin of our species', *Nature Communications* 10 (September 2019): 3406, https://doi.org/10.1038/s41467-019-11213-w.

6 Alan R. Templeton, 'Biological races in humans', *Studies in History and Philosophy of Science Part C: Studies in History and Philosophy of Biological and Biomedical Sciences* 44, no. 3 (September 2013): 262–271, https://doi.org/10.1016/j.shpsc.2013.04.010.

7 Robert L. Kelly, *The Foraging Spectrum: Diversity in Hunter-Gatherer Lifeways*, illustrated edn (Clinton Corners, NY: Percheron Press/Eliot Werner Publications, 2007).

8 Kurzban *et al.*, 'Can race be erased?'

9 Mary E. Wheeler and Susan T. Fiske, 'Controlling racial prejudice: social-cognitive goals affect amygdala and stereotype activation', *Psychological Science* 16, no. 1 (January 2005): 56–63.

10 Kurzban *et al.*, 'Can race be erased?'

11 See, e.g., David Pietraszewski, 'The correct way to test the hypothesis that racial categorisation is a by-product of an evolved alliance-tracking capacity', *Scientific Reports* 11, art. no. 3404 (February 2021), https://doi.org/10.1038/s41598-021-82975-x.

Notes

12 SVT, '"We shall overcome" – kalabaliken i Rinkeby 1992 | Rapport | SVT', YouTube, 4 December 2007, www.youtube.com/watch?v=mQakZce3GhQ.

13 Stanley Weintraub, *Silent Night: The Story of the World War I Christmas Truce*, 1st edn (New York: Free Press, 2001).

14 Daniel Weinstein *et al.*, 'Singing and social bonding: changes in connectivity and pain threshold as a function of group size', *Evolution and Human Behavior* 37, no. 2 (March 2016): 152–158, https://doi.org/10.1016/j.evolhumbehav.2015.10.002.

15 Andrew Bradford Stone, 'Growing Up Soviet? The Orphans of Stalin's Revolution and Understanding the Soviet Self' (PhD thesis, University of Washington, 2012).

16 Hendrik Johannes Theodoor Dekker, *Cycling Pathways* (Amsterdam: Amsterdam University Press, 2021).

17 Joseph Henrich, 'Culture and social behavior', *Current Opinion in Behavioral Sciences* 3 (June 2015): 84–89, https://doi.org/10.1016/j.cobeha.2015.02.001.

18 Ernst Fehr and Ivo Schurtenberger, 'Normative foundations of human cooperation', *Nature Human Behaviour* 2, no. 7 (July 2018): 458–468. https://doi.org/10.1038/s41562-018-0385-5.

11 Metaframing: from difference to higher sameness

1 Frimer, Skitka, and Motyl, 'Liberals and conservatives are similarly motivated to avoid exposure to one another's opinions'.

2 Renström, Bäck, and Carroll, 'Protecting the ingroup?'

3 Hannah Arendt, *On Revolution* (London: Praeger, 1963); Josh Cohen, 'The meaning of anger', *Aeon*, 6 January 2022, https://aeon.co/essays/anger-is-a-state-of-agitated-enervation-that-moves-the-world.

4 Malle, Knobe, and Nelson, 'Actor–observer asymmetries in explanations of behavior'.

5 Johnson and Fowler, 'The evolution of overconfidence'.

6 Raymond S. Nickerson, 'Confirmation bias: a ubiquitous phenomenon in many guises', *Review of General Psychology* 2, no. 2 (1998): 175–220, https://doi.org/10.1037/1089-2680.2.2.175.

7 Trivers, *Deceit and Self-Deception*.

8 Cohen, 'The meaning of anger'.

9 Audre Lorde, *Sister Outsider: Essays and Speeches*, reprint edn (Berkeley, CA: Crossing Press, 1984), 131.

10 Cohen, 'The meaning of anger'.

11 Melinda Miceli, 'Morality politics vs. identity politics: framing processes and competition among Christian right and gay social movement organizations', *Sociological Forum* 20, no. 4 (December 2005): 589–612.

12 Hugo Mercier *et al.*, 'Experts and laymen grossly underestimate the benefits of argumentation for reasoning', *Thinking and Reasoning* 21, no. 3 (August 2015): 341–355, https://doi.org/10.1080/13546783.2014.981582.

13 Mark Alfano, Colin Klein, and Jeroen de Ridder, *Social Virtue Epistemology* (New York: Routledge, 2022).

14 Thomas F. Gieryn, *Cultural Boundaries of Science: Credibility on the Line* (Chicago, IL, and London: University of Chicago Press, 1999).

15 Klintman, *Knowledge Resistance*.

16 Tom McLeish, 'Science + religion', *Aeon*, 21 November 2019, https://aeon. co/essays/its-not-science-vs-religion-but-each-one-via-the-other.

17 cf. Haidt, *The Righteous Mind*.

18 Mike Kent, 'Scientists in Congregations guest post: Life on the Edge', ECLAS, 26 April 2022, www.eclasproject.org/scientists-in-congregations-guest-post-life-on-the-edge.

19 Philip Oltermann, '"At first I thought, this is crazy": the real-life plan to use novels to predict the next war', *Guardian*, 26 June 2021, sec. Books, www.theguardian.com/lifeandstyle/2021/jun/26/project-cassandra-plan-to-use-novels-to-predict-next-war.

20 For example, the Hindu text *Bhagavad Gita* speaks of 'Lokasamgraha', emphasizing actions that benefit the global community. Buddhism also echoes utilitarianism by advocating for the greatest good for the largest number, while the ancient Chinese philosophy of Mohism preaches universal love. In Islamic ethics, the principle of Maslaha focuses on common interests beyond individual groups, while Christianity and Judaism offer teachings that align with the utilitarian outlook on prioritizing basic needs and saving lives. Some Native American philosophies, like the 'Seven Generation Sustainability' principle of the Iroquois Confederacy, also advocate for decisions that protect everyone's needs for generations to come.

21 Jeremy Bentham, *An Introduction to the Principles of Morals and Legislation.* (Farmington Hills, MI: Gale, 2018).

22 William Hazlitt, *The Spirit of the Age: Or, Contemporary Portraits* (London: A. and W. Galignani, 1825), 5; see also Philip Lucas and Anne Sheeran, 'Asperger's syndrome and the eccentricity and genius of Jeremy Bentham', *Journal of Bentham Studies* 8, no. 1 (January 2006): 7, https://doi.org/10.14324/111.2045-757X.027.

23 John Stuart Mill, *The Subjection of Women* (Urbana, IL: Project Gutenberg, [1869] 2008), ebook, www.gutenberg.org/ebooks/27083.

24 Anne Campbell, 'The study of sex differences: feminism and biology', *Zeitschrift Für Psychologie* 220, no. 2 (2012): 137–143, https://doi.org/10.1027/2151-2604/a000105.

25 Sebastian Lippold *et al.*, 'Human paternal and maternal demographic histories: insights from high-resolution Y chromosome and mtDNA sequences', *Investigative Genetics* 5, no. 1 (September 2014), https://doi.org/10.1186/2041-2223-5-13.

26 Brian Harrison, *Separate Spheres: The Opposition to Women's Suffrage in Britain*, 1st edn (Abingdon and New York: Routledge, 2013).

27 Johnson, *God Is Watching You*.

28 Joshua Greene, *Moral Tribes: Emotion, Reason and the Gap Between Us and Them* (New York: Penguin, 2014).

29 Miriam Williford, 'Bentham on the rights of women', *Journal of the History of Ideas* 36, no. 1 (1975): 167–176, https://doi.org/10.2307/2709019.

Notes

30 Philippa Foot, 'The problem of abortion and the doctrine of double effect', in *Virtues and Vices: And Other Essays in Moral Philosophy* (New York: Oxford University Press, [1967] 2002), https://doi.org/10.1093/0199252866.003.0002.

31 David Edmonds, *Would You Kill the Fat Man? The Trolley Problem and What Your Answer Tells Us About Right and Wrong* (Princeton, NJ, and Oxford: Princeton University Press, 2013).

32 Greene, *Moral Tribes*.

33 Greene, *Moral Tribes*.

34 David A. Snow and Robert D. Benford, 'Ideology, frame resonance and participant mobilisation', *International Social Movement Research* 1 (1988): 197–217.

35 Åsa Lundqvist, *Transforming Gender and Family Relations: How Active Labour Market Policies Shaped the Dual Earner Model* (Cheltenham: Edward Elgar Publishing, 2017).

36 Immanuel Kant, *Lectures on Ethics*, trans. Louis Infield (New York: Harper & Row, 1780), 239–240.

37 'Bulletin de La Société Protectrice des Animaux', translated by and quoted in Christophe Traïni, 'The animal rights struggle: an essay in historical sociology', *HAL Open Science* (August 2016), https://shs.hal.science/halshs-02864005.

38 Nick Zangwill, 'Our moral duty to eat meat', *Journal of the American Philosophical Association* 7, no. 3 (September 2021): 295–311, https://doi.org/10.1017/apa.2020.21.

39 World Commission on Environment and Development, *Our Common Future* (Oxford: Oxford University Press, 1987).

40 Peter Scarborough *et al.*, 'Vegans, vegetarians, fish-eaters and meat-eaters in the UK show discrepant environmental impacts', *Nature Food* 4, no. 7 (July 2023): 565–574, https://doi.org/10.1038/s43016-023-00795-w.

41 Ulrich Beck, *World Risk Society* (Cambridge: Polity, 1999).

42 Rune Blomhoff *et al.*, *Nordic Nutrition Recommendations 2023* (Copenhagen: Nordic Council of Ministers, 2023), https://doi.org/10.6027/nord2023-003.

12 Questions, answers, and discussion

1 Ola Persson and Mikael Klintman, 'Framing sufficiency: strategies of environmental non-governmental organisations towards reduced material consumption', *Journal of Consumer Culture* 22, no. 2 (December 2020), 1–20.

2 Robert Plomin, *Blueprint: How DNA Makes Us Who We Are* (Cambridge, MA: MIT Press, 2018).

3 Decontextualized facts, even if true, can mislead. For instance, a graph depicting a slight temperature dip from 1998 to 2012, based on correct NASA data, was used to challenge global warming theories. This misuse of data capitalizes on 1998 being exceptionally warm, thus normalizing subsequent years. Extending the data range reveals a clear warming trend,

highlighting the necessity for comprehensive context to avert knowledge resistance.

4 Mattias Holmgren *et al.*, 'When A+B < A: cognitive bias in experts' judgment of environmental impact', *Frontiers in Psychology* 9 (2018), https://doi.org/10.3389/fpsyg.2018.00823.

5 Maic Rakitta and Jannis Wernery, 'Cognitive biases in building energy decisions', *Sustainability* 13, no. 17 (January 2021): 9960, https://doi.org/10.3390/su13179960.

6 Judith Friedlander and Chris Riedy, 'Celebrities, credibility, and complementary frames: raising the agenda of sustainable and other "inconvenient" food issues in social media campaigning', *Communication Research and Practice* 4, no. 3 (July 2018): 229–245, https://doi.org/10.1080/22041451.2018.1448210.

7 Donald Horton and R. Richard Wohl, 'Mass communication and para-social interaction', *Psychiatry* 19, no. 3 (August 1956): 215–229, https://doi.org/10.1080/00332747.1956.11023049.

8 Scott Curry *et al.*, 'Moral molecules'.

9 Emile Durkheim, *Rules of Sociological Method* (New York: Free Press, [1895] 1982).

10 cf. Lawrence Kohlberg, *The Meaning and Measurement of Moral Development* (Worcester, MA: Clark University Heinz Werner Institute, 1981).

11 Rein and Schön, 'Reframing policy discourse'.

Select bibliography

Abrams, Jamie R. 'The #MeToo movement: an invitation for feminist critique of rape crisis framing'. *University of Richmond Law Review* 52, no. 4 (2022): 749–794.

Alfano, Mark, Marc Cheong, and Oliver Scott Curry. 'Moral universals: a machine-reading analysis of 256 societies'. *Heliyon* 10, no. 6 (March 2024): 1–13. https://doi.org/10.1016/j.heliyon.2024.e25940.

Alfano, Mark, Colin Klein, and Jeroen de Ridder. *Social Virtue Epistemology* (New York: Routledge, 2022).

Arendt, Hannah. *On Revolution* (London: Praeger, 1963).

Atir, Stav. 'Girlboss? Highlighting versus downplaying gender through language'. *Trends in Cognitive Sciences* 26, no. 8 (June 2022): 623–625. https://doi.org/10.1016/j.tics.2022.05.001.

Baldin, Andrea, and Trine Bille. 'The avant-garde consumers: a new perspective on quality evaluations of performing arts'. *Poetics* 97 (April 2023): 101771. https://doi.org/10.1016/j.poetic.2023.101771.

Bargh, John. *Before You Know It: The Unconscious Reasons We Do What We Do* (New York: Penguin, 2017).

Baudrillard, Jean. *The Intelligence of Evil: Or, The Lucidity Pact*, trans. Chris Turner (London and New York: Bloomsbury Academic, 2013).

Beck, Ulrich. *World Risk Society* (Cambridge: Polity, 1999).

Benford, R. D., and D. A. Snow. 'Framing processes and social movements: an overview and assessment'. *Annual Review of Sociology* 26 (2000): 611–639.

Bentham, Jeremy. *An Introduction to the Principles of Morals and Legislation* (Farmington Hills, MI: Gale, 2018).

Berberick, Stevie N. *Reframing Sex: Unlearning the Gender Binary with Trans Masculine YouTube Vloggers* (Lanham, MD: Lexington Books, 2020).

Boström, Magnus. *The Social Life of Unsustainable Mass Consumption* (Lanham, MD: Lexington Books, 2023).

Boström, Magnus, and Mikael Klintman. 'Mass consumption and political consumerism'. In *The Oxford Handbook of Political Consumerism*, ed. Magnus Boström, Michele Micheletti, and Peter Oosterveer (Oxford:

Oxford University Press, 2018), pp. 855–876. https://doi.org/10.1093/oxford hb/9780190629038.013.53.

Boström, Magnus, and Rolf Lidskog, *Environmental Sociology and Social Transformation*, 1st edn (Abingdon and New York: Routledge, 2024).

Boyd, Robert, Herbert Gintis, Samuel Bowles, and Peter J. Richerson. 'The evolution of altruistic punishment'. *Proceedings of the National Academy of Sciences* 100, no. 6 (March 2003): 3531–3535.

Boyer, Pascal. *Minds Make Societies: How Cognition Explains the World Humans Create*, 1st edn (New Haven, CT, and London: Yale University Press, 2018).

Brown, Kenneth G. *Influence: Mastering Life's Most Powerful Skill*, The Great Courses (Chantilly, VA: The Teaching Company, 2013). Audiobook. www.audible.com/pd/Influence-Audiobook/B00FPTSNYQ?action_code=ASSGB 14908011900oH&share_location=pdp.

Bryan, Christopher J., David S. Yeager, and Cintia P. Hinojosa. 'A values-alignment intervention protects adolescents from the effects of food marketing'. *Nature Human Behaviour* 3, no. 6 (June 2019): 596–603. https://doi.org/10.1038/s41 562-019-0586-6.

Burgess, Adam. '"Nudging" healthy lifestyles: the UK experiments with the behavioural alternative to regulation and the market'. *European Journal of Risk Regulation* 3, no. 1 (2012): 3–16.

Campbell, Anne. 'The study of sex differences: feminism and biology'. *Zeitschrift Für Psychologie* 220, no. 2 (2012): 137–143. https://doi.org/10.1027/2151-2604/ a000105.

Campbell, Bradley, and Jason Manning. *The Rise of Victimhood Culture: Microaggressions, Safe Spaces, and the New Culture Wars*, 1st edn (New York: Palgrave Macmillan, 2018).

Bradley, Karin, and Ola Persson. 'Community repair in the circular economy – fixing more than stuff'. *Local Environment* 27, no. 10–11 (November 2022): 1321–1337. https://doi.org/10.1080/13549839.2022.2041580.

Camus, Albert. *The Myth of Sisyphus and Other Essays* (New York: Vintage Books, [1942] 2018).

Carothers, Bobbi J., and Harry T. Reis. 'Men and women are from Earth: examining the latent structure of gender.' *Journal of Personality and Social Psychology* 104, no. 2 (2013): 385–407. https://doi.org/10.1037/ a0030437.

Cesareo, Ludovica, Claudia Townsend, and Eugene Pavlov. 'Hideous but worth it: distinctive ugliness as a signal of luxury'. *Journal of the Academy of Marketing Science* 51, no. 3 (2023): 636–657.

Clark, Kenneth B., and Mamie P. Clark. 'Emotional factors in racial identification and preference in negro children'. *Journal of Negro Education* 19, no. 3 (1950): 341–350. https://doi.org/10.2307/2966491.

Cournoyer, D. E. 'Evaluating claims for universals: a method analysis approach'. *CrossCultural Research* 38, no. 4 (November 2004): 319–342.

Cukier, Kenneth, Viktor Mayer-Schönberger, and Francis de Véricourt. *Framers: Human Advantage in an Age of Technology and Turmoil* (London: Penguin, 2021).

Select bibliography

De Vydt, Michiel, and Pauline Ketelaars. 'Linking consensus to action: does frame alignment amongst sympathizers lead to protest participation?' *Social Movement Studies* 20, no. 4 (July 2021): 439–458. https://doi.org/10.1080/14 742837.2020.1770071.

Dijker, Antonj. M., Robm. A. Nelissen, and Mandym. N. Stijnen. 'Framing posthumous organ donation in terms of reciprocity: what are the emotional consequences?' *Basic and Applied Social Psychology* 35, no. 3 (2013): 256–264.

Douglas, Mary. *Purity and Danger: An Analysis of the Concepts of Pollution and Taboo* (London: Routledge & Kegan Paul, 1978).

Druckman, James N., and Toby Bolsen. 'Framing, motivated reasoning, and opinions about emergent technologies'. *Journal of Communication* 61, no. 4 (August 2011): 659–688. https://doi.org/10.1111/j.1460-2466.2011.01562.x.

D'Souza, Clare. 'Marketing challenges for an eco-fashion brand: a case study'. *Fashion Theory: The Journal of Dress, Body and Culture* 19, no. 1 (February 2015): 67–82. https://doi.org/10.2752/175174115X14113933306824.

Dunbar, Robin. *Friends: Understanding the Power of Our Most Important Relationships* (London: Hachette UK, 2021).

Durkheim, Emile. *Rules of Sociological Method* (New York: Free Press, [1895] 1982).

Edmonds, David. *Would You Kill the Fat Man? The Trolley Problem and What Your Answer Tells Us About Right and Wrong* (Princeton, NJ, and Oxford: Princeton University Press, 2013).

Fairclough, Isabela, and Irina Diana Mădroane. 'An argumentative approach to "framing". Framing, deliberation and action in an environmental conflict'. *Co-Herencia* 17, no. 32 (June 2020): 119–158. https://doi.org/10.17230/ co-herencia.17.32.5.

Foot, Philippa. 'The problem of abortion and the doctrine of double effect'. In *Virtues and Vices: And Other Essays in Moral Philosophy* (New York: Oxford University Press, [1967] 2002), https://doi.org/10.1093/0199252866.003.0002.

Foucault, Michel. *The History of Sexuality*, vol. 1: *An Introduction*, reissue edn (New York: Vintage, 1978).

Frimer, Jeremy A., Linda J. Skitka, and Matt Motyl. 'Liberals and conservatives are similarly motivated to avoid exposure to one another's opinions'. *Journal of Experimental Social Psychology* 72 (September 2017): 1–12. https://doi. org/10.1016/j.jesp.2017.04.003.

Fünfschilling, Lea, and Bernhard Truffer, 'The structuration of socio-technical regimes – conceptual foundations from institutional theory'. *Research Policy* 43, no. 4 (May 2014): 772–791. http://doi.org/10.1016/j.respol.2013.10.010.

Gamson, William A., and Andre Modigliani. 'Media discourse and public opinion on nuclear power: a constructionist approach'. *American Journal of Sociology* 95, no. 1 (1989): 1–37.

Gaskell, George, Katrin Hohl, and Monica M. Gerber. 'Do closed survey questions overestimate public perceptions of food risks?' *Journal of Risk Research* 20, no. 8 (August 2017): 1038–1052.

Genette, Gerard, and Richard Macksey. *Paratexts: Thresholds of Interpretation*, trans. Jane E. Lewin (Cambridge: Cambridge University Press, 1997).

Gieryn, Thomas F. *Cultural Boundaries of Science: Credibility on the Line* (Chicago, IL: University of Chicago Press, 1999).

Goffman, Erving. *Frame Analysis: An Essay on the Organization of Experience* (Boston, MA: Northeastern University Press, 1974).

Greene, Joshua. *Moral Tribes: Emotion, Reason and the Gap Between Us and Them* (New York: Penguin, 2014).

Gross, Matthias, and Linsey McGoey, eds. *Routledge International Handbook of Ignorance Studies*, 2nd edn (Abingdon and New York: Routledge, 2022).

Haidt, Jonathan. *The Righteous Mind: Why Good People Are Divided by Politics and Religion* (New York: Knopf Doubleday Publishing Group, 2012).

Hales, Steven D. *The Myth of Luck: Philosophy, Fate, and Fortune* (New York: Bloomsbury Academic, 2020).

Hamilton, W. D. 'The genetical evolution of social behaviour. I'. *Journal of Theoretical Biology* 7, no. 1 (July 1964): 1–16. https://doi.org/10.1016/0022-5193(64)90038-4.

Harrison, Brian. *Separate Spheres: The Opposition to Women's Suffrage in Britain*, 1st edn (Abingdon and New York: Routledge, 2013).

Hassin, Ran R., ed. *The New Unconscious*, Oxford Series in Social Cognition and Social Neuroscience (Oxford: Oxford University Press, 2007).

Hauser, David J., and Norbert Schwarz. 'The war on prevention: bellicose cancer metaphors hurt (some) prevention intentions'. *Personality and Social Psychology Bulletin* 41, no. 1 (January 2015): 66–77. https://doi.org/10/f6r9qj.

Heinrichs, Harald. 'Aesthetic expertise for sustainable development: envisioning artful scientific policy advice'. *World* 2, no. 1 (February 2021): 92–104. https://doi.org/10.3390/world2010007.

Henrich, Joseph. 'Culture and social behavior'. *Current Opinion in Behavioral Sciences* 3 (June 2015): 84–89. https://doi.org/10.1016/j.cobeha.2015.02.001.

Herrold, Catherine E. 'When promoting democracy, less is more'. *Foreign Policy*, 8 December 2021. https://foreignpolicy.com/2021/12/08/biden-demo cracy-summit-pluralism-promotion-ngos/.

Holmgren, Mattias, Alan Kabanshi, John E. Marsh, and Patrik Sörqvist. 'When A+B < A: cognitive bias in experts' judgment of environmental impact'. *Frontiers in Psychology* 9 (2018). https://doi.org/10.3389/fpsyg.2018.00823.

Humphreys, Ashlee, and Kathryn A. Latour. 'Framing the game: assessing the impact of cultural representations on consumer perceptions of legitimacy'. *Journal of Consumer Research* 40, no. 4 (2013): 773–795. https://doi.org/10.1086/672358.

Hunt, Elle. 'From tofu lamb chops to vegan steak bakes: the 1,000-year history of fake meat'. *Guardian*, 12 January 2020, sec. Life and style. www.theguardian.com/lifeandstyle/2020/jan/12/mock-lamb-chops-vegan-steak-ba kes-history-fake-meat.

Huxley, Thomas. *Evolution and Ethics, and Other Essays* (Urbana, IL: Project Gutenberg, [1893] 2001). Ebook. www.gutenberg.org/cache/epub/2940/pg29 40-images.html.

Jansson, Johan, and Ellen Dorrepaal. 'Personal norms for dealing with climate change: results from a survey using moral foundations theory'. *Sustainable Development* 23, no. 6 (2015): 381–395.

Select bibliography

Johnson, Dominic. *God Is Watching You: How the Fear of God Makes Us Human* (Oxford: Oxford University Press, 2016).

Johnson, Dominic D. P., and James H. Fowler. 'The evolution of overconfidence'. *Nature* 477, no. 7364 (September 2011): 317–320.

Johnson, J. L. '"Meet them where they are": attentional processes in social movement listening'. *Symbolic Interaction* 44, no. 4 (2021): 728–747.

Kabat-Zinn, Jon. *Full Catastrophe Living: Using the Wisdom of Your Body and Mind to Face Stress, Pain, and Illness*, revised edn (New York: Bantam, 2013).

Kahan, Dan M., Hank Jenkins-Smith, Carol L. Silva, Tor Tarantola, and Donald Braman. 'Geoengineering and climate change polarization: testing a two-channel model of science communication'. *Annals of the American Academy of Political and Social Science* 658, no. 1 (March 2015): 192–222.

Kahneman, Daniel. *Thinking, Fast and Slow*, reprint edn (New York: Farrar, Straus and Giroux, 2011).

Kahneman, Daniel, Olivier Sibony, and Cass R. Sunstein. *Noise: A Flaw in Human Judgment* (New York: Little, Brown Spark, 2021).

Kant, Immanuel. *Lectures on Ethics*, trans. Louis Infield (New York: Harper & Row, 1780).

Keene, J. R., P. D. Bolls, H. Shoenberger, and C. K. Berke. 'The biological roots of political extremism: negativity bias, political ideology, and preferences for political news'. *Politics and the Life Sciences* 36, no. 2 (2017): 37–48.

Kelly, Robert L. *The Foraging Spectrum: Diversity in Hunter-Gatherer Lifeways*, illustrated edn (Clinton Corners, NY: Percheron Press/Eliot Werner Publications, 2007).

Klintman, Mikael. 'Apollonian and Dionysian trust in vaccination'. In *Vaccine Hesitancy in the Nordic Countries: Trust and Distrust During the COVID-19 Pandemic*, ed. Lars Borin, Mia-Marie Hammarlin, Dimitrios Kokkinakis, and Fredrik Miegel (London: Routledge, 2024), pp. 21–34.

Klintman, Mikael. *Human Sciences and Human Interests: Integrating the Social, Economic, and Evolutionary Sciences* (London: Routledge, 2018).

Klintman, Mikael. *Knowledge Resistance: How We Avoid Insight from Others* (Manchester: Manchester University Press, 2019).

Krebs, John R. 'The gourmet ape: evolution and human food preferences'. *American Journal of Clinical Nutrition* 90, no. 3 (September 2009): 707S–711S.

Kupferschmidt, Kai. 'Can skeptical parents be persuaded to vaccinate?' *Science*, 27 April 2017. www.sciencemag.org/news/2017/04/can-skeptical-parents-be-persuaded-vaccinate.

Kurzban, Robert, John Tooby, and Leda Cosmides. 'Can race be erased? Coalitional computation and social categorization'. *Proceedings of the National Academy of Sciences of the United States of America* 98, no. 26 (December 2001): 15387–15392.

Lakoff, George. *The ALL NEW Don't Think of an Elephant! Know Your Values and Frame the Debate*, 2nd revised edn (White River Junction, VT: Chelsea Green Publishing, 2014).

Lakoff, George, and Mark Johnson. *Metaphors We Live By* (Chicago, IL: University of Chicago Press, 2003).

Lamont, Michèle. *The Dignity of Working Men: Morality and the Boundaries of Race, Class, and Immigration* (Cambridge, MA: Harvard University Press, 2009).

Larsson, Jörgen, Simon Matti, and Jonas Nässén. 'Public support for aviation policy measures in Sweden'. *Climate Policy* 20, no. 10 (January 2020): 1305–1321.

Lasko, Emily N., Abigale C. Dagher, Samuel J. West, and David S. Chester. 'Neural mechanisms of intergroup exclusion and retaliatory aggression'. *Social Neuroscience* 17, no. 4 (August 2022): 339–351.

LeBlanc, Steven A., with Katherine E. Register. *Constant Battles: The Myth of the Peaceful, Noble Savage*, 1st edn (New York: St. Martin's Press, 2003).

Lee, Katharine, Saffron O'Neill, Leda Blackwood, and Julie Barnett. 'Perspectives of UK adolescents on the youth climate strikes'. *Nature Climate Change* 12, no. 6 (June 2022): 528–531.

Lehner, Matthias, Jessika Luth Richter, Halliki Kreinin, Pia Mamut, Edina Vadovics, Josefine Henman, Oksana Mont, and Doris Fuchs. 'Living smaller: acceptance, effects and structural factors in the EU'. *Buildings and Cities* 5, no. 1 (June 2024): 215–230.

Loomba, Sahil, Alexandre de Figueiredo, Simon J. Piatek, Kristen de Graaf, and Heidi J. Larson. 'Measuring the impact of COVID-19 vaccine misinformation on vaccination intent in the UK and USA'. *Nature Human Behaviour* 5, no. 3 (March 2021): 337–348.

Lorde, Audre. *Sister Outsider: Essays and Speeches*, reprint edn (Berkeley, CA: Crossing Press, 1984).

Lukianoff, Greg, and Jonathan Haidt. *The Coddling of the American Mind: How Good Intentions and Bad Ideas Are Setting Up a Generation for Failure* (New York: Penguin, 2018).

Lundqvist, Åsa. *Transforming Gender and Family Relations: How Active Labour Market Policies Shaped the Dual Earner Model* (Cheltenham: Edward Elgar Publishing, 2017).

Marlowe, Frank W. 'Hunter-gatherers and human evolution'. *Evolutionary Anthropology: Issues, News, and Reviews* 14, no. 2 (2005): 54–67.

McCarthy, John D., and Mayer N. Zald. 'Resource mobilization and social movements: a partial theory'. *American Journal of Sociology* 82, no. 6 (May 1977): 1212–1241.

Mill, John Stuart. *The Subjection of Women* (Urbana, IL: Project Gutenberg, [1869] 2008). Ebook. www.gutenberg.org/ebooks/27083.

Mill, John Stuart. *Utilitarianism*, ed. George Sher, 2nd edn (Indianapolis, IN: Hackett, 2002).

Mills, C. Wright. *The Sociological Imagination*, 40th anniversary edn (Oxford: Oxford University Press, 2000).

Moore, George Edward. *Principia Ethica* (Buffalo, NY: Prometheus Books, 1903).

Murch, Kevin B., and Daniel C. Krawczyk. 'A neuroimaging investigation of attribute framing and individual differences'. *Social Cognitive and Affective Neuroscience* 9, no. 10 (October 2014): 1464–1471.

Select bibliography

Newkey-Burden, Chas. 'More fast-food chains are offering plant-based food – but should vegans be celebrating?' *Guardian*, 7 January 2020, sec. Life and style. www.theguardian.com/lifeandstyle/shortcuts/2020/jan/07/more-fast-food-chains-are-offering-plant-based-food-but-should-vegans-be-celebrating.

Nickerson, Raymond S. 'Confirmation bias: a ubiquitous phenomenon in many guises'. *Review of General Psychology* 2, no. 2 (1998): 175–220.

Nietzsche, Friedrich. *Ecce Homo: How One Becomes What One Is*, reissue edn (Oxford: Oxford University Press, [1908] 2009).

Nietzsche, Friedrich. *Twilight of the Idols and the Anti-Christ: Or How to Philosophize with a Hammer*, ed. Michael Tanner, trans. R. J. Hollingdale, reissue edn (London: Penguin Classics, [1889] 1990).

Ophir, Yotam, and Kathleen Hall Jamieson. 'The effects of media narratives about failures and discoveries in science on beliefs about and support for science'. *Public Understanding of Science* 30, no. 8 (November 2021): 1008–1023.

Panero, James. 'Radical un-chic'. *New Criterion*, December 2007. https://new criterion.com/article/radical-un-chic.

Park, Jihye, and Wenhan Li. '"I got it FIRST": antecedents of competitive consumption of a new product'. *Journal of Retailing and Consumer Services* 73 (July 2023).

Persson, Ola, and Mikael Klintman. 'Framing sufficiency: strategies of environmental non-governmental organisations towards reduced material consumption'. *Journal of Consumer Culture* 22, no. 2 (December 2020), 1–20.

Pietraszewski, David. 'The correct way to test the hypothesis that racial categorisation is a by-product of an evolved alliance-tracking capacity'. *Scientific Reports* 11, art. no. 3404 (February 2021).

Pinker, Steven. *The Better Angels of Our Nature: Why Violence Has Declined* (New York: Viking Adult, 2011).

Plomin, Robert. *Blueprint: How DNA Makes Us Who We Are* (Cambridge, MA: MIT Press, 2018).

Prooijen, Jan-Willem van. *The Psychology of Conspiracy Theories*, 1st edn (New York: Routledge, 2018).

Rein, Martin, and Donald Schön. 'Reframing policy discourse'. In *The Argumentative Turn in Policy Analysis and Planning*, ed. Frank Fischer and John Forester (Durham, NC: Duke University Press, 1993), 145–166.

Rosling, Hans, Anna Rosling Rönnlund, and Ola Rosling. *Factfulness: Ten Reasons We're Wrong About the World – and Why Things Are Better Than You Think* (New York: Flatiron Books, 2018).

Rousseau, Jean-Jacques. *Discourse on the Origin of Inequality* (Mineola, NY: Dover Publications, [1755] 2004).

Russo, Francine. 'Like humans, apes are susceptible to spin'. *Scientific American*, 1 July 2015.

Sacks, Oliver. *Musicophilia: Tales of Music and the Brain*, 1st edn (New York: Knopf, 2007).

Sandel, Michael J. *What Money Can't Buy: The Moral Limits of Markets*, reprint edn (New York: Farrar, Straus and Giroux, 2013).

Select bibliography

Sapolsky, Robert M. *Behave: The Biology of Humans at Our Best and Worst*, illustrated edn (New York: Penguin, 2017).

Sapolsky, Robert M. *Why Zebras Don't Get Ulcers*, 3rd edn (New York: Holt Paperbacks, 2004).

Sartre, Jean-Paul. *The Words: The Autobiography of Jean-Paul Sartre*, trans. Bernard Frechtman, 1st edn (New York: George Braziller, 1964).

Scarborough, Peter, Michael Clark, Linda Cobiac, Keren Papier, Anika Knuppel, John Lynch, Richard Harrington, Tim Key, and Marco Springmann. 'Vegans, vegetarians, fish-eaters and meat-eaters in the UK show discrepant environmental impacts'. *Nature Food* 4, no. 7 (July 2023): 565–574.

Schopenhauer, Arthur. *Parerga and Paralipomena: A Collection of Philosophical Essays* (New York: Cosimo, [1851] 2007).

Scott Curry, Oliver Scott, Mark Alfano, Mark J. Brandt, and Christine Pelican. 'Moral molecules: morality as a combinatorial system'. *Review of Philosophy and Psychology* 13 (August 2021). https://doi.org/10.1007/s13164-021-00540-x.

Scott Curry, Oliver Daniel A. Mullins, and Harvey Whitehouse. 'Is it good to cooperate? Testing the theory of morality-as-cooperation in 60 societies'. *Current Anthropology* 60, no. 1 (February 2019): 47–69. https://doi.org/10.1086/701478.

Singer, Peter. *Life You Can Save* (London: Picador, 2009).

Smedley, Audrey, and Brian D. Smedley. 'Race as biology is fiction, racism as a social problem is real: anthropological and historical perspectives on the social construction of race'. *American Psychologist* 60, no. 1 (January 2005): 16–26.

Smelser, Neil J. *Theory of Collective Behavior* (New Orleans, LA: Quid Pro Books, 2011).

Smith, Adam. *The Theory of Moral Sentiments*, 2nd edn (London: A. Millar, 1761), https://books.google.se/books?id=bZhZAAAAcAAJ.

Smith, Eric Alden, and Brian F. Codding. 'Ecological variation and institutionalized inequality in hunter-gatherer societies'. *Proceedings of the National Academy of Sciences* 118, no. 13 (March 2021): e2016134118.

Snow, David A., E. Burke Rochford, Steven K. Worden, and Robert D. Benford. 'Frame alignment processes, micromobilization, and movement participation'. *American Sociological Review* 51, no. 4 (1986): 464–481.

Soneryd, Linda, and Göran Sundqvist, *Science and Democracy: A Science and Technology Studies Approach*, 1st edn (Bristol: Bristol University Press, 2023).

Svenfelt, Åsa, Noha Baraka Wadha, and Vishal Parekh, 'Sustainable consumption futures: according to whom?' *Sustainability: Science, Practice, and Policy* 20, no. 1 (December 2024).

Tajfel, Henri. *Human Groups and Social Categories: Studies in Social Psychology* (Cambridge: Cambridge University Press, 1981).

Tang, Yi-Yuan, Britta K. Hölzel, and Michael I. Posner. 'The neuroscience of mindfulness meditation'. *Nature Reviews Neuroscience* 16, no. 4 (April 2015): 213–225.

Thaler, Richard H., and Cass R. Sunstein. *Nudge: The Final Edition* (New York: Penguin, 2021).

Select bibliography

Traïni, Christophe. 'The animal rights struggle: an essay in historical sociology'. *HAL Open Science* (August 2016). https://shs.hal.science/halshs02864005.

Trivers, Robert. *Deceit and Self-Deception: Fooling Yourself the Better to Fool Others* (New York: Penguin, 2011).

Tversky, A., and D. Kahneman. 'The framing of decisions and the psychology of choice'. *Science* 211, no. 4481 (January 1981): 453–458.

Walt, Stephen M. 'Morality is the enemy of peace'. *Foreign Policy*, 13 June 2024. https://foreignpolicy.com/2024/06/13/gaza-ukraine-ceasefire-war-peace-morality/.

Wardlaw, Malcolm J. 'History, risk, infrastructure: perspectives on bicycling in the Netherlands and the UK'. *Journal of Transport and Health* 1, no. 4 (December 2014): 243–250.

Weinstein, Daniel, Jacques Launay, Eiluned Pearce, Robin I. M. Dunbar, and Lauren Stewart. 'Singing and social bonding: changes in connectivity and pain threshold as a function of group size'. *Evolution and Human Behavior* 37, no. 2 (March 2016): 152–158.

Wheeler, Mary E., and Susan T. Fiske. 'Controlling racial prejudice: social-cognitive goals affect amygdala and stereotype activation'. *Psychological Science* 16, no. 1 (January 2005): 56–63.

Wiesel, Elie. *The Gates of the Forest* (New York: Knopf Doubleday Publishing Group, 1966).

Wild, Geoff, Vonica J. Flear, and Graham J. Thompson. 'A kin-selection model of fairness in heterogeneous populations'. *Journal of Theoretical Biology* 565 (May 2023): 111469.

Zangwill, Nick. 'Our moral duty to eat meat'. *Journal of the American Philosophical Association* 7, no. 3 (September 2021): 295–311.

Index

Index

Index